mBraining

"Using your multiple brains to do cool stuff"

Over the last decade, the field of Neuroscience has discovered we have complex and functional brains in both our heart and gut. Called the cardiac and enteric brains respectively, scientific evidence is emerging that these neural networks exhibit intelligence and wisdom.

Now scientific knowledge is finally catching up with deep insights from esoteric and spiritual traditions informing us for thousands of years about these three powerful intelligences. Using methodologies from NLP (Neuro Linguistic Programming), Cognitive Linguistics and Behavioral Modeling, and informed by the latest Neuroscientific discoveries, the newly emerging field of mBIT (multiple Brain Integration Techniques) has codified a powerful system for communicating with and integrating the wisdom and intelligence of your multiple brains.

Written in an easy to read and entertaining style, this is a highly accessible guide to understanding the scientific basis of your gut intuitions, heart-felt emotions, and head-based creative powers. *mBraining* coaches readers in achieving greater success and happiness in a world of massive change.

mBraining

"Using your multiple brains to do cool stuff"

GRANT SOOSALU AND MARVIN OKA

www.mbraining.com

First Published 2012

Contents

mBraining

"Using your multiple brains to do cool stuff"

mBraining

"Using your multiple brains to do cool stuff"

Introduction

The exciting new field of mBIT

This book is a surprise... It evolved itself into existence over the last two years as we discovered and then pulled together a wide range of leading-edge neuroscience research findings on the enteric (gut) brain, the cardiac (heart) brain, and the cephalic (head) brain. We didn't originally intend to write a book when we first started our informal yet exciting dinner conversations about the topic. As behavioral modelers, we were fascinated by the latest findings in neuroscience and their implications and applications to human performance. As we continued to explore what neuroscience was discovering about each of the different *'brains'* (neural networks), we were struck by two insights that eventually led to this book you're now reading.

The first insight was that the practical significance of the scientific findings was not explicit in the original papers. These published articles were simply reports on the research itself and its technical findings. From our perspective as behavioral modelers, however, we could immediately see the profound implications and applications for personal development, human performance, and as you'll discover in this book, for how to live with greater wisdom and authenticity in life.

The second insight was that over the course of studying over six hundred research papers and articles, we noticed how each had approached their specific topic in a specialized and isolated manner. There were numerous studies on the gut brain, *or* the heart brain, *or* the head brain. There were literally no studies done on the integration of all three neural networks and how they communicate and interact with each other for optimal human functioning. Again, as behavioral modelers, we instinctively began to integrate and synthesize these disparate research findings into a bigger picture and an operating framework with practical value for improving how we live our lives.

Working from these two insights, what emerged over time is a whole new field of behavioral change techniques and frameworks. More importantly, what's formed from this process is a generative structure and exciting new platform for exploring what's possible for us as human beings, both individually and collectively as a society.

We called the specific suite of methods for working with our three brains '*mBIT*', which stands for '*multiple Brain Integration Techniques*', and we named the overall process for working with our three brains '*mBraining*'. Developed through behavioral modeling informed by neuroscience research, we believe mBIT has something to offer that is both startlingly new and valuably old. It's new in that the insights and methods provided bring far greater precision and transformational power to existing approaches to personal development and behavioral change. In fact, the neuroscience-based principles you'll learn in this book explain why certain techniques from any personal development approach work when they do, and why they don't when they simply don't. What we are proposing here, though, is also old or ancient. It's old in the sense that the applications we recommend in this book are aligned with what many esoteric and spiritual practices have been saying for two and half thousand years or more. Ancient wisdom was and is wise for valid reasons, and science is just beginning to catch up and validate the neuro-structures behind much of the sage advice from past teachings.

What this book is about

Every book is a reflection of the biases of the author(s), and this book is no exception. We could have written this book as simply a collection of self-help techniques; however we chose to do something much more with it.

So here are a few points about how this book was written that may be helpful to keep in mind when reading:

- We wrote this to be a source book for those wanting to reference the foundational underpinnings of mBIT and *mBraining*. We didn't write this book to be a popular self-help book with overly simplified explanations for a general audience. We consciously chose to write this book for people like us who are keenly interested in leading edge material and who want depth of knowledge.
- The flavor of the book is a blend of neuroscience-based research with practical applications for wise living. We have attempted to make the scientific material accessible for the majority of our readers while still keeping its technical precision and edge. We've also done our best to put in some light-hearted humor where we can (mostly because we don't

like reading dry or boring books ourselves).

- We deliberately chose to develop mBIT and *mBraining* by starting first with what scientific research has found or has proven. This then informed our behavioral modeling research activities for developing competency-based techniques and behavioral insights. The format and structure of the chapters reflects this competency-based orientation.

- We also deliberately chose to call our approach *'multiple'* brain integration techniques (*m*BIT) and not *'three'* brain techniques because we believe additional complex neural networks that function as *'brains'* or intelligence centers may eventually be discovered in the future. This will likely happen once science directs its technology, processes, funding and methods towards detecting and measuring them. When this occurs, the field of mBIT and *mBraining* will evolve accordingly.

- It's our belief as the authors of this book and the developers of this emerging field that the world does not need yet more methods for doing its current paradigm more effectively or efficiently. It doesn't need *'improvement'* on the status quo. What's needed instead is a transformational and generative change in consciousness. To achieve this collectively, it starts individually. Subsequently, much of this book is structured along an evolutionary framework we call the *'mBIT Roadmap'*. As you'll discover in this book, the main purpose for working with your multiple brains is not so you can *'do more'* in life, but instead the aim is to live your life from your highest authentic expression and to live with greater wisdom in all your decisions and actions.

As we began in our behavioral modeling research to uncover and explore more deeply the numerous undesirable consequences that arise when people are not aligned and integrated in their multiple brains, we began to see why and how individuals and societies create their current challenges. We also saw why so many people find it difficult to make any real and lasting change in their lives. As you'll learn in this book, for real, deep, generative change to occur it takes all of your brains working together, aligned and in the right sequence. And that makes mBIT and *mBraining* a good news story. It combines the *'what'* to do with the *'how'* to do it, and even suggests a meaningful *'why'*.

Given all of this, we want this book to be more than a technical resource guide. As a reference source for an emerging field, it has something to say. Aligned within our own hearts, guts and minds, as the authors of this book and the developers of this field, we're proud to unashamedly say that mBIT and *mBraining* are ultimately about making a difference in the world. This new field aims to do this by facilitating higher orders of meta-consciousness that lead to greater wisdom in decision-making and in the actions of individuals, groups, communities, and societies.

We'd also like to say that this is not some form of *'pie in the sky'* idealism. As you'll discover in this book, our aim is pragmatic, practical and very accessible to everyone right now. The latest findings in neuroscience lay out the map, behavioral modeling research provides us with the journey's route, and mBIT and *mBraining* give us the means and tools to start travelling now. So let's start journeying together to make a real and significant difference in our individual worlds and in the world at large. What it will take is simply openness, desire, practice and experimentation. And oh yes, it'll also take your willingness to have some fun while you do cool stuff with your multiple brains. So if you're ready for that now, roll up your metaphorical sleeves, and let's take the journey both back in time followed by swift fast forward to where cutting edge neuroscience meets advanced behavioral modeling.

Welcome to the exciting new field of mBIT and *mBraining!*

Grant Soosalu & Marvin Oka

March 2012

mBraining

"Using your multiple brains to do cool stuff"

Chapter 1

Neuroscience meets ancient wisdom

"The important thing in science is not so much to obtain new facts as to discover new ways of thinking about them."

Sir William Henry Bragg

The year is 2009, and in a laboratory at the University of Pennsylvania, a stainless steel cannula is slowly and carefully inserted into the arm of an experimental subject. Laying on a gurney amidst a dazzling array of high tech medical scanners, the subject is in a deep meditative trance. This is subject sixteen of a total of twenty-six men and women partaking in an advanced scientific study. Twelve of the twenty-six people are advanced meditators, each of them having actively practiced meditation or prayer for more than fifteen years. The other fourteen subjects are controls, normal people with no meditation experience who will be used as comparisons against the advanced meditators.

Subject sixteen, randomly selected from the group, is instructed to rest for ten minutes with her eyes shut. As the ten minutes draws to a close, a lab-coated medical technician slowly injects a radioactive tracer through the cannula into her bloodstream. The solution of Technetium-99 courses its way into her brain where it perfuses throughout the delicate structures of the cranial cells and neural networks. Gently, the subject is wheeled into a SPECT brain imaging machine. This is a huge Picker-Prism 3000XP triple-headed rotating gamma camera; a gleaming, buzzing, rotating monster of high tech wizardry that is used to peer inside a person's head and show details of the structures and processes involved in their brain.

The results from the scan make their way to the computers used to store and analyze the complex data from all twenty-six subjects. Over the coming weeks, the imaging data will be combined and statistically mapped using advanced mathematical techniques. Laterality indexes will be computed, statistical parametric mappings calculated and cerebral blood flow results produced. Conclusions will be drawn and inferred from these results.

Great news

Fast forward to the end of 2009, researcher Dr. Andrew Newberg and his colleagues have just heard the great news. It's worth celebrating. Their paper, entitled *'Cerebral blood flow differences between long-term meditators and non-meditators'* has just been accepted for publication by Elsevier Science in the prestigious journal *'Consciousness and Cognition'*. The conclusions stated in the article:

> "The Cerebral Blood Flow of long-term meditators was significantly higher ($p < .05$) compared to non-meditators in the prefrontal cortex, parietal cortex, thalamus, putamen, caudate, and midbrain. There was also a significant difference in the thalamic laterality with long-term meditators having greater asymmetry. The observed changes associated with long-term

meditation appear in structures that underlie the attention network and also those that relate to emotion and autonomic function."

Yes, after thousands of hours of exacting procedures and study, with the use of millions of dollars of advanced high tech R&D equipment, Andrew and his colleagues have just announced to both the willing subjects of their study and the scientific world at large, they've found strong evidence that meditation changes the structure of the brain related to attention, emotion and the control of the autonomic nervous system.

Finally, science is beginning to prove that the process of meditation, of focusing on mindfulness, compassion and loving-kindness, changes both behavior and mood and ultimately the structure of the neural networks of the brain.

Circling back

But let's backtrack for a moment a couple of thousand years. In a serene garden in a remote countryside in the high Himalayas, a wizened monk, seated in lotus posture, swaying gently and rhythmically, is imparting a deep wisdom and knowledge to the students arrayed in concentrated attention at his feet.

The saffron robed monk declaims, "To awaken, sit calmly, letting each breath clear your mind and open your heart. The heart is like a garden. It can grow compassion or fear, resentment or love. Those who are pure in heart and single in purpose are able to understand this most supreme truth."

The monk gently looks into the eyes of each person before him and continues, "To understand everything is to forgive everything, and forgiveness begins with focusing your mind, focusing your breath, focusing your heart. To calmly abide is the key. To sit calmly as each breath clears your mind and transforms your world. This is the secret of peace. This is the secret of existence."

Yes, as the circle of time cycles round, we're now coming back, with our billions of dollars of R&D funding, with the aid of SPECT, PET and fMRI brain scanners, and with electron microscopes and multi-modal EEG devices, to finally know what was known in essence by the spiritual sages more than 2500 years ago. We are finally learning with fine grained scientific detail, what esoteric traditions have maintained for thousands of years about how we can embody and express the highest qualities of being human. It's an exciting time to be alive; a time when science and ancient wisdom meet. A time when we can really begin to review, inform and advance our knowledge about what it is possible for humans to do with the powerful tools of their minds and bodies.

Ancient wisdom

Sage advice about how to generate and access deeper levels of wisdom can be found across nearly all spiritual disciplines and in many philosophical views.

"And wanting what's precious

you do what distorts your being.

The sage knows this in his gut,

And is guided by his instinct

and not by what his eyes want."

Tao Te Ching

"Knowledge coupled with a warm heart brings wisdom."

Dalai Lama

"The way is not in the sky. The way is in the heart."

Buddha

"Educating the mind without educating the heart is no education at all."

Aristotle

"That which is false troubles the heart, but truth brings joyous tranquility."

Rumi

"The body is the instrument of the mind... The mind is an instrument of the heart."

Hazrat Inayat Khan

You might ask "What's common across these ancient traditions that leads to a greater level of wisdom in their counsel?" Well, as you'll learn in this book, much comes from where and how they source their wisdom. For example, ancient Chinese Taoist philosophy maintains there are three minds, intelligences or energy

19

centers within the body known as the Three Tan Tiens. The Upper Tan Tien is located within the head brain, the Middle Tan Tien is located in the heart and the Lower Tan Tien in the abdomen.

The Enneagram on the other hand is a mystical system based in part on a synthesis of ancient Sufi wisdom. It describes how we prevent our spiritual growth via ego fixations derived from three centers: head, heart and gut.

Gurdjieff, an Armenian born philosopher mystic, spent decades in the late 1800's traveling in Asia Minor and the far east studying with numerous spiritual communities and seeking deep esoteric knowledge. Gurdjieff claimed we all have three brains: an intellectual brain, an emotional brain and a body-ruling moving/instinctive brain.

The notion that we have three souls or intelligences also features in a huge cross-section of the world's religions. It can be found in Kahuna the native Hawaiian occult tradition as a notion of a *'lower self'*, a *'middle self'* and a *'higher self'*. Jewish Kabbalah similarly has a spiritual conception with three distinct levels of soul. The shamans of Mongolia, Siberia and Central Asia say that all humans possess three souls, the *'suld'* soul, the *'suns'* soul and the *'ami'* body soul. In addition, many tribal peoples such as the Nupe in Africa, the Native American Lakota Sioux, the Inuit Eskimos, the indigenous Taiwanese Puyuma, and the Hmong Chinese aborigines all claim that humans have three souls. In a review of the last 100 years of ethnographic data, researchers Frecska, Moro and Wesselman found that a tripartite concept of soul was the rule rather than the exception in aboriginal spiritual traditions. And when you think about it, wouldn't the notion of a *'soul'* be a primitive way of making sense of and expressing the concept of an intelligence operating within us?

Three intelligences

Notice the pattern here with all these spiritual and esoteric traditions? They all seem to indicate there are three intelligences located within the human body that can be accessed, communicated with, and channeled toward wiser living.

So what do all these ancient philosophies with their esoteric practices have to do with you? Well, a lot, actually — assuming of course you want to live life more fully, more authentically and more meaningfully — something not so easy to do in today's world.

Stressful living

You see, we live in a day and age of massively accelerating change and a world filled with untold stressors. More than ever, just getting through daily living leads to stress and burn out.

Work-life balance has become a major issue for many people as they try to juggle the economics of practical living against the authenticity of doing a job that has real meaning. What about you? Is there something you'd truly rather be doing than your current job? Is your heart really in the work you do to make a living?

In the end though, it seems many people feel they're stuck in a situation where no matter what decisions they make, it all ends up the same. Decisions appear to take them out of the pan, but end up leading them straight into the fire.

As an example, it's a common experience with divorce, for a person to leave one partner only to find the same relationship issues still active with the next. And of course, as your overall happiness and wellbeing go down you begin to wonder "is that all there is?" and you may end up asking "so really, what's it all about?"

In the end, you begin to question your identity, who you are, why you're here, and what's your purpose. We all hunger for meaningfulness, especially as our current decisions and actions don't seem to be getting us anywhere fast.

It's how you respond

Popular personal development and new age sayings do attempt to come to our rescue: "It doesn't matter what happens, it's how you respond that counts," they advise. This ultimately is true, but *'how'* exactly are we to *'respond'*? What specifically are we supposed to do?

And traditional folk wisdom often seems contradictory:

"Follow your heart"
"Follow your gut"
"Follow your instincts"
"Use your head"
"Use your intuition"
"Trust your gut"
"Be true to your heart"
"Don't let your emotions override your head"
"Don't lose your head, think it through"
"Go with your gut response"

What the... What are we supposed to do with all this apparently contradictory advice? Our answer is: *'do them all'*.

Because, as you'll learn in this book, there's no contradiction when you begin to understand the principles behind our work with *'multiple Brain Integration Techniques'*, or mBIT for short.

mBIT is based on startling insights from leading edge research in the neurosciences that show we have more than just the brain in our head. Indeed, we have a head brain, a heart brain and a gut brain. And in the upcoming pages we'll explore these brains in detail and you'll learn techniques and strategies for how to communicate with them and integrate and align them to respond to the world with a wisdom that is simply not possible through the head brain alone.

Heading into trouble

Over the last few hundred years, the world has had a fascination and obsession with science, technology and head based rational thinking. The power of science and its benefits to our lives have driven ongoing and accelerating change throughout our society.

It can be argued however, we've largely focused on and elevated head based rational cognition over more traditional heart focused and intuitive gut based ways of knowing to our detriment. It seems if we can't explain something in head based objective terms, we denigrate or ignore it.

As we'll attempt to show in this book and in the research we'll share, this head based way of living and decision-making is out of balance and causing problems. And we suggest it has led to many of the modern global-social issues that have arisen today from decisions made without the benefits of multiple brain wisdom.

Just look around… in the world today, unfettered greed and lack of awareness of systemic consequences has led to:

- Environmental degradation
- Overpopulation
- Unbridled consumerism
- Stress and health issues
- Accelerated change without meaningfulness, just keeping up the pace
- Work life imbalance
- Social fragmentation; people are no longer connected in meaningful ways even though we have more ways to communicate than ever before

- Inflexibility, lack of acceptance and compassion leading to violence, wars, global conflict
- Unethical corporate behavior
- Collapse of financial systems due to either greed, lack of diligence or outright corruption

Our world is out of balance, out of alignment and we need to find a way to bring back some integrated wisdom to how we are living on our planet. We need a way to integrate our head based knowledge with heart-felt values and deep intuitions. A way that is strongly based on valid science, yet informed by thousands of years of insightful wisdom. And we'd like to suggest that way is mBIT.

So what is mBIT?

Ok, so what's this thing called mBIT we keep talking about, other than a rather cool sounding name?

[*BTW: we could have chosen a name that was far more staid and conventional, but funnily enough our hearts just couldn't get into anything that boring…*]

As the title of this chapter indicates, mBIT is where the neurosciences meet ancient wisdom. And it has everything to do with you and the way you experience living your life. Sure this is a **bold** statement, but stick around and see if you agree by the time you've finished reading this book.

We'll make quite a few bold statements along the way, but we have an abundance of scientific evidence to back up our claims. And that scientific evidence is often surprising, if not sometimes out and out shocking.

24

Point to your brain

For instance, take a moment now from your reading and point to your brain with your finger. OK, we're not silly; we know you probably did nothing of the sort and have just kept on reading. So just imagine having done it for now. If you are like most people reading this, you probably pointed or imagined pointing to your head. If you did, you'd be only partially correct.

I I **Cool Fact:** You have more than one brain. You have at least 3!

What? Yes! Three brains. And in order to help you appreciate your three amazing brains and how to use them, let's first clarify what constitutes a brain.

- Large numbers of neurons and ganglia, including sensory neurons and motor neurons
- Neural cells with inter-neurons; neurons re-entrantly interconnecting with other neurons
- Support cells and components such as glial cells, astrocytes, proteins, etc.
- Functional attributes: perceiving/assimilating information, processing information, memory storage and access
- Able to mediate complex reflexes via an intrinsic nervous system (i.e. it doesn't need the head brain to direct it, it functions even in the complete absence of the head brain)
- A chemical warehouse of neurotransmitters (those found in the head brain are also found in the gut and heart brains)

Clearly the brain in your head is the reference model for this. But where else do we see the very same criteria and structure present? Yes as we've intimated, in both the heart and the gut.

The heart brain

In 1991, Dr. J. Andrew Armour in his pioneering research on neuro-cardiology, introduced the concept of the functional brain in the heart. His work revealed that the heart has a complex intrinsic nervous system sufficiently sophisticated to qualify as a *'brain'* in its own right.

The heart's brain meets all the criteria specified above for a brain including several types of neurons, interneurons, neurotransmitters, proteins and support cells. Its complex and elaborate neural circuitry allows the heart brain to function independently of the head brain and it can learn, remember, feel and sense.

There are somewhere between 40,000 and upwards of 120,000 neurons in the heart brain. This number varies between people and can change across the course of a lifetime. The heart brain can also grow new neurons and make new neuronal connections. It can learn and change. This is an amazing fact that we'll come back to later as its implications are huge.

The heart brain secretes and uses neuro-hormones such as dopamine and norepinephrine, once thought to only exist in the head brain. Importantly, the heart also secretes oxytocin, commonly referred to as the love or bonding hormone, and concentrations are found to be as high in the heart as those in the head brain. Oxytocin has been shown to be involved in cognition, tolerance, adaptation and the learning of social cues.

Getting to the heart of the matter

Ok, so there's a brain in the heart. But what about intelligence?

Scientists John and Beatrice Lacey, in over 20 years of research, discovered that the heart communicates with the cranial brain in ways that significantly affect how we perceive and react to the world. The Laceys found that the heart has a logic that frequently diverges from the direction of the autonomic nervous system and appears to send meaningful messages to the head brain that affect an individual's behavior.

More recent research by Dr. Rollin McCraty and others at the Institute of HeartMath Research Center in California have shown that the heart has a powerful intelligence that is involved in processing and mediating a range of important and complex behaviors.

Of course, as we pointed out at the beginning of this chapter, for thousands of years across many esoteric and spiritual traditions, the heart has been seen as the intelligent center and source of emotions, values, courage and certain kinds of wisdom. So finally neuroscience is catching up, meeting and aligning with traditional understandings, but adding some very powerful new insights and distinctions. It also now provides objective evidence to what were previously unsubstantiated notions. Pretty damn cool and exciting hey!

| | **Cool Fact:** You have a complex and intelligent brain in your heart.

[BTW: *you know, even if you don't feel comfortable calling the heart brain a brain, you'll have to agree based on scientific findings, it's a complex neural network that displays its own form of intelligence. So, throughout this book we will use the terms 'brain', 'neural network' and 'intelligence' interchangeably and as best suited to the points we are making.*]

The discovery of the gut brain

If you visit your local Medical Centre and ask your friendly GP to tell you about the gut brain, (also known as the enteric brain), it's highly likely they'll tell you they've never heard of it unless they've had exposure to the specialized area of gastroenterology.

As a social experiment, we did just this to check how widely disseminated the recent re-discovery of the gut brain has become. Yes, you saw that correctly... *'re-discovery'*. Because the enteric brain was originally discovered over a 100 years ago, and then somehow got lost in the annals of medical science, so that today few doctors have learned about it in medical school. One of the doctors we queried was amazed to hear about this brain in the gut, and even more amazed when we showed her Dr. Michael Gershon's ground-breaking book *'The Second Brain: Your Gut Has a Mind of Its Own'*. Dr. Gershon is one of the leaders in the newly emerging field of neurogastroenterology, and his book is being hailed as "a quantum leap in medical knowledge" and that it provides "radical new understandings about a wide range of gastrointestinal problems."

But before we explore the newly released findings about the gut brain, let's take a trip back to the late 1800's. There, in a primitive laboratory in a bleak and fog enshrouded London, two medical researchers, Bayliss and Starling were uncovering details about the gut that were startling.

Working with dogs, they found that the gut could continue to function and digest food even when the nerves from the spinal cord were severed. They discovered a complex *'local nervous mechanism'* in the gut and attributed the ability of the gut to function autonomously to the intrinsic plexus of nerve cells and fibers that can be found throughout the visceral system. Over on the Continent, the German biophysiologist Ulrich Trendelenburg was finding detailed evidence that confirmed the work of Bayliss and Starling.

Then in 1907, an incredibly influential clinician, researcher and writer Byron Robinson M.D. published his monumental book 'The Abdominal and Pelvic Brain'. The book was over 700 pages long and contained more than 200 detailed illustrations of the enteric nervous system — the little brain in the gut. We've included one of his beautifully depicted images below so you can see what was lost to common medical knowledge. Because alas, for reasons unknown, the discovery of the gut brain went unheeded by medical schools and its evidence and knowledge disappeared into the dark recesses of history, only to re-emerge with the re-discovery of the enteric (gut) brain over the last 15 years.

| | **Cool Fact:** You have a complex and intelligent brain in your gut that contains over 500 million neurons and has the equivalent size and complexity of something like a cat's brain.

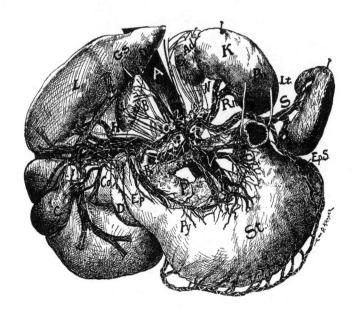

ABDOMINAL BRAIN AND COELIAC PLEXUS

Ok, that's our historical tour over for the moment. Fast forward to 1998 and neurobiologist and M.D. Dr. Michael Gershon has just published '*The Second Brain*'. This book is the culmination of over a decade of research and discovery by Dr. Gershon and his colleagues around the world.

Getting to the guts of it

The gut brain contains over 500 million neurons located in the sheaths of tissue lining the esophagus, stomach, small and large intestines, colon and bowel. It sends and receives nerve signals throughout the chest and torso and innervates organs as diverse as the pancreas, lungs, diaphragm and liver. The gut brain is a vast chemical and neuro-hormonal warehouse and utilizes every class of neurotransmitter found in the head brain. Major neurotransmitters found in the enteric brain include serotonin, dopamine, glutamate, norepinephrine and nitric oxide. According to Dr. Gershon over 95 percent of the serotonin used throughout the body and brain is made in the gut.

Brain peptides and endorphins have also been found in the gut. And here's an interesting fact, the gut is a large source of benzodiazepines, which are psychoactive chemicals used in popular drugs such as Valium and Xanax. Indeed, it's been found that in times of massive acute stress, the gut produces sufficient benzodiazepines to calm and sedate the head brain, down-regulating the cognitive and emotional stress response. Our gut literally shuts the head brain down so it doesn't freak out too much. This is also why sometimes we 'choke' with emotion. The gut brain co-innervates the esophagus and can stop the head brain from swallowing food during times of danger and high stress.

Diseases of the head brain also affect the neurons in the gut and heart brains. Patients with Alzheimer's and Parkinson's diseases often suffer from constipation due to the same damage to their gut brains as is occurring in their cranial brains. And according to Dr. Wood, chairman of the department of physiology at Ohio State University, there is a growing body of evidence that suggests that autoimmune diseases like Crohn's disease and ulcerative colitis may involve the gut brain.

The gut can learn

The gut brain can learn. Dr. Gershon tells the story of an Army sergeant who was a male nurse in charge of a group of paraplegics. With their lower spinal cords destroyed, the patients would get fecally impacted, so at 10:00 A.M. every day, without fail, the patients got enemas. At one point, the sergeant was rotated off the ward and his replacement decided to give the enemas only after compactions occurred. According to Gershon, "At 10:00 the next morning, everyone on the ward had a bowel movement at the same time, without enemas." The sergeant had nicely trained their colons.

A less colorful and entertaining example of gut nervous system learning is described by Dr. Wood. His evidence comes from Hirschsprung's disease, a genetic defect that deprives the last section of the colon of nerves. And without these nerves the patient can't defecate. According to Dr. Wood, a German surgeon successfully removed this defective portion of the colon from 300 patients and attached the adjacent piece to the anus. Except this piece of colon knows nothing about toilets, having lived its life further upstream. Yet within 18 months, it learns to go to the toilet successfully, indicating that the enteric nerves have learned a new function.

A final example of the effects of learning on the gut comes from research just published that describes how psychological and emotional traumas experienced over a lifetime such as the death of a loved one, divorce, natural disasters, accidents and physical or mental abuse contribute to adult irritable bowel syndrome (IBS). IBS is a chronic functional gastrointestinal disorder and research suggests it is caused by changes in the nerves and muscles that control sensation and motility of the bowel. According to Dr. Saito-Loftus from the Mayo Clinic, her research indicates that trauma may sensitize the brain and gut leading to IBS and suggests that the enteric brain learns and becomes over-sensitized by traumatic experiences.

Plasticity in the gut brain

The gut brain can also grow new neurons. Research reported in a recent issue of The Journal of Neuroscience shows that the adult human enteric nervous system can generate new neurons. Known as neurogenesis — the formation of new neurons — this is a powerful and cool finding, not least because it may soon be used to treat patients who suffer from gastrointestinal disorders caused by an absence or loss of neurons in the gut.

| | **Cool Fact:** Your gut brain exhibits plasticity and can learn, form memories, take on new behaviors and grow new neurons.

Evolutionary development

The enteric and cardiac brains are ancient in evolutionary terms. The enteric brain has been discovered in sea slugs, sea cucumbers and spineless helminthes (a type of parasitic worm). Sea cucumbers are echinoderms, a part of the chordate phylum, and have been found to have a sophisticated enteric nervous system.

When you think about it this makes sense. As life developed on the planet, the first organisms were single celled and then multi-cellular creatures that floated around in the ocean, moving towards food and away from danger. As they developed more complexity they needed a neural network, an intelligencing system, to process the information required to obtain, digest and assimilate food, to track for danger and safety and to move within their environment. This nervous system, linked to what in organisms like sea cucumbers is basically a tube designed for feeding and replication, became the enteric brain in higher organisms. It predates the head brain and central nervous system.

Development in the womb

Fascinatingly, the development of our brains during gestation mirrors evolutionary sequencing. As the fetus begins to grow, cells form that will eventually become the various brains. A neural plate first forms and then rolls into a neural tube. This tube eventually becomes the spinal column and goes on to generate the cephalic head brain. However, at the point where the edges of that neural plate meet and form the tube an outpoaching called the neural crest forms and this develops and begins the process of generating the gut brain as the crest derived cells colonize the developing gut.

So before the neural tube has elongated and rolled up to form the encephalon and ultimately the complete head brain, the gut brain has begun forming and populating the visceral region. Along the way, as the neural tube develops there is another outpoaching of what ultimately becomes the vagus nerve system and this forms the cardiac plexus and the innervation of the heart.

So in summary, developmentally the gut brain forms first in nature and in the womb, followed by the heart and then the head brains.

|| **Cool Fact:** The gut brain is primal. It develops both evolutionarily and in the womb before the heart and head brains.

Ok, you might be thinking "so what's so cool about that?" Well, read on...

So what?

The enteric brain is primal. It's primal in your physical development and it's primal to your very existence as a life form. Even more significantly, you will discover through mBIT that your enteric brain's functioning intelligence is primal to your very identity. It is the intelligence that is at the core of your deepest sense of self... your subconscious sense of who you are and who you are not. It's also the intelligence that is at work dealing with all core identity-based issues and motivations such as needs for safety, protection, maintaining boundaries, and what you will physically or psychologically internalize or reject. It's not much different to what a sea cucumber needs to do. In short, your enteric brain is primal to who you are. All right, we told you this was cool, and there'll be much more to digest on this in Chapter 2.

Knowing in your gut

It is known from ancient Chinese historical records that the great sage Li Shizhen, a famous physician from the Ming Dynasty, was a skilled medical practitioner with a great love for medical books. Now, it's said that in his home town there was a rival physician who was both incompetent and ignorant, but who owned a huge collection of medical books he used to show off his supposed wealth of knowledge.

As the story goes... one day at the end of a long and wet rainy season, the rival doctor ordered his servants to lay out his collection of medical books in the courtyard to dry. Pacing back and forth in front of the collection he primped and preened in an all too obvious display of both himself and his knowledge.

Passing through the courtyard, Li Shizhen stopped, loosened his clothing and dropped down next to the books. The physician, seeing Li Shizhen laying with his belly exposed to the sun, rushed over and asked, "Hey, what are you doing there?"

Li Shizhen responded, "I also want to get some sunshine for my books."

His rival asked, "But where are your books then?"

Li patted his belly and said, "All my books are in here."

Li Shizhen's humorous yet insightful rejoinder tells us a lot. It talks deeply about how true knowledge depends not on how many books you own, but on how much knowledge you have digested. Now isn't that interesting…

It is a common expression to talk about *'digesting an idea'*. You often hear people say things like "I need to digest that fact," "I can't swallow that notion." What's that about? Why is knowledge and understanding linked linguistically and metaphorically to gustatory experience? What's going on here? As you'll see, these are not just figures of speech.

Deep insights from neuro-linguistics

In the early 1970's, John Grinder and Richard Bandler based at the University of California, and drawing on work from a diverse range of fields including General Semantics, Transformational Grammar, Ericksonian Hypnosis and Systems Theory, created a powerful synthesis they called Neuro Linguistic Programming or NLP for short. Using the methodology of Behavioral Modeling (more on this below), NLP developed models for human communication, learning and behavioral competence amongst others.

Science Digest reported that NLP: "could be the most important synthesis of knowledge about human communication to emerge since the explosion of humanistic psychology… It may be the ultimate behavioral engineering tool."

NLP provides a set of models, skills and techniques for thinking and acting effectively in the world, through which you can change, adopt or eliminate behaviors in yourself and others.

Most importantly for us, one of the many principles that NLP provided is the insight that how people use language is a direct representation of what is happening in their neurology. As NLP points out, "very little of human communication is metaphorical, language is a literal description of deep unconscious process." What this means is that we can listen to natural and common expressions and unpack the underlying neurological processing represented within.

In terms of evidence for multiple intelligences outside of the head brain, common expressions such as:

- "Listen to your gut wisdom"
- "Trust the intelligence of your heart"
- "Follow your heart"
- "Use your gut intuition"
- "Trust your gut"
- "Be true to your heart"
- "My gut is telling me there's something wrong"
- "Deep in my heart I know"
- "Go with your gut response"

These expressions all indicate in their neuro-linguistics that intelligence, wisdom and intuition are occurring in the regions of the heart and gut. This is a powerful insight and backs up the message from ancient esoteric traditions.

Cognitive linguistics

In 1980, at the University of California, two young linguists published a book that rocked the field of linguistics to its core and created a whole new and exciting field called Cognitive Linguistics.

In their book, '*Metaphors We Live By*', Professor George Lakoff and Dr. Mark Johnson demonstrated that much of language and thought is grounded in metaphor and that metaphor and associated aspects of mind are embodied. What does this mean?

When Lakoff and Johnson claim that mind and language is '*embodied*' they are saying that human cognition depends on and deeply uses the sensorimotor system and emotions. An example might help explain this more simply. According to Lakoff a statement such as "She gave me a warm greeting" is based on an underlying conceptual metaphor that '*Affection is Warmth*', and that this cognitive concept is embodied in an actual physical experience and a corresponding neural network mapping. We literally feel and experience affection as warmth. So the linguistic expressions we use to communicate and make sense of our world are representations of our ongoing unconscious experience of the world. As Lakoff puts it, "We are neural beings. Our brains take their input from the rest of our bodies. What our bodies are like and how they function in the world thus structures the very concepts we can use to think. We cannot think just anything — only what our embodied brains permit."

[*BTW: Notice the similarity here to the powerful ideas from NLP, cool hey, science meets the progeny of behavioral modeling.*]

Lakoff and Johnson's insights and theories were initially controversial and at first hotly debated throughout the halls of linguistic and psychological science. However, in the intervening period since 1980, and with the use of brain imaging tools, neural network simulations and other powerful technologies, the ideas from Cognitive Linguistics have been largely proven out. Metaphor and cognition really is embodied. And in the case of our example above, researchers at Yale University recently found that subjects holding a warm cup of coffee in advance were more likely to evaluate an imaginary individual as warm and friendly than those holding a cold drink. This of course is predicted by the conceptual metaphor that affection is warmth.

| | **Cool Fact:** Thought and language are largely metaphorical and embodied. Our language deeply represents underlying neural and behavioral processing.

Ok, that's interesting, but really... so what? Well, here's what's really cool and useful about this: you can use what's called *'linguistic corpus analysis'* to unpack and infer the underlying neurological processes and competencies that are being referenced by the words people use. You can take common expressions and parlance, folk-wisdom if you will, and use it as a tool to guide behavioral modeling. And this is one of the many methodologies we've employed to create mBIT. Sound interesting? Well read on.

The power of behavioral modeling

In our efforts to properly research and develop mBIT as a practical suite of tools, we needed to draw upon more than just scientific findings from a plethora of research reports. We needed to field test our techniques for *'real life'* effectiveness. We also needed to uncover what really happens for people at the unconscious level when working with their three brains.

To help us with this, we reached for a highly pragmatic and penetratingly insightful field known as Behavioral Modeling. Classed as a behavioral technology for human performance, Behavioral Modeling is a methodology for identifying and codifying any form of human ability (thinking abilities, emotional abilities, physical abilities, and ways of being).

Behavioral Modeling has been used to great advantage by a wide range of corporate businesses, government agencies, sports teams, sales teams, market research companies, educational institutions, and of course behavioral researchers.

What makes Behavioral Modeling so powerful and insightful is that it is able to map a person's unconscious processes that often they're not able to consciously articulate themselves. This remarkable capability gave us a way to develop, test and refine our mBIT techniques with a direct focus on its behavioral effectiveness. We needed mBIT to be much more than a theoretical model, we wanted it to be a practical set of techniques that anyone can use to create powerful results.

So really, what's mBIT?

Ok, let's get back to the question we posed earlier, *'what's mBIT?'* (ah, so you thought we'd not remembered that question hey?)

Well, it's all about *mBraining* – using your multiple brains in an integrated and powerful way. mBIT is a set of concepts, principals and techniques for aligning and integrating your multiple brains. It's powerful. And it brings an incredible depth and precision to many other personal development fields such as NLP, Positive Psychology, Meditation modalities, Yoga, Kinesiology and the various mind-body disciplines. mBIT explains how and why many of their techniques work, when they do, and what's missing when they don't.

We have three separate intelligences operating in our bodies and these can end up in antagonism to each other, can have various patterns, habits and learned propensities. Knowing the core competencies of each of your brains allows you to leverage and communicate with and between your multiple brains in ways that previously may have only occurred crudely, by happenstance or by accident.

mBIT brings science to traditional wisdom, and utilizes behavioral modeling informed by the latest advances in neuroscience. We hope you're as excited by this as we are. And in the following chapter we'll roll up our sleeves and drill into the details of the mBIT framework and the prime functions of each of the brains.

mBraining

"Using your multiple brains to do cool stuff"

Chapter 2

mBIT
Prime Functions

The *'so what?'* test

While we love intriguing scientific insights, in the end what gets us really excited are practical and pragmatic applications in the real world. It only cuts the mustard if it meets our *'so what?'* test.

With what science was saying about our multiple brains, all we had to do was begin looking around and using our skills in NLP and Behavioral Modeling to start generating incredibly practical and impactful tools and techniques for change.

In our work with Executives in leadership positions, as well as working with Coaches, Educators, Counselors, Health Practitioners and Organizational Change Facilitators, the implications and applications of mBIT were right in front of us. It was everywhere we looked. Blindingly obvious once we'd been alerted and attuned to it; like the proverbial scales falling from our eyes, a huge number of peoples' professional and life issues were issues of alignment and integration between their multiple brains. We'd even go so far as to say the most significant and critical core issues that people face are due to how they are utilizing their three brains in ways that are inappropriate to their outcomes.

If someone is dealing with real life issues, what they'll ultimately be dealing with are issues of alignment or integration of identity, safety, boundaries, meaning, courage, action, connection and values. These are all functions of our three brains. As you'll discover in this chapter, each of your brains has a set of prime functions and unless you utilize these functions appropriately and in the correct sequence, you run into problems and difficulties.

So the significance of mBIT is that we now have powerful models and techniques to help align and integrate your three brains to produce wise decisions and actions in your life.

mBIT Guiding Principal: Prime Functions

In order to really fulfill the '*so what?*' test, you need to understand the prime functions of the three brains.

It's an important guiding principal for working with your multiple brains to understand that each of the brains has its own prime function. Each brain has a fundamentally different form of intelligence; they utilize different language, have different goals and operate under different criteria. In other words, your head, heart and gut have different ways of processing the world, of communicating, operating and addressing their own concerns and domains of expertise.

We discovered these differences through a process of examining divergent domains and looking for common factors and convergent evidence. Using behavioral modeling informed by the latest neuroscientific evidence, we analyzed data from:

- Neurological evidence from each brain network
- Functional disorders of brain regions and pathologies of the head, heart and gut regions

- Neuro-linguistic analysis of common sayings, folk wisdom and web based linguistic corpora
- Cognitive linguistic research on conceptual metaphor
- Esoteric wisdom from fields such as Traditional Chinese Medicine, Taoism, Enneagram, Spiritual Disciplines, Gurdjieff, etc.
- Research with clients and behavioral modeling of skills and competencies

What we found from all this is an overwhelmingly consistent pattern showing how these different brains have clearly distinct prime functions and underlying core competencies. In hindsight they are obvious and intuitive, which you as the reader will be able to validate in your own personal experience. So what are they?

mBrain Prime Functions

Heart Brain Prime Functions
- Emoting
- Relational Affect
- Values

Gut Brain Prime Functions
- Mobilization
- Self-Preservation
- Core Identity

Head Brain Prime Functions
- Cognitive Perception
- Thinking
- Making Meaning

[*BTW: Please note, we are not saying these prime functions are limited only to the particular brain they're associated with. Obviously the head brain, with its approximately 100 billion neurons is far more complex than either the heart or gut brains and is involved in all functions at some level. However, the evidence from our behavioral modeling work indicates that each neural network is a key or prime driver for the functions it's involved with. Note also that behavioral modeling is concerned with pragmatism and developing practical and usable models. The ultimate criterion for the validity of a model is whether you can achieve repeatable results through its implementation. What we have done is used the latest scientific evidence to inform our behavioral modeling efforts.*]

About the head brain...

In many ways the prime functions of the head brain are obvious, they involve the mental cognitive functions of logical thinking and include the processes of reasoning, perception and how we make meaning. Thought processes involve mental imagery, language expression, abstraction and symbol manipulation. The main job of the head is to intellectually make sense of the world and to provide executive control.

About the heart brain...

The heart is the seat of love and desires, goals, dreams and values. When you are connected to something you feel it and value it in your heart. When you hear that someone '*wears their heart on their sleeve*' you intuitively know that this does NOT mean that they are too logical. Instead, this is saying that they show their emotions, desires and intentions too obviously and readily.

If you say something is heartfelt, you aren't saying it's intellectually concise. And when you look at the language patterns of the heart, they express notions of love, connection, kindness and their converse. The prime functions of the heart intelligence involve salience, affection and relational issues such as a deep sense of moral rightness as compared to rule based ethics.

About the gut brain...

Due to its evolutionary history, the gut brain is responsible at a core level for determining what will be assimilated into self and excreted from self. It must determine what is required to maintain health and wellness in the system and decide whether molecules ingested into the stomach will be absorbed or excreted. Indeed, research has shown that more than 80 percent of our immune cells are located in the gut, and the enteric brain is intimately involved in managing immune function.

The prime functions of the gut are around protection, self-preservation, core identity and motility. Back when evolution was at the stage of complexity of sea cucumbers and worms, organisms only had a neural processing system of an enteric brain. This intelligence was used to detect threats and food in the environment and move away from danger and towards food. The gut brain maintains boundary detection and mobilization. In humans it is expressed as motivation, gutsy courage and a gut-felt desire to take action (or not).

</== Discovery Exercises: Exploring the Prime Functions ==/>

Time for some exercises for you to explore and discover the prime functions of your three brains for yourself and how they operate in your world.

1. As you read the following statements, work out where each of these is processed and experienced in your body, and which is the main operating intelligence/brain:

47

- I really need to think this one through
- I swallowed my fear and got moving
- I understand what you're saying more clearly now
- I really love that
- It was a gutsy and courageous thing to do
- What's the logic behind that?
- I really appreciate what you did for me
- I really want to forgive her
- I'm fed up with it, enough is enough

Did you notice that the different statements evoked different qualities of responses within you and that these responses originated in the regions corresponding with the appropriate brain?

2. Remember a time when you were:

- Gutsy and courageous

Take a moment and fully re-experience this. Now, remember a time when you were:

- Filled with love and kindness

Take another moment to fully re-experience this. And now, remember a time when you were:

- Logical and clear headed

Notice what's different in your subjective experience between the three scenarios. Notice the difference in *'what'* you are processing. Now notice what's different in *'how'* you are processing them. Finally, notice the location in your body of *'where'* you are processing them.

With even a moderate degree of self-awareness most people are able to sense the differences between these three experiences. If you are one of the small number of people who are not able to detect any difference then you will benefit greatly from the Awareness Exercises throughout the book.

3. Think of a decision you've made where there were several complex factors to consider but you made an effective decision anyway. Become aware of which of the intelligences you used to make the final decision. Was the ultimate decision based only on head logic? Did you go with your heart? Or was it your gut instinct that had the final call? And was there a consensus between all your brains?

    Now contrast that with a decision that didn't go well in the end. One where it seemed like a good idea at the time, but with the benefit of hindsight you now realize you made a poor decision. Which of your brains was involved in that and in what sequence? Which intelligence did you not listen to or attend to? Is there a difference in this situation compared to the successful decision?

Back to the so what - Implications for life issues

Now that you know there are three different neural networks in play, each with their own intelligence, and each with its own prime function, the significance of these findings becomes more apparent. In our experience, there are five major classes of issues that arise for people when their brains are not aligned or integrated fully. These are known amongst mBIT practitioners as mBIT Integration Constraints.

The five classes of mBIT Integration Constraints are:

1. When one intelligence is used to the exclusion of the others

2. When one intelligence swamps or overrides the others

3. When one intelligence is used inappropriately to do the job or prime function of the others

4. When one or more of the three intelligences are in conflict or antagonism with each other

5. When the intelligences are working together but are used in the wrong sequence

The easiest way to help you understand how these issues play out is to explore some real life case studies, with names and identifying details changed to protect anonymity, except in the case of public figures.

Case study - Craig C

On the surface Craig is a relatively successful executive. He occupies a senior position in a large organization and is valued for his insights and analytical skills. Craig came to us because, though his life appears to be successful on the surface, he suffers from an inability to form deep and lasting relationships both at work and in his personal life. In the work context, Craig is highly regarded by his peers and fellow team members, but during our mBIT coaching session together he admitted, "I think one of my challenges is I don't have a lot of passion as a leader. I'm not a very passionate person. To be honest, I don't think I really inspire my team very much. I'm really good at quickly seeing what needs to be done, but in many ways I don't seem to be included in the way the team relates together. I just don't feel this team spirit thing everyone talks about. I seem to be missing something, but I don't know what it is."

Craig's issue is a classic case of the head intelligence being used to the exclusion of the heart and gut intelligence. Without the use of heartfelt skills of connection, desire, and passion he is unable to build and form strong emotional bonds with people. There is no heart in what he does, or how he does it. People notice this unconsciously and can't relate to him easily. Inspiration requires heart based intelligence, which Craig lacks.

Craig also made the comment that, "Sometimes it's hard to get motivated. I know what to do, and I'm good at it. But getting moving isn't always easy." Once again, his over reliance on his preferred head intelligence means that he lacks engagement with the gut intelligence required for motivated action. A challenge for Craig is that without the integration with his heart and gut brains he can be prone to experiencing a sense of meaninglessness to life. With people like Craig, they can end up finding themselves living inauthentically, since the decisions in their lives are not connected to their own deep values. In our experience, people who live mostly from their heads at the exclusion of the other two brains can be very adept at rationalization and will come up with valid sounding reasons at maintaining their status-quo, but deep down when and if they manage to connect with their other two intelligences they get a sense that all is not right.

Case study - Jason T

What happens when one of your brains swamps or constantly overrides another? Jason T, a 36 year old Executive Assistant in a large multinational, requested mBIT executive coaching but his conversation soon turned to an issue currently close to his heart – Relationships. "I'm finding it hard to focus on my work these days, cause I just had a really tough break up with my girlfriend of the last 2 years. I'm starting to wonder if there's a bit of a pattern in my life. I've already been through 2 previous marriages. You know the saying *'love is blind'* — such a great saying, and I'm really beginning to see that maybe it's the truth. I meet a woman, fall in love and my heart tells me to trust her, to believe everything she tells me... and yet my head is there on the other side cautiously observing, and sometimes there's a small voice in my gut saying *'hey, watch out, there's something not quite right here'*. But what do you do? At the end of the day you have to go with your heart, it's a delicate thing, easily broken — but you have to risk it. And once you've taken that decision you just have to put it behind you and stop worrying!"

In Jason's case, he uses his heart's desire for love and connection to swamp or override the messages and intelligence of both his head and gut. It leads to a pattern of bad relationship decisions. He got married young, and his first marriage ended after 3 years when his wife left him for greener pastures. It didn't take long and he fell in love on the rebound and married after only one year. That marriage lasted a bit longer since after his first learnings, he tried harder and did all he could to keep it together. But he'd chosen someone he was not overly compatible with. His last relationship didn't even get to the marrying stage. With Jason we got him to realize the pattern of swamping he was doing, and helped him through mBIT processes to balance and integrate all the intelligences from his multiple brains.

Case study - Melissa R

Knowing when and how to trust your gut is a common issue for a lot of people. The gut has wisdom and can be deeply intuitive, but only within the areas of its prime functions. When you try to use your gut to do competencies that are the purview of one of the other brain's prime functions you can end up with serious problems in your life. As Rob Gordon says in the movie '*High Fidelity*', "I've been listening to my gut since I was 14 years old, and frankly speaking, I've come to the conclusion that my guts have shit for brains." Of course, if you use your gut brain inappropriately that's what you'll get.

Melissa R, a HR Manager in her mid 30's, came for mBIT coaching because of issues to do with compulsive behavior and over-eating. She opened with, "Something's wrong with me, I just can't seem to help myself. I just can't control myself. I'm not an obsessive person, or anything like that. It's just that I can't stop eating. If I see a box of cookies, I'll eat them all. But I'm like that in everything I do."

Melissa is someone who uses her gut brain to track for her values, something that would normally be done intelligently by the heart. Instead of heartfelt desires, she is filled with hunger for things, life and experience. She eats them up until she's had her fill. She arrived in our office, larger than life and voraciously ready to work on her issues. Salience and importance are tracked through her life via gut based functions rather than her heart intelligence. This leads to over-indulgence, compulsions and a challenge with control.

However, it's not that Melissa uses her gut intelligence to do every prime function. She certainly uses her heart to do connection, empathy and other heart based emotions. It's just that she uses her gut to determine what she wants in life and what is important to her (which is normally a prime function of the heart intelligence). The way her gut does this is through the sense of hunger and satiation. We asked her about this and she responded, "Yes! I really do feel loving and connected with people. And sure I feel that in my heart. But the funny thing is, I tend to flit from friend to friend. I can't stay with any of them for very long. It's like I get my fill, and then I need a break from them. I don't have a problem with that, but I know at times it causes issues with some of my closest friends." You see, Melissa really does connect and process relational affect with her heart brain, but what's salient and valued is processed as hunger. So she'll be larger than life when connecting with people as she tries to consume them and their friendship. But once she is satiated, as happens with a gut hunger, she no longer finds connecting with them important and she'll move on to her next compulsive experience. She's a classic example of using one brain to do a prime function of another.

In an Organizational context, the use of the gut to do heart based intelligence is often evidenced in the CEO who has a voracious hunger for growth and expansion. They typically have a high risk appetite with a strong bias for action and pursue mergers and acquisitions with a passion. They usually have the biggest office, the best clothes, the largest watch and most powerful car, regardless of miles per gallon. They use people like fodder, and as their direct reports burn out they replace them without much remorse. To them, humans really are resources to consume.

Case study - Francesca A

Francesca was a complex case and demonstrates the two integration constraints of conflict between intelligences and how sequencing between the brains is crucial.

Francesca wasn't happy. It's not that she was angry or upset about anything in particular, it's just that she was suffering from a mild depression and a sense of hopelessness. She explained, "I'm stuck. I feel trapped. I hate my job, but what can I do, it pays well, and I need to pay for the kids in private school, the mortgage and you know in many ways it's a good job in that it's a good company to work for, I have good job security and I'm working with a good team. But to be really honest, I'd rather be doing something else. I've always wanted to be a landscape gardener, but I just can't see how to get started and make a living out of that. It would take so long and be way too risky to quit my job and go out on my own with that sort of thing. I used to think I was so creative, but now I wonder if I really ever had it. I feel so dumb, just doing the same job day after day. And I used to think I was a real high achiever, but now... I don't know, I just don't know what I'm good at, if anything. Oh, other than paying the bills."

Let's unpack the syntax (the structure and flow) of Francesca's *mBraining* processes. In mBIT this is called neural syntax mapping. For Francesca, her head recognizes the need for economic security and so chooses a job based on reasons like good pay, good security, etc. However, her heart is not fulfilled and wants to pursue a more passionate endeavor. She would much rather be a landscape gardener allowing her to express her creativity. But her heart, gut and head are in conflict.

When thinking about this, her gut feels the insecurity of economic risk and survival issues and the fear this engenders prevents her from taking action on her heartfelt passion. This leads to cognitive dissonance and a diminishment of her core identity leading to even more gut anxiety. Ultimately this leads to a lower head based self-image and a loss of heart and self-confidence. This

55

mBraining - Using your multiple brains to do cool stuff

experience is unfortunately an all too familiar pattern for many people. As they get more stuck and depressed they spiral downward feeling trapped and unable to drag themselves out of the spiral.

[BTW: While you don't need to know the following, you might find it interesting to note that in mBIT practitioner training we technically document the neural syntax coding for this in two ways. The first is in a linear form such as:

[Hd] >> [Ht s-] >> [Hd s-] >> [Gt s-] >> [Hd s-] >> cycle back to [Ht s-]

i.e. [Head thoughts] leads to [Heart symp. -ve response] leads to [Head symp. –ve response] leads to [Gut symp. –ve response] leads to [Head symp. –ve response] loop back to [Heart symp. -ve response]

The second way to document this sequence is what is known as an **mBIT neural syntax map**, shown in the following diagram:

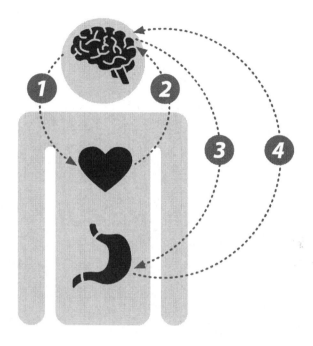

The antidote for Francesca involved designing and installing a new neural processing sequence using what we call the mBIT Roadmap and the mBIT Foundational Sequence, which you'll learn in detail in the coming chapters. In essence, what we did was get Francesca to first connect with her heart intelligence to deeply access her passions and values then move to her head intelligence to find creative and ecological strategies for manifesting these values. The next step in the sequence involved dialog with her gut intelligence to connect with courage and take action in a way that was safe, secure and smart. Finally she integrated back with her heart to inspire and link with the experience in a deeply valued way, and fully appreciate her sense of herself in taking action.

What do dreams know of boundaries - heart over gut

We'd like to finish this section on mBIT alignment issues by sharing a sad but fascinating story about what happens when your three brains are not used in integrated ways.

Amelia Earhart was a pioneering aviatrix who set numerous speed and distance records and was the first woman to fly solo non-stop across the Atlantic. Her inspirational story is depicted powerfully in the movie *'Amelia'* and tells of her amazing life and untimely death.

Amelia is famously quoted as saying, "Everyone has oceans to fly, if they have the heart to do it. Is it reckless? Maybe. But what do dreams know of boundaries?"

Amelia's passion, her dream and her ongoing heartfelt goal was to fly further and longer than anyone had ever done. She wanted to be the first woman to fly around the world and she knew that it would be reckless and dangerous. But she followed her heart, ignoring and downplaying her gut brain messages about risk, boundaries and danger. "What do dreams know of boundaries?" Whoa! Not wise or ecological to her life.

She is also on record as saying, "Please know that I am aware of the hazards. I want to do it because I want to do it."

'Want' is heart based; desire, want, dreams, passionate goals and aspirations are all mediated by heart prime functions. You see, she overrode her knowledge of the risks and recklessness of her goals, at a cost of her life.

In the final leg of her around the world flight, after having spent 32 tiring, dangerous and lonely days in flight, she was finally lost at sea, never seen again. A sad and tragic end to a beautiful and inspirational person. Beware the costs of not integrating your three amazing brains, or using them in ways that don't serve you.

Aligning your three brains: The mBIT roadmap

We've been talking all along about the alignment and integration of your three brains. However, we've found that for many people, this generates a bunch of questions like:

- "How do I know if and when I need to align my three brains?"
- "How do I get them to align and integrate if they are not already?"
- "What do I do if they don't want to align?"
- "Once I get them aligned, now what?"
- "Why should I bother in the first place?"

In order to answer these questions, we've developed the mBIT Roadmap. It is an explicit framework that outlines a clear developmental path when working with your three brains.

When to align

Before we get into the details of the roadmap, it might be worthwhile taking a short detour to summarize when you should align your three brains. While in some ways you want your three brains aligned and integrated everywhere, everytime, there are some contexts in which it is essential that your three brains are working together.

There are 9 broad contexts in which you want to ensure your brains are aligned:

1. Goal/outcome-setting

2. Decision-making

3. Problem-solving

4. Motivation and action-taking

5. Harnessing your intuition

6. Cultivating understanding and perspective

7. Relationships

8. Personal development, learning and behavioral change

9. Health and wellbeing

Signs and indicators you aren't aligned

And some of the clues that will alert you when your brains are not aligned or integrated are:

- You experience internal conflict within yourself between your thoughts, feelings and actions
- You've not acted upon your dreams, goals and plans
- You do unwanted behaviors or habits and don't know why or have difficulty in stopping
- You find it difficult to make a decision(s)
- Something within you is making it difficult for you to motivate yourself to take action
- You sabotage yourself from achieving your goals
- You chronically experience disempowering emotional states such as frustration, depression, anger, anxiety, etc.

The high level roadmap

Alignment and integration requires a number of steps and functions. It needs communication between your three brains and this must be performed in an optimal sequence. The three brains need to be brought into congruence and this is done through what we call the 'Highest Expression' of each of your brains' prime functions. All of this needs to be facilitated through a framework of wisdom.

Now, that's a lot of dense and deep information, so let's take a journey through the mBIT Roadmap to get a better understanding of how it works.

In summary, the mBIT Roadmap consists of:

Wisdom

Highest Expression

Creativity (cephalic brain)
Compassion (heart brain)
Courage (enteric brain)

Congruence

Communication

Communication

Assuming you have recognized the need and value of aligning and integrating your three brains, the first step is to establish communication with your brains and facilitate communication *between* each of the brains.

Remember, each brain speaks to you in different languages and in different ways as related to their prime functions.

In order to facilitate communication with and between each of the brains, you'll need to develop the skills in the upcoming chapters.

Congruence

This is about alignment between the brains. The flip side of this is to eliminate any conflict between the brains, and ensure they are in agreement and supporting each other in their functions toward a common outcome.

In order to facilitate this, you will need to work with NIE's (Neural Integrative Engagements) and NIB's (Neural Integration Blocks) — more about this in later chapters.

Highest Expression

Now that all of the brains are in alignment from the Congruence stage, you want to ensure each neural network is functioning in its most optimized state. We call this optimized state the '*Highest Expression*' of each brain's intelligence.

Note that there isn't a single, definitive Highest Expression for each brain that is universally true for everyone in all contexts. However, while there may be different Highest Expressions for different people and in different contexts, we lovingly propose the following generic yet generative set that serves as a powerful foundation from which you can start to explore, apply and work with the majority of life issues.

The Highest Expressions of the three brains are:

- Head brain – **Creativity**
- Heart brain – **Compassion**
- Enteric brain – **Courage**

[BTW: *the Highest Expressions of creativity, compassion and courage come from a synthesis of ancient wisdoms, behavioral modeling and practical experience. We didn't just pull them out of our gut brains! Oh, and we kind of like the fact it's the 3 C's model of Highest Expressions, makes it easier to remember…*]

Creativity

What we mean by this is not just lateral thinking or thinking outside the box. We mean the creative process by which you continually generate new lines of thinking that are authentic expressions of who you are. It's about how you bring forth and construct your own subjective reality and thereby create your world. It's about being conscious of how you choose to make meaning of anything. It's about coming from the consciousness of being at choice, of being the author of your life, and for living authentically regardless of your circumstances.

Compassion

Many people may use the word '*love*' instead of compassion for the heart brain's Highest Expression. We deliberately chose the word '*compassion*' as it involves both love and a manner of relating to yourself and others.

Compassion is made up of two words, '*co*' meaning together and '*passion*' meaning an intense or strong feeling. It encompasses both love as a virtue along with conscious intention for deep levels of social connection. Compassion transcends a mere selfish focus on self and activates a desire to alleviate the suffering of others. Though it's important to note that care and love towards others do share their origins with care and love for oneself.

As a form of loving-kindness, compassion is an active expression of love that connects, values, relates to and appreciates the oneness in us all.

Courage

As you've now learned, the prime functions of the gut brain are to physiologically maintain your sense of core identity (physically govern what is '*you*' versus '*not you*'), keep you safe from harm or danger, and mobilize you into action or immobilize you as needed (fight, flight, or freeze). Subsequently, the gut brain's Highest Expression of its innate intelligence can be called gutsy courage.

Courage is your ability to act in the face of fear. It's about you (identity) taking action (mobilization), despite being afraid (conditions of perceived danger, lack of safety, risk, threat of harm).

Without courage, we would not be able to act upon our dreams and goals. We would not be able to live an authentic life as we'd be too afraid to do anything unknown, uncertain, or unfamiliar. Without courage, change from the status quo would either be impossible or be by accident.

With gutsy courage, however, your gut brain is able to express your deepest sense of self by empowering you to act in ways that are true to who you really are.

Wisdom

This is the payoff for working with your three brains to get them aligned and integrated. This stage is about the practical applications of mBIT to the issue(s) you are working on.

Wisdom is not a specific thing but rather an emergent quality that is the result of harnessing the perspectives and insights from all of your brains when they are functioning at their Highest Expressions of intelligence.

The wisdom that emerges from aligning and integrating your three brains is now applied to your issue(s) in areas such as decision-making, action-taking, problem-solving, harnessing your intuition, reflection and learning, etc.

Remember that a major contributor to the emergence of wisdom at this level is not simply due to the Highest Expressions, but comes from aligning and integrating your brains in an optimally effective sequence i.e. the mBIT Foundational Sequence (coming up in Chapter 4).

Wrapping it up

So in summary, the mBIT Roadmap is a simple yet powerful framework for aligning and integrating your three brains. It enables you to quickly harness their intelligence for wiser and authentic living at your highest level of being.

The mBIT Roadmap provides a structure for the process of:

1. Establishing communication with your three brains

2. Aligning them so each is fulfilling its prime functions congruently as appropriate to the task-at-hand

3. Ensuring each is operating from its Highest Expression, and

4. Applying those Highest Expressions for greater wisdom in decision-making and action-taking

With all that now explicitly outlined, in the following chapter, we'll continue to explore the next level of distinctions needed to work with your three brains. You'll learn about each brain's detailed core competencies through which they operationalize their prime functions and you'll learn about the two modes in which your brains can operate.

mBraining

"Using your multiple brains to do cool stuff"

Chapter 3

Core *mBrain* Competencies

The mBIT Roadmap gives you a simple yet powerful structure to align, integrate and apply your three intelligences to practically any issue or goal. The rest of the chapters in this book step you through each stage on the roadmap in more detail. Before we can do that however, we need to introduce you to an additional set of distinctions we affectionately call '*the mBIT core mBrain competencies*' that provide you with a remarkable degree of precision and insight when working with your multiple brains.

The mBIT core *mBrain* competencies

Understanding the core *mBrain* competencies helps you quickly recognize how each brain is fulfilling its prime function via manifested behaviors. You'll then be able to discern if those behavioral expressions are optimizing or detracting from your ability for wise living and overall wellbeing. If each or any of your brains are operating in suboptimal states, you'll know what needs to be facilitated within yourself so each brain can fulfill its prime function at the highest level.

We want to alert you up front that there's a fair amount of technical information in this chapter. We'll do our best to keep it easy to understand and digest. And while you don't need to know all the details of the technicalities behind the core competencies framework to work with it, you do need to know the main organizing principles underlying the core competencies; especially if you want to have precision when facilitating yourself or others along the mBIT Roadmap.

The value of having even a small bit of technical understanding can be best explained by analogy. Imagine two people; one person who knows almost nothing about how their computer works compared to someone who at least knows the basic workings of how computers store and process data.

The first person can still use their computer, however only at a very basic level. In contrast, the second person understands that a computer has a hard disk with a certain memory storage size, working memory (RAM) that does not permanently store things, and that their computer can process digital information in a multitude of forms such as text, numbers, images, graphs, sounds and music, etc.

With this knowledge, the second person is able to not only do more with their computer but also do things quicker, easier and more enjoyably. The person without this knowledge would not realize they needed to save their work before finishing, that their work was retrievable in the future because it was stored, or that they can also create, store and manipulate photos, images, movies, sounds and music.

The first person would be amazed to see the second person watching a movie or listening to music on their computer. And while the first person would be able to do this once they became aware of the capability, they would still be limited to just those functions because they don't really understand how computers can do all this and more. The second person has many more choices and much more potential for working with their computer to productive ends.

Similarly, by understanding some of the basic physiological principles that underpin how your brains operate will provide you with a much greater capacity for working with them. For instance, now that you know about the prime functions of each brain from the previous chapter, doesn't it make a difference to how you relate to each brain and how much more insightfully you can work with them?

So relax, it's easy

We'd like to re-state that you don't need to know every detail in what's about to follow. Just as how in our example the second person didn't need to be a full blown computer techno-geek to use their computer well, they only needed to know some key principles of how their computer works in order to work with it effectively.

With that in mind, you may wish to skip over some of the more detailed technicalities in this chapter. We are providing them for those '*neuro-techno-geeks*' like us who do like technical content. What's important, though, is you understand the main principles behind the core *mBrain* competencies so you can work with them effectively. These will be highlighted for you so you can quickly digest them in case you skim over the more detailed content.

Ready? Ok, here we go...

The role of your autonomic nervous system

In order to work effectively with your three brains, it helps to understand the role of your Autonomic Nervous System (ANS) and how it affects the quality of the way your brains function. For example, your heart brain may be attempting to fulfill its prime functions in a particular situation by emotionally expressing either sadness or joy. These are two very different expressions that are based on the same prime function. What accounts for the difference? And what can we do to shift from a debilitating expression to a more empowering one? To answer these questions, we need to look to your ANS.

Your nervous system has two major divisions, the voluntary and the autonomic. The Voluntary System is mainly concerned with movement and sensation. The Autonomic Nervous System on the other hand is responsible for control of involuntary and visceral bodily functions. The functions it controls include:

- Cardiovascular
- Respiratory
- Digestive
- Urinary
- Reproductive functions
- The body's response to stress

It's called *'autonomic'* because it operates largely automatically and outside of conscious control. It's divided into two separate branches — the sympathetic and parasympathetic. These two branches work in a delicately tuned, reciprocal and (usually) opposing fashion. Simplistically, the sympathetic system can be considered to be the *'fight or flight'* system. It allows the body to function under stress and danger. The parasympathetic system is the *'feeding and fornicating'* arm. It controls the vegetative functions of feeding, breeding, rest and repose. The parasympathetic system also provides constant opposition to the sympathetic system to bring your total system into balance or homeostasis.

In times of danger or stress, the sympathetic system, which has a very fast onset and response, kicks in and gets you moving to handle or resolve the situation. The slower acting parasympathetic system begins to operate after the danger has passed, and brings you back to normalcy. Without the opposing function of the parasympathetic system your body would stay amped up, burning energy and fuel and eventually exhaust itself.

[BTW: an easy way to remember which of the two systems is which, is to remember that 'para' means beside or beyond, and therefore the parasympathetic system works beside or beyond the sympathetic to bring it back to alignment. So just remember, sympathetic does fight/flight and the parasympathetic kicks in beyond the stress to bring you back to normal.]

Why is this important?

The reason you want to know about the sympathetic and parasympathetic systems is because they innervate the heart, gut and head. There are major connections between the head brain hemispheres, the cardiac brain, the enteric brain and these sympathetic and parasympathetic arms of the ANS. And as the two ANS components work in opposing ways, the dominance of one or the other leads to very different modes of processing throughout our multiple brains.

In the gut, parasympathetic activity enhances intestinal peristaltic movement promoting nourishment during quiescence, whereas sympathetic activity inhibits such activity during times when physical exertion requires catabolic (energy) mobilization. Parasympathetic activity generally slows the heart, whereas sympathetic activity accelerates it.

You'll notice here that a powerful functional principle of opponent processing is operating for autonomic control across your total system. Your brains can function in ways that are sympathetic dominant, parasympathetic dominant, or some combination of the two, but that each of these systems typically opposes the other. You can see this opponent processing clearly at work by examining details of what each system activates.

Sympathetic activation

Activation of the sympathetic nervous system has the following effects:

- Dilates the pupils and opens the eyelids
- Stimulates the sweat glands
- Dilates the blood vessels in the large skeletal muscles
- Constricts the blood vessels in the rest of the body
- Increases heart rate
- Relaxes and opens up the bronchial tubes of the lungs
- Contracts the sphincter of the bladder and the bladder wall relaxes
- Shuts down and inhibits the secretions in the digestive system
- Can lead to involuntary defecation
- Is associated with Right Hemisphere activation and dominance in the head brain

Parasympathetic activation

Activation of the parasympathetic nervous system has the following effects:

- Constricts the pupils
- Activates and increases the secretion of the salivary glands
- Decreases heart rate
- Stimulates the secretions of the stomach
- Constricts the bronchial tubes and stimulates secretions in the lungs
- Stimulates the activity of the gastro intestinal tract
- Is involved in sexual arousal
- Is associated with Left Hemisphere activation and dominance in the head brain

[BTW: *For those readers who have studied NLP, notice that the activation effects above are important sensory cues and can be used to refine your calibration of another person and allow you additional distinctions about which arm of the autonomic system is activated.*]

So what?

The really interesting thing about these sympathetic and parasympathetic activation processes is that while they normally operate in opposition to each other, they don't always have to. In certain circumstances they can operate in patterns where one, the other or both are dominant in chronic patterns. What you'll also see shortly is that when your brains are operating in sympathetic or parasympathetic dominance, they have access to differing psychological qualities and core competencies.

ANS Balance

parasympathetic ---→ ←--- *sympathetic*
parasympathetic ----------→ **sympathetic**
parasympathetic ←--------- *sympathetic*
parasympathetic ←--- ---→ **sympathetic**

Physiological coherence - balance between the systems

The diagram above summarizes the four modes that your system can operate in. In the top mode, when your two systems are in balance and harmony, when you are in a powerful state known as physiological coherence (more on this coming up in the next chapter), you are able to respond optimally to the world. This mode is connected with feelings of joy, happiness, peace and relaxation.

Sympathetic dominance

In the next mode, your sympathetic system is dominant. This is the stress and danger response and in this mode you have access to competencies that typically serve you to respond via fight and flight processes such as anger, aggression, defensiveness and avoidance. It can be linked to lifestyle patterns of stress, such as taking on too much work, or worrying excessively about things you can't control.

Parasympathetic dominance

In the third mode, your parasympathetic system is dominant. As we've seen above, this is the mode that quietens and settles your neurophysiology. It's normally designed to bring you back to homeostasis after a sympathetic dominant experience. However, in certain circumstances parasympathetic dominance can be chronically activated and lead to withdrawal, depression, despair and down regulation of all your vital functions. People in this state have essentially given up and are living with a sense of helplessness and hopelessness. Poor diet, toxic metals and chemicals in our food, water and air can lead to issues of parasympathetic dominance.

Parasympathetic over-dominance can also activate in acute stress situations as an overreaction to an intense sympathetic response, and lead to what is called parasympathetic rebound. This leads to the *'freeze'* response and in really extreme cases can cause the heart to stop completely and result in death. This is what causes people to literally die of fright, fear and shock.

Mixed dominance

In some cases, a person can have both sympathetic and parasympathetic systems operating in high states of activation. When these are in relative balance, the snapshot that the person presents is somewhat similar to the first mode described above. However, with this mixed dominance mode, the system is in what's called a *'meta-stable state'* and can flip rapidly from one state to the other. The two systems are in effect maxed out and fighting one another. So the dominance can rapidly oscillate from one extreme to the other.

Some researchers suggest this mode may be associated with bipolar disorder and involve rapid changes from a manic phase to deep depression. Certainly this mode is not a healthy one and is representative of diminished control in the system.

I I **Cool Fact:** The sympathetic and parasympathetic dominance of your ANS controls the operating modes of your three brains and influences the core competencies they evince.

Finding the *mBrain* Core Competencies

Ok, let's recap. The latest advances in neuroscience have uncovered we have three intelligent neural networks and these brains can operate in sympathetic or parasympathetic dominated modes. As highlighted in Chapter 2, armed with these insights and using them to inform the process of behavioral modeling we looked for convergent evidence across multiple divergent domains in order to codify how our multiple brains communicate, integrate and function to generate our reality.

We discovered that each brain has a series of prime functions and that these are operationalized through a set of core competencies for each brain. As you'll see, because of the ANS involvement in how the brains operate, we also found that the competencies grouped naturally together along the dichotomous axes of sympathetic versus parasympathetic dominance and the balance of the two. Once we put these competencies into an organized structure, we were stunned with what was explicitly displayed before us.

The evidence suggested that the core competencies associated with and leveraged by each brain are:

Heart Brain - Core Competencies

Predominantly Parasympathetic	<<	Balanced/Coherent	>>	Predominantly Sympathetic
Emotional Numbness	<<	**Peace/Forgiveness**	>>	Anger
Despair	<<	**Hope**	>>	Desperation
Sadness/Sorrow	<<	**Joy**	>>	Delirious/ Manic/Hysterical
Blind Trust	<<	**Trust**	>>	Distrust
Loneliness	<<	**Connection**	>>	Guarded
Emotionally Unaffected	<<	**Appreciation/ Gratitude**	>>	Obligation
Uncaring /Apathy	<<	**Compassion**	>>	Vengefulness
Emotionally Disengaged	<<	**Equanimity/ Emotional Security**	>>	Jealousy/Envy/ Emotional Insecurity
Indifference	<<	**Love**	>>	Hate
Self-focused	<<	**Generosity**	>>	Greed/Avarice
Emotional Blindness	<<	**Emotional Truth & Wisdom**	>>	Fickle Heart/ Lying Heart/ Emotional Deceit

Aimlessness	<<	**Passion** **(Dreams/Aspirations** **/Values/Purpose)**	>>	Obsession

Gut Brain - Core Competencies

Predominantly Parasympathetic	<<	Balanced/Coherent	>>	Predominantly Sympathetic
Lust	<<	**Hunger/Satiety**	>>	Disgust
Sedation/ Hibernation	<<	**Action/Gut** **Motivation/Drive**	>>	Impulsiveness
Habit/Habituation	<<	**Will-Power**	>>	Compulsion/Urges
Fear- Freeze/Withdrawal	<<	**Courage**	>>	Fear-Fight/Flight (note: caveat sympathetic rebound for freeze)
Lethargy/Depression	<<	**Relaxed/Calm**	>>	Anxiety
Self Preservation	<<	**Wellbeing**	>>	Self Damage
"Dumb shit"	<<	**Gut Intuition**	>>	Gut Turmoil

Head Brain - Core Competencies

Left hemisphere (Parasympathetic)	<<	Balanced/Coherent	>>	Right hemisphere (Sympathetic)
Orienting Through Time	<<	**Being Present**	>>	Atemporal
Dissociation	<<	**Meta Consciousness/ Meta Cognition**	>>	Subjective Reality
Singular Reality	<<	**Balanced Perspective/ Integrated View**	>>	Simultaneous Multiple Realities
Mental-Looping	<<	**Flow States**	>>	Mental/Subjective Jumping
Convergent Thinking	<<	**Creativity**	>>	Divergent Thinking
Fixation	<<	**Curiosity**	>>	Mentally Scattered
Logical-Structured Learning	<<	**Transformational/ Generative Learning**	>>	Survival/ Streetwise Learning

[BTW: Note that we are not suggesting that these competencies and states are the only ones each intelligence is controlling and manifesting. Humans are incredibly complex and adaptive creatures and can pretty much generate almost any behavior they desire in a multitude of ways. It is always possible to use a tool inappropriately and so we don't deny the potential for someone to have learned to use one of their neural networks in ways that is not usual and even not optimal for that neural network. However, the list above is what we found from common-factor analyzing the results of our behavioral modeling and the research evidence. We would *like to suggest these are the competencies that are core to each intelligence in the sense that they cohered out of the evidence and that at minimum, this is what each brain does. And we'd also like to suggest from our experience that more often than not, these are the key states and competencies pragmatically useful for generative change.*]

Linking back

Let's now integrate your learnings by linking these core competencies back to the mBIT prime functions so you can get a strong sense of how the functions are operationalized through the competencies listed above. Once we've done that we'll move onto a whirl-wind tour through some of what we think are the coolest and most impactful pieces of evidence we've uncovered in our research. We'll also zoom into some examples of how to use the core competencies and a case study so you can see how they play out in real life. Sound good?

As you remember, one of the prime functions of the heart intelligence is relational affect. This is about deeply connecting with people, and the states and heartfelt emotions associated with that. Looking at the list of core competencies above for the heart, can you see how a number of them represent the competencies, skills and states required to perform relational affect and connection? Competencies such as trust, connection, appreciation and compassion are obviously all key to building intimate and meaningful relationships. And conversely, the sympathetic dominant competencies of distrust, guardedness, vengeance and jealousy destroy positive heart connection and lead to damage of close relationships. (And aren't some people really competent at that?)

With the gut, a really important prime function is mobilization. Notice how hunger, drive, courage and will-power are all part of how you achieve movement in your life. It can require guts to take action, especially in fearful or uncertain situations. On the other side, the parasympathetic competencies of sedation, freezing, lethargy and withdrawal can keep you stuck in situations to your detriment.

If we turn now to the head, one of the prime functions is obviously thinking and I'm sure you'll recognize how creativity, balanced perspective and meta-consciousness are required for optimal thinking about life. When one or all of these competences are missing or performed unskillfully, you'll see that your thinking can end up muddled or out of synch with reality, causing you major issues and headaches.

So how can you use this?

To fully appreciate the value of knowing about the core *mBrain* competencies, it helps if you recognize they're more than just a list. The competencies are a navigational map, and as a map they're a tool to help you know what you need to facilitate within yourself (or others) to effectively align your multiple brains at high levels of functioning.

As a diagnostic tool

Used as a diagnostic tool, the competences help you discern:

- Which brain is at the center of your issue, or how all your brains are either supporting or conflicting with each other
- Whether that brain's behavioral expression is overly sympathetic or parasympathetic, and therefore what mode is required to balance it back into a more optimized, coherent state

- What solutions will and won't work for you given the mode your brains are functioning in
- What should be the ideal or more coherent behavioral expression of each brain from which to better deal with your issue

As an alignment tool

Used as an alignment tool, the competencies help you to determine:

- What combinations of behavioral expressions across all brains prevent or enable alignment and integration
- What combinations of ideal or more coherent behavioral expressions for each brain enable you to address your issue more wisely, effectively and authentically

How does this work?

So how can you use the core competencies framework to do all of this? First of all when you look at the listings they're sorted into their related neural networks. By identifying which of the competencies most matches your subjective experience, related to the issue you are working on, you will quickly know three things:

1. Which brain(s) is expressing it's intelligence in relation to your issue

2. The subsequent set of prime function(s) that are in play

3. The mode (sympathetic, parasympathetic or coherent /balanced) in which the competency is being expressed

How do you know this last point? Because the competency listings are laid out in the order of:

[over-dominance of parasympathetic] **<< [coherent/balanced state]** **>>** [over-dominance of sympathetic], (reading from left to right).

Once you have identified the above, this now informs you about:

- What solutions will work for you or not (e.g. you cannot ask someone who is in an overly parasympathetic fear-freeze response to start taking action and doing something different)
- What is needed to move toward a more coherent balanced state of functioning (e.g. in the previous example above, you will need to gently engage their sympathetic system first)
- What is the idealized coherent-balanced state you are after as a benchmark goal (i.e. the center competency listed in the grouping you are working with)

The core *mBrain* competency listings are also laid out in a general flow of sequence. This layout enables you to plot out a possible developmental path for yourself (or others) by seeing if the progression of coherent-balanced states would be useful for you to embody in your daily living.

Now let's examine a Case Study example from our action research to see how all this plays out in the world at large.

Case Study - Mary J

Twenty-three year old Mary J came reluctantly for mBIT coaching at the instigation of a good friend. Mary's issue was that she simply couldn't get motivated in life, she was aimlessly drifting and saw no point to activities such as goal setting and life planning even though her friend was pushing her to try and make more out of her life.

Exploring the background of Mary's life, it turned out that several years before she had suffered intense rejection from her father when he fell in love and married a new partner who was jealous, controlling and resentful of his close relationship with his daughter. To compound the issue, Mary's father was a sole parent who'd brought Mary up by himself after Mary's mother died when she was six.

In a separate background information check with Mary's friend, she elaborated, "Mary has always been the apple of her father's eye and up until this new woman, he has meant everything to her, but after the marriage, thanks to this manipulative woman, he took away his love and started being harsh and distant with Mary. Poor Mary, she's so heart-broken by her Dad and I really feel she's been quite damaged in her self-esteem. I'll tell you, her ability to connect with men is gone. But it's more than that, she just doesn't seem to connect with life anymore. She used to be so motivated. She had plans for her life. She's such an intelligent person and was going to Uni, going to have a career. But since her Dad got married, she just seems to be lost and drifting. She does nothing with her life. It's so sad, and I really wish I could help."

In exploring these issues with Mary, she agreed that since she was estranged with her father, she'd lost all motivation in life and in particular given up on her dreams, goals and purpose. In discussion on the subject she stated, "I can't find anything I want to do with my life. I really don't see the point of having a purpose. I mean, what's the point." Mary readily agrees she is doing nothing with her life and is aimless. Compounding Mary's issue is that since the problem

84

began, her weight has ballooned and she focuses on food and comfort eats to her detriment.

Applying the core competencies framework, it becomes easy to see that the main competencies that relate to Mary's situation are heart-based:

1. **Love** - Connection, closeness, bonding

2. **Passions** - Values, dreams, goals, purpose

Her heart brain, in being triggered into a strong parasympathetic dominance or negative state associated with the first competency (love and connection) has lost the ability to perform the balanced/coherent aspect of the second (passions and values). Suffering from the loss of love and connection has resulted in an *mBraining* state in which she now has no *'desire'* to attend to values, dreams and purpose. From an mBIT perspective, this is not at all surprising.

If the intelligence that is responsible for the two competencies is put into a negative spiral (in Mary's case, her heart intelligence), it will do poorly at either of the skills. In essence, Mary has become *'closed hearted'* and has *'hardened her heart'* in order to protect herself and this strategy is congruent with the over parasympathetic dominant state of her heart brain.

Further analysis through the core competencies framework also explains how without the passion, dreams and desires to focus her, she now lacks motivation via her gut brain to do anything with her life. The framework also shows us how this parasympathetic dominance leads her into lustful states around hunger and why she then compulsively over-eats.

</== Discovery Exercise: Self-awareness ==/>

In this discovery exercise you'll learn to use the core *mBrain* competencies framework as a tool for self-awareness around how your brains are functioning in a real life context.

Awareness

1. Identify a goal, decision or issue you are having a challenge with.

2. Become aware of your subjective experience and take an inventory of what is occurring for you in your head, heart and gut.

3. Put a word label on your main subjective experience (e.g. sad, confused, scared, etc.). You may have several words to describe your overall state as one, two or all three of your intelligences may be actively expressing themselves regarding your issue.

Discovery

4. Look through the core *mBrain* competencies listings and find the competency(s) that match or come closest to matching your word label(s).

5. Note which intelligence(s)/brain(s) your issue resides in, and do a self-assessment on which prime function it is trying to fulfill. If your issue spans more than one brain, reflect on the nature of the conflict occurring between the two intelligences and the related prime functions. What insights can you glean here?

Diagnosis

6. Now examine which modes are more dominant for the competencies in play. Are you functioning more in the sympathetic or parasympathetic mode? Reflect on this. What are the implications for being too aroused/stressed or too inhibited/withdrawn? Is this a pattern for you in other areas of your life with similar issues?

7. Explore options for how you might be able to activate your arousal or relaxation responses accordingly to counter-balance the current behavioral expressions (competencies) in play.

Balance

8. Identify the coherent/balanced state that is in the middle of the set that your currently active competency belongs to.

9. Explore what this coherent-balance state would be like for you in experience. Use this as a benchmark for you to manage your sympathetic-parasympathetic systems.

The more fully developed '*how*' for fulfilling step 9 above can be accomplished through the use of the mBIT Roadmap and its related skills and techniques; and this is what will be covered in the rest of this book.

Remember that your three brains can each operate in four different modes of functioning:

*   Sympathetic dominant (arousal/stress states)

- Parasympathetic dominant (inhibited/withdrawn states)
- Meta-stable (both sympathetic and parasympathetic in overdrive and fighting each other)
- Coherent-Balanced (optimum functioning)

The core *mBrain* competencies framework enables you to quickly determine how each of your intelligences are functioning in relation to your issue, and what specific coherent-balanced state might be needed. The mBIT Roadmap is what will enable you to do something with this information by aligning and integrating your brains as they each function from optimally coherent-balanced states. When this occurs... magic happens!

So what's the evidence?

As you know, we poured over numerous scientific research papers, articles and monographs (well over 600 of them! And for a complete listing of suggested readings and references, in case you want to read them for yourself, see: www.mbraining.com). We also looked at the neuro-linguistic and cognitive linguistic analyses of the teachings from numerous spiritual disciplines, philosophies and hundreds of common sayings. We conducted action-research workshops working with live subjects and through Behavioral Modeling began to develop the list of core competencies of the three brains.

In this section, which you can skip over without losing any of the power of our findings and models, we're going to share what we feel are the coolest and most impactful of the findings. There's some really amazing stuff amongst this. Some things that made us go *'wow!'* So as we've said, if you're into *'neuro-techno-geek'* stuff, then roll up your sleeves and let's get going.

Heart Brain

>> Personality changes after heart bypass surgery

There's a large body of research that shows heart bypass surgery can lead to personality changes, including anger, mood swings, irritability, sadness, irrational behavior, lashing out, detachment, feeling emotionally flat, feelings of loneliness and a general loss of interest in goals or purpose. This is supported by copious anecdotal reports from bypass recipients, spouses and family members on support web forums where comments such as the following are common:

> "My husband just had a triple bypass and he is not the same person he was. There are a great deal of changes in his personality. I really don't know this other person, he flys off the handle for no reason and he does not remember things like he did before the surgery. He seems less interested in anything."

> "I too had a triple bypass and suffer from the after effects. The first couple of years I had outbursts in which I lashed out at my wife and children. I said horrid things which make my heart ache thinking about. I am now going into my ninth year post and things HAVE improved but I am a different man than before the surgery. My ability to feel joy has been damaged and I constantly live with the fear, not of my death, but of leaving my family in a bad place."

> "My husband had a bypass over 6 years ago. Afterwards, he became distant, irritable, lost joy in life, forgot how to laugh, did not make eye contact, and the worst, had rages on a daily basis over practically nothing. He began to tell lies, misrepresent reality, and generally find something to complain about on a

daily basis. His only love became food, much of which he wasn't supposed to eat, and he gained much too much weight. He lost all of the sweetness he had before the bypass."

There are also numerous reports of similar personality changes after heart attacks.

The message from the evidence: The heart is connected with competencies around its prime functions of connection, passion, values and emotional processing, and when it has suffered physical damage or degradation, it downshifts into negative modes. What you can see above is evidence of a stress/sympathetic response in some people, and a parasympathetic over-reaction in others.

>> Despair, depression, hopelessness and apathy are linked with heart disease

The emotions of despair, hopelessness, apathy and clinical depression are all associated with a strikingly increased risk of coronary artery disease, heart attack, fatal heart attack, and sudden cardiac death. There are numerous studies with huge cohorts that confirm this finding. In one study with over 63,000 participants it was found that clinical depression was significantly correlated with increased risk of cardiac events.

Research has also shown that high-grade carotid artery blockage is associated with depressive symptoms and that depressive symptoms are relieved by carotid artery stent placement.

The message from the evidence: The heart processes emotional experiences and chronic parasympathetic dominant competencies such as despair and apathy can do damage to the heart over long time periods. The fact that removing blockages in the heart via stents leads to removal of depressive feelings indicates that the heart is definitely involved in processing and regulating emotional affect. It is likely that the depressive symptoms are the heart brain's way of trying to let the head and gut brains know that something is not right within the physical heart. It's also attempting to down-regulate behavior via mood in order to conserve energy and oxygen to the constricted blood vessels within the heart.

>> Negative emotions such as anger and hostility can damage the heart or lead to coronary heart disease

In a converse manner to the above, numerous studies have shown that negative emotions of anger and hostility can damage the heart. For example in a large meta study, researchers in London comprehensively reviewed 25 previously published clinical studies of coronary artery disease risk in healthy populations, as well as another 19 studies of patient volunteers with existing coronary artery disease. Those patients who scored highly in terms of anger and hostility were nearly 20 percent more likely to develop new coronary artery disease or experience heart attacks when compared to the patients who had very low hostility and anger scores. This comprehensive review confirms the findings of earlier studies that chronic anger and hostility are associated with an increased risk of coronary artery disease and heart attacks, even when other preexisting risk factors are controlled for.

The message from the evidence: The heart is deeply involved in and impacted by the processing of sympathetic dominant emotions such as anger and hostility. It is not just a pump, but an intelligent processing system that is affected by the types of experiences, actions and emotions it is performing.

>> Suppressing anger can be harmful to the heart

A newly published study has found that heart disease patients who suppressed their anger had nearly three times the risk of having a heart attack or dying over the next 5 to 10 years. The study followed 644 patients with coronary artery disease and monitored them over a period of approximately six years. The results indicated a significant risk from how the subjects processed and handled anger.

The message from the evidence: A key core competency of the heart is peace/forgiveness and its sympathetic converse, anger. Over-dominance of the stress response of anger can do physical damage to the heart.

>> Low emotional intelligence and negative expressiveness are linked to heart disease

Research shows that facets of emotional intelligence such as decreased ability to use and regulate emotions as well as frequency of negative expressiveness are associated with increased incidence of coronary heart disease. In one recent study, fifty six patients with coronary heart disease and an equal number of controls with no indications of heart disease were assessed for components of emotional intelligence such as emotion perception, emotion regulation, emotion expression and use of emotions. The results demonstrated that facets such as decreased ability to use and regulate emotions as well as frequency of negative expressiveness were associated with a significantly higher incidence of coronary heart disease, even when other risk factors were controlled for.

The message from the evidence: The heart is involved in processing emotional intelligence and expression and when it is forced to process and enact negative competencies, it leads to damage to the structure of the heart.

>> Positive emotions are an antidote to heart disease

While negative emoting is damaging to the heart, the opposite is also true. Being happy, enthusiastic and contented is the best antidote to heart disease says a major new study. Karina Davidson, professor of medicine and psychiatry at the Columbia University Medical Centre, who led the study, suggested that the results indicate it is possible to help avert heart disease by enhancing positive emotions. The study involved following the health of 1,739 healthy adults over a period of 10 years. Positive affect from the experience of pleasurable emotions such as joy, happiness, excitement, enthusiasm and contentment was measured in the subjects. Those people with high positive affect were significantly less likely to suffer from heart disease over the period.

The message from the evidence: As the research keeps showing, the heart is not just a simple organ made of a pump and some plumbing, it is a deeply intelligent system involved in processing emotional intelligence, and the modes in which it consistently operates have long term impacts on its health. The research also shows the types of affective processing that the heart brain is involved with, such as pleasure, joy, enthusiasm and contentment.

>> Trust your heart - emotions may be more reliable when making choices

A new study suggests the adage *'trust your heart'* may be true for consumers. Research indicates that when making a decision you might be better off letting heart-felt emotions guide you. "If one buys a house and relies on very cognitive attributes such as resale value, one may not be as happy actually purchasing it," report the researchers from Columbia Business School, University of California and Duke University. They state, "Our results suggest that the heart can very well serve as a more reliable compass to greater long-term happiness than pure reason."

The message from the evidence: The heart has an intelligence and wisdom with respect to your values and what is true and important for you within your current world view. You can learn to trust it.

>> Heart awareness and intuition

A new study published recently in the journal Psychological Science, shows that intuition from hunches and listening to your heart can assist in decision-making, but the quality of this can vary from individual to individual. The research shows that trustworthiness of intuition is strongly influenced by what is happening physically in our bodies and how attuned we are to this.

To investigate how different bodily reactions influence decision-making, Dr. Barnaby Dunn, of the Brain Sciences Unit in Cambridge, England and his co-authors asked study participants to learn how to win at a card game they had never played before. The game was designed so there were no obvious strategies to follow and instead players had to follow their hunches. While playing the game, each participant wore a heart rate monitor and a sensor that measured the amount of sweat on their fingertips. Most players gradually found a way to win at the game and they reported having relied on intuition rather than reason. Subtle changes in the players' heart rates and sweat responses affected how quickly they learned to make the best choices.

Interestingly, the quality of the advice their bodies gave them varied. Some people's instincts were spot on and they mastered the game quickly. Other people's bodies told them exactly the wrong moves to make and they learned slowly or never found a way to win. Dunn and his co-authors found the link between hunches and intuitive decision-making to be stronger in people who were more aware of their own heartbeat. So for some individuals being able to '*listen to their heart*' helped them make wiser choices. According to Dr. Dunn, "What happens in our bodies really does appear to influence what goes on in our minds."

The message from the evidence: The heart has an intelligence and can attune to cues from the head brain, gut brain and the environment to make distinctions about subtle cues that would otherwise be ignored by conscious reasoning. The better the relationship between your head and heart, and the more you are consciously attuned to the messages from your heart, the better your intuitions will be.

|| **Cool Fact:** The greater your awareness of the signals from your heart the better the intuition, intelligence and wisdom it will provide.

>> Personality changes in heart transplant recipients

There is a growing body of evidence that recipients of heart transplants can experience marked changes in personality that parallel the personality of the original heart donor. These changes include attitude, temperament, patience levels, philosophies, tastes in food and music, changes in tastes in art, sexual, recreational, and career preferences.

In one study of 47 transplant patients, six percent reported a distinct change of personality due to their new hearts. In another study, Dr. Gary Schwartz, professor of medicine at the University of Arizona found definitive evidence of 70 cases in which recipients inherited traits of their donors. He stated that, "The stories we have uncovered are very compelling and are completely consistent."

One of the most widely known cases of a heart transplant patient who inherited personality changes from her donor is that of Claire Sylvia. She received a heart and lung transplant in the mid 1970's from an eighteen year old male who'd been in a motorcycle accident. None of this information was known to Claire due to strict privacy laws that prevented recipients from knowing about their donors.

However, some time after the operation, Silvia began having dreams about her heart's original owner and she developed new and intense cravings for beer, chicken nuggets, and motor cycles; all things she didn't enjoy or desire prior to the surgery. Claire's experience is documented in her biography '*A Change of Heart*' and makes fascinating reading as she describes how she went about finding her donor's family and learning that her new tastes and cravings matched exactly those of the original owner of her heart.

Other documented cases have been perplexing and sometimes extreme. In one case, a 47 year old man received the heart from a 17 year old boy and suddenly picked up an intense fondness for classical music. The boy whose heart had been donated was killed in a drive-by shooting, still clutching his violin case in his hands. In another graphic case, a 56 year old college professor received the heart of a 36 year old police officer. The officer had been shot in the face whilst arresting an unkempt, unshaven drug dealer. Sometime after the transplant, the professor became plagued with dreams in which he saw the face of Jesus, followed by a bright flash of light and then felt an intensely painful burning sensation in his face. At the time he reported his dreams to the researchers, the professor had no knowledge of who his donor was, or how the donor had died.

The message from the evidence: The heart has a neural network that can process experiences, store memories and is associated with interests, values, passions and aesthetic preferences and desires. When the heart is transplanted into a recipient, the heart brain and its '*personality*' and memories go with it.

There is a large body of scientific evidence that proves that cardiac neural networks can reconnect and be re-innervated by the autonomic nervous system in the months after heart transplantation. However, the research indicates not all recipients manage to reconnect to the brains of their new hearts, and some recipients can take years for the connections to occur.

This supports the idea that the personality changes some recipients experience are likely due to early and comprehensive reconnection of the heart brain of their new hearts to the central nervous system and explains how the heart can begin communicating information to the head brain leading to perceived changes in aspects of personality, passion and preferences.

>> Heart rate variability

Autonomic nervous system dysfunction is thought to play a significant role in emotional and psychological conditions such as anxiety, apathy, depression, phobias and Post Traumatic Stress Disorder (PTSD). Studies have shown that low Heart Rate Variability (HRV) is associated with these disorders. HRV biofeedback training in which subjects learn to adjust their breathing rate to a resonant frequency and thereby increase their HRV has been successfully used to reduce symptoms of these conditions.

The message from the evidence: The heart is intrinsically involved in the emotions/competencies of anxiety, apathy, phobia and stress and this shows up in measures of Heart Rate Variability, (which we will cover in much more detail in the coming chapters). When biofeedback is used to train breathing rate and thereby educate the heart brain to allow it to operate in a more resonant or coherent state, the resultant emotional processing and signaling between the heart and head changes. Learning to change heart rate and heart brain response changes emotional processing.

>> Neuro-linguistic evidence

Heart language is found in numerous cultures across the world and the heart as a soul/intelligence appears in almost every language and every corner of history. The Thai language has more than 500 heart language terms. The Lao people have so many common heart expressions that they are considered to be a *'people of the heart'*. The Lomwe of Africa also use heart language to express emotion and character, while the Llongots of the Philippine highlands speak of the heart as an organ of feeling. Heart language is found throughout Mexican, French, Italian, Chinese and Hebrew. Indeed, in Hebrew literature, *'people without heart'* translates literally to *'people without understanding'*.

So what's the evidence from English? Let's examine some neuro-linguistic evidence in English for the heart's core competencies. Here's a representative sampling of neuro-linguistic examples from common parlance:

- "Put your heart at rest" [peace]
- "My heart was filled with hope" [hope]
- "She lost heart" [despair]
- "It made my heart sing" [joy]
- "She spoke from the heart" [trust/honesty]
- "Our hearts were like one" [connection]
- "We had a heart to heart talk" [connection]
- "With heartfelt appreciation" [appreciation/gratitude]
- "She is soft hearted" [compassion]
- "My heart goes out to you" [compassion]

- "A heart burning with love and desire" [love]
- "I'll always hold her close in my heart" [love]
- "Let your heart be your guide" [emotional truth/wisdom]
- "Listen to the wisdom of your heart" [emotional truth /wisdom]
- "Follow your heart's desires" [passion/dreams/values]
- "It was my heart's dream" [passion/dreams/values]

The message from the evidence: What you can clearly see is that there are specific competencies that are expressed and presupposed both metaphorically and literally within these common examples from linguistic corpora.

For your own educational purposes, you might like to grab a pen and paper and write down as many heart based sayings and normal utterances you can think of. You might also like to start noticing *'heart language'* in everyday conversations, in songs, movies and the language you hear around you throughout the day.

Gut Brain

>> Effects of massage produce/release deep emotions, core identity issues and abreactions

Pierre Pallardy, a world-renowned osteopath, dietician and physical therapist, in his work on gut instinct and how to create harmony between the head and gut brains, relates how when massaging and manipulating a patient's abdomen, he frequently observes that deep-rooted emotions and traumas are released and surfaced. In Pallardy's opinion, deep abdominal work can at times be akin to the processes of psychotherapy and psychoanalysis. He claims that both Freud and Jung, the fathers of psychotherapy, used the technique of simultaneously placing their hands on a patient's head and abdomen during consultations and that there are records that Freud would massage a subject's abdomen during treatment. Pallardy describes in his own work how massaging the gut seems to tap into previously hidden wellsprings of the deep subconscious and can sometimes release lost memories and recollections.

In the fields of remedial and relaxation massage therapy it is common knowledge that massage of the abdomen and stomach can lead to strong emotional release and reactions. In our own massage training we were taught that we store a lot of emotions in our stomach and visceral region and that great care should be taken when massaging the gut. The trainers were adamant that work on this area should be done gently and for only a very short period otherwise strong emotional abreactions can occur in people who have deeply repressed or unresolved life issues. These insights were backed up during our research by evidence from web forums like massageprofessionals.com, in postings entitled *'Why do so many therapists avoid belly work?'*, where comments from massage practitioners stated that "Abdominal work is rarely covered in most basic massage courses because of the possibility of emotional abreactions… It is the emotional center of the body, and clients are very sensitive, or can even become embarrassed should they have an emotional release."

Additional evidence for the gut being linked to core emotions and identity issues comes from ancient Chinese Taoist practices. Chi Nei Tsang (CNT) is a specialist massage technique for the abdomen and internal organs that is derived from the Taoist tradition. Taoist philosophy maintains that memories of our deep emotions reside in the gut. CNT aims at re-establishing wellbeing and happiness by relaxing the belly. CNT associates emotions such as anxiety, fear, worry, and sadness with different areas of the viscera. For example, massaging the large intestine can help relieve negative emotional charges, and massaging the stomach can get rid of anxiety.

The message from the evidence: What this tells us is that if the gut was only responsible for digesting food, absorbing molecules and secreting waste then a deep massage would likely just lead to warm nice feelings in the gut or perhaps a good fart or two. The fact that massage therapy can lead to the release of intense emotional and identity issues, tells us that the gut brain is involved in far more than food and flatulence. It also indicates that emotions such as fear and anxiety are associated with gut intelligence.

>> Crohn's disease, gut response and emotions

Crohn's disease is a chronic inflammatory gastrointestinal disorder involving abdominal pain, diarrhea, vomiting and weight loss. During flare-ups of the condition it can be extremely debilitating. Research has shown there is heightened negative emotional response in people with Crohn's disease due to aberrant feedback from the gastrointestinal system that changes the intensity of feelings of negative emotions such as anxiety, disgust, fear and resentment.

It is well documented that patients in the active (flare-up) Crohn's phase experience more intensely reported emotions and that electrogastrogram (EGG) signal levels from their gut increase correspondingly. EGG is used to measure nerve signal activity in the viscera and is the equivalent for the enteric brain of what an EEG is for the head brain.

In one fascinating study, negative emotionally salient films were presented to participants with Crohn's disease in both the active and silent phases of the condition and their emotional and physical responses were compared to normal subjects. Physical responses were determined by measuring EGG, heart rate and electro-dermal activity. After each film was presented, the subjects also reported emotional intensity and valence. The results showed that only the active Crohn's group showed a significant increase in subjective arousal for negative emotions and a corresponding increase in EGG activity. The researchers concluded that aberrant feedback from the gastrointestinal system changes the intensity of feelings of negative emotions and that information from the gut appears to be involved in the capacity for fine tuning feelings.

Crohn's Disease sufferers also report that that the converse is true — strong emotions such as anxiety, disgust, stress, anger and resentment often send them into bad flare-ups. This evidence is backed up by research findings that visceral signals map onto head brain areas associated with emotion.

The message from the evidence: The condition of the gastrointestinal tract affects the gut brain and influences the emotions it is involved in expressing and processing. When we say that someone who shows little emotion in the face of danger has *'guts'*, we are literally describing how their gut brain is modulating their emotional response, and not just their mental discipline.

The electrogastrogram results support this idea since as patients with active Crohn's phase experienced more intense emotions, their EGG levels increased significantly. In contrast, there was no correlation between EGG levels and emotional arousal in the silent phase patients.

The evidence about the types of emotions that become exacerbated by active Crohn's also shows which emotional core competencies the gut brain is responsible for.

>> Liver disease associated with increased anxiety and phobic anxiety

It is well documented that liver disease is associated with an increase in anxiety and phobic anxiety feelings and behaviors, regardless of the etiology or cause of the damage to the liver. The liver is comprehensively innervated by the enteric brain and is also considered to be a key component of the visceral intelligence by healing modalities such as Traditional Chinese Medicine and along with the gall bladder is said to be involved in courage, decision-making and moods such as irritability.

The message from the evidence: The gut brain is involved in the competencies of courage and its converse anxiety. When components of the enteric nervous system are damaged, they are unable to function in a coherent manner and generate states to alert the head brain that all is not well within the system.

>> Personality changes of celiac disease sufferers

Celiac disease is an autoimmune disorder of the small intestine that leads to intolerance to gluten protein in the diet. Celiac symptoms include chronic diarrhea, cramping, bloating, weight loss and malnutrition. Celiac sufferers report changes in personality when they are living gluten free and not experiencing the symptoms of the disease. When impacted by gluten they are depressed, anxious and lacking motivation. When gluten free they are calm, relaxed, motivated and energized. As one sufferer reported on the online forum celiac.com, "Now I am calm and have clarity.....with a bit of sassiness! But also find I can be less tolerant of ignorance too. I have goals and maintain certain projects around the house that give me that sense of accomplishment… where before, I'd start and stop and not go back to it."

The message from the evidence: Personality and emotions are linked at a core level to the gut's enteric brain. When the enteric brain is struggling to cope with a diseased state in the gut, it cannot operate in a balanced state and therefore is unable to enact the competencies of motivation and action. The graphic changes in celiac sufferers from the active phase to when they are gluten free, shows just how impactful the enteric nervous system is in regulating core competencies.

>> IBS and anxiety

Irritable bowel syndrome (IBS) is a disorder of intestinal hypersensitivity and altered motility, usually exacerbated by stress. Research shows that up to ninety percent of people with IBS have a chronic psychiatric disorder, typically anxiety and/or depression. It is also associated with panic disorder and PTSD.

Several studies have provided evidence of abnormal autonomic nervous system activity in IBS, and the results indicate that IBS patients have greater sympathetic activity during both waking and sleep (a finding we'll come back to in the next chapter). Functional brain imaging studies have identified abnormal brain responses to visceral stimuli in IBS patients suggesting that IBS involves a dysregulation of the communication between the central and enteric nervous systems. This fits with the pattern of anxiety and hyper-vigilance that IBS sufferers display.

The message from the evidence: Once again we see evidence of the gut brain's core competencies around anxiety, lethargy and their converse calmness, wellbeing and energy. You can clearly see that the gut brain is intrinsically involved in regulating emotions such as anxiety, panic and some forms of depression. The research also supports the concept that autonomic balance is crucial to coherent operation of the brains and that when under stress by the internal or external environment, our neural networks end up in sympathetic over-dominance.

>> IBD and emotional helplessness

Inflammatory Bowel Disease (IBD), an inflammatory condition of the colon and small intestine, is sometimes associated with or precipitated by emotional abuse, stress and despair connected with extreme guilt, fear and helplessness. One study reported evidence that some sufferers can experience complete remission from the disease after separating themselves from abusive relationships and seeking counseling. As one researcher stated, "It is the sense of helplessness in coping with abuse that is identified as the trigger for their pathology."

The message from the evidence: The gut brain is deeply involved in core identity issues, and when a person suffers emotional and physical abuse, it impacts the patterns and responses of this neural network. Fear, helplessness, guilt and anxiety are all mediated by the intelligence of the gut. They are responses that send a message to the head and heart brains that all is not well at a core level and you need to do something to change your situation and your world.

>> Intestinal micro-biota, probiotics and anxiety

Our gut flora, also known as micro-biota (the millions of bugs and organisms in our gut) play a massive role in mediating our entire immune response. The human gastro-intestinal tract houses the bulk of the human immune system, between 70 to 85 percent of it. And this gut flora aids and abets our innate immune system by improving the function of our mucosal immune system and providing a physical barrier to invading pathogenic micro-biota.

There is now a growing body of research that shows that the micro-biota in the gastro-intestinal tract can influence emotions and behavior. Equally there's a huge amount of evidence that in turn, perturbations of behavior such as stress can change the composition of the micro-biota.

Further studies have shown that infection of the gut with pathogenic organisms leads to increased anxiety behaviors. And in the reverse of this, research has proven that probiotic bacteria (good bugs) have antidepressant effects and can help ease anxiety symptoms.

The message from the evidence: The enteric nervous system is intimately involved in managing the immune function of the gut, and is intricately entwined with the micro-biota populations used in the gut to aid digestion and wellness. A system that is out of balance and unwell leads to anxiety, which can be alleviated by ingestion of a dose of good probiotic bacteria. This evidence proves the gut is closely involved in emotional processing of anxiety and its converse.

>> Personality changes after gastric banding surgery

Gastric banding is a relatively safe and simple surgical procedure in which an adjustable band is placed around the top part of the stomach to constrict it and thereby limit the amount of food that can easily be ingested. Research on personality changes after gastric banding shows that recipients can experience a decrease in traits such as insecurity and sensitivity and a significant increase on obsessive traits such as orderliness and dominance. There is also a significant increase in exerting more control in their lives.

The message from the evidence: What a surprise that the gut brain, when it experiences massive constriction, becomes obsessive and feels the need to exert more control over the situation it finds itself in. I'm sure that if someone bound you tightly, you'd start obsessing and feeling the need for control, and you'd also have to down-regulate your sensitivity to cope with the constant pressure. In any case, you can see from the evidence that the gut brain is involved in regulating control, dominance, security and orderliness in your environment and life. This aligns with the prime functions of the gut intelligence.

>> Anterior cingulate cortex, insula, cognitive dissonance and motivation

The enteric nervous system connects to the head brain via the vagus nerve and neurophysiological research has conclusively demonstrated that gut brain signals from the vagus are processed in two major regions of the head brain — the Anterior Cingulate Cortex (ACC) and the Insula.

The ACC is strongly involved in motivation, conflict monitoring, error detection, reward anticipation, decision-making, empathy and emotion. It is also involved in regulating blood pressure and heart rate (the heart brain also connects to the head via the vagus nerve). In addition, the ACC is critically involved in processing the emotional component of visceral pain sensation. Visceral hypersensitivity is a characteristic of Irritable Bowel Syndrome and other functional gastro-intestinal disorders. Studies also show that enteric stimulation and gut hypersensitivity cause increased activity in the ACC as measured by brain imaging, while at the same time causing an associated increase in anxiety and hypervigilance.

The Insula on the other hand is believed to process convergent information to produce an emotionally relevant context for sensory experience. The anterior part of the Insula is related to olfactory, gustatory and visceral autonomic function. As an example, people

107

with Irritable Bowel Syndrome have been shown to have abnormal processing of visceral pain in the Insular.

Further evidence for the role of the ACC in gut based emotional consciousness comes from studies of brain injuries. Damage to the ACC is associated with a variety of emotional disturbances. In human beings, damage to the ACC can cause Akinetic Mutism. Patients with this condition suffer from a profound lack of motivation despite being able to perceive the world and understand language. They will not initiate actions and they will hardly respond when spoken to.

Cognitive dissonance is an uncomfortable feeling caused by holding conflicting ideas simultaneously. It is usually felt in the gut region. Brain imaging studies have shown that cognitive dissonance engages the ACC and the anterior region of the Insula. In addition, the activation of these regions tightly predicted participants' subsequent attitude change as a result of the experimentally generated dissonance.

The message from the evidence: The gut brain connects directly to the regions of the head brain that are involved in motivation, dissonance, conflict, safety, reward and decision-making and these same regions are also responsible for processing visceral feelings and signals. The evidence from Akinetic Mutism strongly supports the mBIT model of the gut being intrinsically involved in motivation. You can see from all of this evidence the clear links to the gut prime functions and competencies.

>> Gut wisdom - moral judgment, ethics and the gut

Are the gut and gut wisdom involved in moral judgment? Can sweet-tasting substances trigger kind, favorable judgments about other people? What about substances that are disgusting and bitter?

The results of a recent study show that bitter tastes and embodied gustatory experiences do affect moral judgment and can certainly make people more judgmental.

Researchers at City University, New York, asked 57 volunteers to rate how morally questionable a set of scenarios were on a scale of 1 to 100. These included situations such as a man eating his already-dead dog, and second cousins engaging in consensual sex. Before and halfway through the exercise, participants were given a bitter drink, a sweet juice or water. Those who drank bitter drinks were much harsher in their judgments than those who drank water, giving scenarios a score on average 27 percent higher.

In other research, disgust was induced in participants in a series of experiments by using bad smells, recall of physically disgusting experiences and video inductions. The results showed conclusively that gut based feelings of disgust influence moral judgment even when it is extraneous to the action being judged. The data also indicated that the role of disgust in the severity of moral judgments depends on participants' sensitivity to their own bodily sensations. As the researchers concluded, the results "indicate the importance and specificity of gut feelings in moral judgments."

While most of us have been taught that ethical thinking, decisions and behavior is a product of logic and reason, and devoid of emotions and feelings, there is now a growing scientific consensus that moral judgments are based largely on intuition and gut feelings about what is right and wrong. In a series of experiments at the University of Toronto, subjects were placed into interactions with an anonymous partner where they had two options, treat their partners fairly or lie to them. If they decided to lie, they would gain at the expense of their partners. Before making the decision to cheat or be fair, half the test participants were encouraged to think rationally about the situation and ignore their emotions. Given this advice, the majority, a whopping 60 percent analyzed the situation and concluded they should cheat. The other half of the participants were advised to make their decision based on *'gut feelings'*. Out of this group, only 27 percent of them lied and cheated their partners. The results indicate that focusing on gut feelings leads people to make more ethical decisions compared with rational decisions alone.

The message from the evidence: The gut has an intelligence and wisdom. You can learn to trust your gut instincts and your gut brain will provide you with greater insight and better moral judgment.

>> Food, mood, personality, taste, smell and feelings

There is an incredibly large and diverse body of research that links food, mood, personality, taste and feelings — backing up the claim that the gut brain, responsible for processing gustatory taste, is also deeply associated with our processing of related emotional and personality functions. For example, taste-related terms like bitter, spicy, sour, and sweet are often used in normal discourse to characterize personality and behavior and the manner in which people both relate and differ from each other. People are called *'bitter'* when they have a disposition that is angry and vengeful. And we say someone is a *'sour'* person when they are overly negative, pessimistic and unfriendly.

Such metaphors are especially common when considering sweet tastes. Many of the most common expressions for romantic partners and helpful prosocial people are sweetness related, such as *'honey'*, *'sugar'* and *'sweetie'*. These metaphors aid communication, but as we described in Chapter 2, theories of conceptual metaphor from the field of Cognitive Linguistics show that such metaphors are deeply embodied. And research recently completed at North Dakota State University has provided strong supporting evidence for this.

In a series of five studies, Dr. Brian Meier and his colleagues showed that individual differences in the preference for sweet foods predicted prosocial personalities, prosocial intentions, and prosocial behaviors. The experimental results also showed that momentarily savoring a sweet food, versus a non-sweet food or no food, increased participants' agreeableness and helping behavior.

Another fascinating finding that's emerged over recent years, is that taste buds have been found throughout the gastro-intestinal tract and not just on the tongue. The gut brain is literally tasting food as it moves throughout the digestive process and obviously using that information to aid nutrient extraction and determining what will be absorbed into body and self.

Amazingly, taste buds have also been found in the lungs, meaning we are actually tasting the air we breathe. Indeed, during development of the enteric nervous system in the embryo, the neural crest cells that colonize the foregut, emigrate out into the lung buds and give rise to ganglia and neural tissue within the airways. The gut brain really does innervate much of the torso and visceral area, and taste is one of its key sensory mechanisms and (as we'll see in the following chapter), one of the key ways in which it communicates with the other two brains.

In terms of the effect of food and taste on emotion and behavior, research has also demonstrated that suppressing emotion leads to comfort eating and eating sweet foods such as chocolate or apples elevates mood. In the case of chocolate, it has been found to both induce joy, and serve as a means to temporarily repair negative mood.

Backing this up, new Australian research has found that sweetened beverages help people under stress control aggressive responses and be less argumentative. Participants had their natural levels of aggression tested, and were then required to fast before being given a lemonade drink sweetened with either glucose or a sugar-free placebo. They were then provoked by another individual and were given the opportunity to retaliate. Participants were significantly less easily provoked when given the sweet drink compared to those receiving the placebo.

Anger is typically felt in the heart, but agitation, rage and aggression are felt in the gut — fight and flight are gut mediated reactions. So sugar, soothing the gut brain, decreases sympathetic signals from the gut to the head and heart brains and thereby modulates anger and aggression.

In a final look at the effects of taste and smell, it is well documented in the research literature that anosmia, the loss of smell, leads to depression and emotional blunting. Conversely, depression can cause a loss or decrease in the sense of smell in turn. Smell is used by our brains to inform the gut about the safety of food being ingested and about the complex chemical makeup of the incoming bolus, so that the gut brain can best digest it. Obviously, smell is a key sensory signal for the enteric nervous system.

What is most fascinating is the recent research on smell and anxiety (a gut core competency) that shows anxiety in humans can be communicated through smell and can influence risk-taking behavior. When people are anxious they release a chemical signal that's detectable unconsciously by those close to them. Researchers in a recent study collected sweat from people as they completed a high-rope obstacle course, and then tested the effect of that sweat on study participants as they played a gambling game. They found that gamblers risk-taking behavior was significantly affected when exposed to sweat collected from anxious people compared to that from non-anxious riders of an exercise bike.

The message from the evidence: The gut and its taste preferences are a vital and intrinsic component of core self and personality. Changing the state of the gut brain through the use of food, taste and smell, changes mood, influences emotion and ultimately changes behavioral responses.

|| **Cool Fact:** You have taste buds throughout your gut and even in your lungs.

>> Neuro-linguistic evidence

Now let's examine, some neuro-linguistic examples of gut brain competencies from common parlance:

- "I hunger for that" [hunger/compulsion]
- "I find that disgusting behavior" [disgust]
- "I have a fire in my belly for action" [action/gut motivation]
- "I'm hungry for success" [action/gut motivation]
- "He had the intestinal fortitude needed for the job" [will-power]
- "It was a gutsy move" [courage]
- "It really took a lot of guts to do that" [courage]
- "There was a peace deep in my gut" [relaxed/calm]
- "I had a calm feeling in my gut" [relaxed/calm]
- "I have a healthy appetite for life" [well being]
- "Deep in my guts it felt right" [gut intuition/wisdom]
- "You need to trust your gut instinct" [gut intuition/wisdom]

- "Listen to the inner voice of your gut" [gut intuition /wisdom]

The message from the evidence: What you can see, once again, is that there are specific competencies that are expressed and presupposed both metaphorically and literally within these common examples from linguistic corpora.

Head Brain

As we know, the head brain has two separate, but connected hemispheres and has approximately 100 billion neurons. It is far more complex than either the heart or gut brains. Like those two brains, its processing mode is also influenced by sympathetic and parasympathetic dominance so that the left hemisphere is dominant when the nervous system is under parasympathetic control, and the right hemisphere is dominant when the sympathetic arm is in ascendance.

Because of its primacy and massive complexity, the head brain is obviously involved in every aspect of human behavior. So it would take a book in itself, and probably several books, to detail the competencies that entail head brain control. For pragmatic purposes, and informed by our behavioral modeling work, we have chosen the *'hemispherical specialization brain model'* as the best way to approach the head and its core competencies, and in particular we have focused on what appear to be the competencies that emerge when the two hemispheres are in a balanced or centrally coherent/flow states.

Starting with the work of Dr. Roger Sperry and Dr. Michael Gazzaniga in the 1960's on split-brain patients, it has become known that the two hemispheres of the brain are specialized for certain functions or capacities. While the research in the intervening years has been somewhat controversial, especially with some of the commercially popularized interpretations of that work, overall there is now broad scientific agreement on the sort of processing each hemisphere is responsible for.

Left Hemisphere Competencies

- Verbal tasks
- Logic and problem solving tasks
- Analytical time sequence processing
- Detailed processing
- Positive or approach-related emotions

Right Hemisphere Competencies

- Nonverbal tasks
- Spatial tasks
- Discriminating shapes
- Global holistic processing
- Understanding/processing metaphor
- Music and tonal processing
- Facial recognition
- Negative or withdrawal-related emotions

As you can see, the hemispheres perform very different types of processing and depending on task and context, each hemisphere will be more active than the other. Research however, clearly supports the notion that competencies such as creativity are performed with both hemispheres working together and not solely by one of the hemispheres alone. Additionally, research done on states of *'flow'* also suggests that cross-hemisphere synchronization and coherence between brain regions are key components for triggering these states.

The message from the evidence: When your system becomes overly sympathetic or parasympathetic dominant, the related hemisphere of the brain also becomes dominant and this can lead to ways of thinking or experiencing the world that are limited or restrictive through one mode of processing alone.

>> Neuro-linguistic evidence

Some neuro-linguistic examples of head brain competencies from common parlance:

- "Use your head and be more logical will you" [logic/cognition]
- "We put our heads together and did some original thinking" [creativity]
- "I need to wrap my head around it" [meta cognition]
- "I was lost in my imagination" [flow]
- "I looked at it from both sides" [balanced perspective]
- "My mind is filled with curiosity" [curiosity]
- "Learning has given me a head start in life" [generative learning]

The message from the evidence: As with the heart and gut examples, you can see there are specific competencies expressed and presupposed both metaphorically and literally within these common examples from linguistic corpora.

Putting it into practice

Now, with all this fascinating and powerful evidence informing your understandings of the competencies and functions of your three brains, it's time to refocus on the pragmatic use of this knowledge. In the following chapters we'll take a look at how to use the core *mBrain* competencies to facilitate generative behavior and change as we continue our journey along the mBIT Roadmap.

mBraining

"Using your multiple brains to do cool stuff"

Chapter 4

Communicating with your *mBrains*

Wisdom

Highest Expression

Creativity (cephalic brain)
Compassion (heart brain)
Courage (enteric brain)

Congruence

Communication

When we first learned about the brains in our heart and gut we immediately knew there must be ways in which the three brains communicate with one another and facilitate system level control of our total organism. It's blindingly obvious our brains will not, and do not, operate in isolation from each other. They are intimately connected via nerve channels and plexi and must communicate back and forth via these and other mechanisms.

So we started examining the latest neuroscientific evidence on how the brains communicate, plumbed the depths of ancient traditions for insights to assist us, and used the resultant foundation to directionalize our behavioral modeling work. We also found a comprehensive body of material in the fields of biofeedback and personal development well validated by scientific research.

In this chapter you'll learn models for how your *mBrains* communicate and techniques for how to enhance that communication. These skills and processes will then be used in Chapter 5 to align and generate congruence between your head, heart and gut intelligences.

mBIT Principle: Most signals flow upwards

One of the first principals you need to know is that the majority of nerves connecting the heart and gut brains to the head flow upwards. The enteric and cardiac brains communicate with the cranial brain via the vagus nerve. Approximately ninety percent of these vagal nerve fibers are afferent sensory nerves, meaning they travel into the head brain, communicating the state of the viscera to it. Only ten percent provide communication signaling in the other direction from head to heart and gut brains.

This explains a lot about how difficult it can be to consciously alter the states of your heart and gut intelligences. Have you ever been nervous and experienced butterflies or nausea in your gut, perhaps before having to do a performance or public speaking? If you have, how difficult was it to use the thoughts in your head to calm your gut? In our experience, trying to talk to or convince your gut to settle down and feel normal is damn near impossible. Words and thoughts just don't translate to the language of the heart and gut easily. You can't talk your heart and gut brains into or out of things. And it's easy to see why, there's only a very small communication channel from head to gut and heart. And these two brains don't normally communicate via words. They speak in a different language, as we'll see later in this chapter.

However, the fact that ninety percent of the vagus signals travel upwards means the heart and gut can easily affect the processing of the head. If you've ever had a gut ache or been badly constipated, you'll know just how much your gut can alter your moods, thoughts and feelings.

The idea that signals from the vagus nerve have strong impacts on head brain thinking and processing is also strongly supported by research showing electrical stimulation of the vagus nerve can ameliorate depressive symptoms in patients who've been unresponsive to other forms of treatment. It can also increase or induce symptoms of anxiety and depression in others. This is not surprising, as we discussed in the previous chapter, depression and anxiety are gut brain competencies, so artificially generating signals in the vagus channel up to the head is likely to amplify the resultant head-based experiences of these gut-mediated affective states.

Felt-sense - what the body knows...

Dr. Eugene Gendlin, the developer of a powerful therapeutic technique called *'focusing'*, states in his excellent book of the same

121

name, that, "there is a kind of bodily awareness that profoundly influences our lives and that can help us reach personal goals. So little attention has been paid to this mode of awareness that there are no ready-made words to describe it." He calls this set of body feelings and bodily awareness a *'felt-sense'*.

A felt-sense represents and encompasses everything you think, feel and know about any situation or subject at a given time, and communicates this to you as a total bodily experience. In mBIT terms, we can see this as the heart and gut brain attempting to communicate their ideas and knowledge to your conscious (head) awareness.

As Dr. Gendlin points out, "Since a felt-sense doesn't communicate itself in words, it isn't easy to describe in words... It is a physical sense of meaning." When examining any problem situation in your life, Gendlin says that the felt-sense is, "the broader, at first unclear, unrecognizable discomfort, which the whole problem (all that) makes in your body... It is how your body carries the whole problem."

In a way, a felt-sense is the integration of all the signals and messages from the unconscious parts of your head brain, your heart brain and your gut brain, and is experienced as a broad set of sensations throughout your body.

In Dr. Gendlin's focusing method, he gets clients to talk internally with the felt sense, asking it questions about what it means, what its qualities are and what it's telling them. Problems are resolved by tuning into the wisdom of the *mBrains* and acknowledging and utilizing their intelligence and intentions.

Communicating with the gut

Listening to the gut

"Experience taught me a few things. One is to listen to your gut, no matter how good something sounds on paper."

Donald Trump

Listen to the neuro-linguistics in Donald Trump's statement. It's a common way of expressing how we receive intuitions and messages from our gut brain. Your gut sends messages to your head and heart. Biology text books say that the gut communicates via:

- Hunger signals and meal initiation
- Satiety signals
- Taste signals
- Muscle tension
- Visceral sensation

Now, we know that taste is a key sensory modality for the gut. As we described in the previous chapter, it's recently been discovered the gut has taste buds throughout the gastro-intestinal tract and not just on the tongue. The notion that the gut brain communicates to the head via tastes is also backed up by the neuro-linguistics of common statements such as:

- "the bitter taste of failure"
- "the sour taste of anger"
- "the metallic taste of fear"
- "the sweet taste of success"

Yes, it's certainly true, and you can verify this in your own experience. And given that cognitive linguistics has proven just how much of our metaphorical language is embodied, we can see why we would experience gut-based messages about danger, fear, etc. as taste signal messages that are available to conscious awareness.

Even though these scientifically validated communication mechanisms listed above are certainly important and interesting, what's more intriguing are the signaling processes suggested by esoteric literature and backed up by behavioral modeling, which include:

- Hungers, lusts, cravings for foods and satiety signals
- Motivation signals and visceral feelings of attraction, compulsion and repulsion
- Fear signals and visceral feelings of safety and threat e.g. fear, apprehension, foreboding, nagging, etc.
- Peristalsis — swallowing, choking, burping, vomiting, flatulence, excreting
- Kinesthetic/gut visceral sensations e.g. anxiety, butterflies in the stomach, cramping, gut rumblings, unsettled stomach, heartburn, etc.
- Physical movement (including physical hesitation)
- Gut/Gastro-intestinal tract (GIT) health issues, immune system issues
- Diaphragmatic breathing
- Belly laughing
- Guttural sounds
- Quiet/small voice and simple words
- Gut-based language
- Tastes/smells

- Moral disgust and physical disgust, distaste and stench/dis-smell
- *'Felt-sense'* and body/torso sensations
- Dreams/visions

While many of these communication mechanisms are not yet fully scientifically validated, notions are finally starting to form within the halls of neuroscience that there's legitimacy in these insights. This is evidenced by comments like this one from Dr. Pankaj Jay Pasricha from the Stanford University School of Medicine, "The gut isn't just a pit stop where foods are made usable. It is also a signaling station that keeps the body in tune of what's about to happen. It's not surprising," says Dr. Pasricha. "It's surprising that it took us so long to find out."

As Dr. Pasricha points out, and as we described above, "The gut and the brain are hardwired together by the vagus nerve, which runs from the brain to the body's internal organs. In addition, the gut has its own nervous system that is relatively independent. So the communication between the gut and the adult brain is elaborate and bi-directional, and changes in the gut are signaled directly to the brain."

The gift of fear

Gavin de Becker has been described as America's leading expert on violent behavior. He is a specialist in security issues and consults to top Hollywood stars, government agencies and leading politicians on how to detect and control risk and danger.

In his thought provoking book *'The Gift of Fear'*, he talks about the power of intuition, gut instincts and other survival signals that can protect you from violence and danger. He suggests that nagging visceral feelings of hesitation, fear, anxiety, doubt and suspicion are truly gifts that can save your life. He makes an important distinction between unwarranted fear signals and '*true fear*' and that you can learn to tell the difference between them and gain real wisdom from the messages they provide.

As de Becker points out, "Trust that what causes alarm probably should, because when it comes to danger, intuition is always right... Intuition is always learning, and though it may occasionally send a signal that turns out to be less than urgent, everything it communicates to you is meaningful." In terms of danger signals, de Becker believes there is a hierarchy or ranking of importance and urgency. He suggests that, "The intuitive signal of the highest order, the one with the greatest urgency, is fear; accordingly, it should always be listened to. The next level is apprehension, then suspicion, then hesitation, doubt, gut feelings, hunches, and curiosity. There are also nagging feelings, persistent thoughts, physical sensations, wonder and anxiety. Generally speaking, these are less urgent. By thinking about these signals with an open mind when they occur, you will learn how you communicate with yourself."

The quiet, small voice

The esoteric literature, and this is confirmed by our behavioral modeling work, often describes communications from both the gut and heart as a "small, quiet voice." This voice needs silence to be heard and apparently only talks in short sentences and with simple words. It also uses metaphor and symbolism rather than literal statements. From an mBIT perspective, we suggest this voice is the cranial brain's way of interpreting and representing the subtle signals coming from the other two brains and of presenting it to consciousness in language. It is a powerful part of intuition and needs to be nurtured for it to flourish in your life.

In Japanese culture, there is a term called *'haragei'*. This word has no direct equivalent in English, but can be loosely translated as *'stomach art'*. The word *'hara'* means belly or guts, it is the point in the center of the body that provides physical and emotional balance and involves connotations of intuition and feeling. Haragei then is the practice of using *'hara'*, of using visceral communication. It is beyond logic. It's about instinct, courage and wisdom.

In his deeply intriguing book *'The Unspoken Way – Haragei: Silence in Japanese Business and Society'*, Michihiro Matsumoto describes how haragei is practiced in the silence or pauses within verbal communication. According to Matsumoto, in Japan, senior business executives are able to reference decisions made with haragei as equally valid as logic and bottom-line accounting methods. Interestingly, (and you'll see the importance of this later in this chapter), Matsumoto says that, "To practice haragei, you must learn to breathe correctly."

Dreams as messages

It is common folk wisdom that eating a meal filled with rich and complex food just before sleeping leads to nightmares and poor quality sleep. But is there any truth to this assertion? Does the gut brain communicate to the head during sleep and dreaming and is that why if we eat immediately before going to bed we end up with disturbed sleep? Are dreams messages from the enteric or heart brains? Let's find out.

RGM sleep - the evidence

Every night, as you sleep, your head brain goes through periods of what is known as REM (Rapid Eye Movement) sleep. REM sleep is a normal stage of sleep, occurs approximately every 90 minutes on average, and is associated with the act of dreaming. It's believed by many neuroscientists and sleep researchers to be an integral part of the learning process and plays a major role in the integration of memory, experience and knowledge. A recent study at the University of California, using brain scans, showed that during REM sleep, memories are being reactivated, put in perspective and integrated. It was demonstrated that REM sleep acts like a form of overnight balm, soothing the emotional experiences of the previous day.

Fascinatingly, the gut brain also goes through a process akin to REM sleep, only in the gut this is known as RGM (Rapid Gut Movement) sleep. Approximately every 90 minutes, while you sleep, the gut goes through periods of RGM. It is suggested by some researchers that this is a time when the gut and head are communicating and integrating the knowledge and experiences of the day. Based on this insight, it is likely that dreams are important ways in which the gut brain communicates to the head brain and allows intuitions and '*gut wisdom*' to surface into consciousness. As the esoteric wisdom traditions maintain, your dreams contain messages from your gut and heart.

|| **Cool Fact:** Just as the head brain performs REM sleep each night, the gut undergoes RGM sleep, and it's likely this is the gut brain dreaming and communicating.

TCM and dreams

In Traditional Chinese Medicine (TCM) it is suggested the gut communicates about its state through dreams and when it's infected with intestinal parasites the dreams have specificity about what sort of parasite exists in the gut. Ancient Taoist TCM texts say that, "When one has small intestinal parasites, one will dream of crowds; when one has long intestinal parasites, one will dream of fights and mutual destruction."

What do IBS patients dream about?

So what does current medical science have to say about this?

It is well known that patients with bowel disorders often show abnormal REM sleep. For example, those with *'gut dysbiosis'*, an abnormal microbial mass in the gut, experience sleep disorders amongst their many symptoms. As discussed in the previous chapter, numerous studies also confirm that Irritable Bowel Syndrome (IBS) patients display alterations in intensity and duration of REM sleep, along with associated disturbances in normal gastric functioning during sleep as measured by electrogastrogram (EGG).

In terms of dreams, research suggests that chronic gastrointestinal disorders such as IBS can influence the nature of dreams. One study found that significantly more patients with Irritable Bowel Syndrome and Inflammatory Bowel Disease, not surprisingly, dreamt about their bowels. Obviously, the gut brain is sending strong messages to the head brain and these influence the content and process of dreaming.

According to Joy Ainley, a behavior change specialist who writes an excellent blog (www.painsinthebutt.com) about Crohn's disease and Ulcerative Colitis research, "Dreams are the mind's way of communicating its interpretation of current situations to us. They are usually a call for us to take action, *'Do something to make this situation different'*. In the case of the bad dreams described on the Crohn's discussion thread, there are extreme physical and emotional sensations being experienced with Crohn's and the mind is responding by calling for action to alleviate them. In the case of the dreams experienced by people with Crohn's who are in physical pain and feeling bloated, the interpretation of dreams of being pregnant, being in labor and undergoing a caesarian operation without anesthesia is quite straight forward... the gut is calling out to its owner to find a means to end this pain."

Dreams that saved a life

In early 2011, Oprah Winfrey decided she wanted to run an issue of her magazine solely devoted to the power of intuition and how to tap into gut instincts. Her magazine editors and researchers began searching for true and verifiable stories about people whose lives had been saved by hunches and messages from their deep intuition. What they found are some amazing stories, and these are detailed in the August 2011 issue of *O, The Oprah Magazine*, but the one that really stands out for us, is the experience of Trisha Coburn.

Trisha was 46 years of age and living a successful, healthy life, when one night she had an intense and disturbing dream that ultimately saved her life. In the dream she was standing at a barbed-wire fence and a group of frail and scary people on the other side were trying to tell her something in a language she couldn't comprehend. For the next couple of weeks she had the same dream recurringly, and each time the number of people in the dream increased and looked more and more desperate. The dreams were so disturbing she would wake up crying. She knew something was wrong.

So Trisha called her doctor and scheduled a full physical workup. But the results came back negative and her doctor was convinced Trisha was healthy and over-reacting. Still the dream came back, this time with 100 people, all wailing, screaming and pleading in their strange language. A few days after that, the same dream occurred one last time, but in this dream the fence was empty, there was no one there.

This was so disturbing to Trisha she went immediately to her doctor again and asked him what he thought was the deepest place in the human body. After he told her it was the colon, she demanded a colonoscopy. Even though her doctor was against it because she had no symptoms and no family history of colon cancer, Trisha insisted.

And fortunately for Trisha, she listened to the messages from her dreams. During the colonoscopy the gastroenterologist found aggressive and fast moving cancer throughout her colon. Her life was saved. A message from her gut brain that all was not well, communicated via dreams, allowed her to find the cancer and have it removed before it killed her. The surgeon later told her if she'd waited another two months, the prognosis would have been grim.

What a chilling and powerful story about the power of dreams for tapping into your deep gut wisdom!

Heart transplant evidence and the specificity of messages

Now here are some more amazing and somewhat spooky pieces of evidence about messages received from dreams. These however, are about dream messages from the heart and what is most fascinating is the level of specificity that must be contained in heart brain memories for the messages to contain such incredible details. We hope you find them as intriguing as we did when we first read them.

As described in the last chapter, after a heart and lung transplant operation, dancer Claire Sylvia discovered that her new organs were not the only thing she inherited. As detailed in her fascinating biography 'A Change of Heart', one night, five months after her operation, Claire woke from a vivid and entrancing dream. In her dream, she met a man named Tim L. and formed a strong bond with him. As the dream unfolded, it became time for Tim to leave, and just before he did, Claire and Tim kissed and during the kiss, Claire inhaled Tim into her and awoke, knowing that she and Tim would be together forever.

This dream was so vivid, unusual and exhilarating that on awakening, Claire felt as if she'd finally integrated her new heart and lungs within her. She says she woke up knowing that Tim L. was her donor and that parts of his spirit and personality were now within her. This deep sense of knowing started her on a quest to find out who her donor really was and after months and months of frustrated research and searching she finally made contact with his family. And the kicker to the story... the donor's real name was Tim LaSalle.

What an amazing story! Definitely worth reading. It's also backed up by medical research that shows that severed vagus nerves can, after several months, reconnect and re-innervate the cardiac nervous system of the new heart. Obviously, in Claire's case, her new heart connected strongly and was able to send messages in her dreams to help her accept and integrate her new heart brain.

Finally, here's another heart chilling and incredible story from the literature on personality changes after heart transplants. In this example, an eight year old girl received the heart of a ten year old girl, but sometime after the transplant, the young recipient began to have vivid nightmares about an attacker and a girl being murdered. Concerned about her young daughter, the mother took her to a psychiatrist who became convinced that with nightmares so detailed and real they appeared to be genuine memories. The psychiatrist recommended they contact the police, and presciently, it turned out the ten year old donor had been murdered.

According to the literature, the recipient's violent reoccurring dreams were so vivid and accurate, and she was able to describe the events of the horrible encounter and the murderer with such detail, police were able to apprehend and convict the killer. An incredible story that makes you wonder just how much intelligence and specificity the heart brain and its memories have.

[*BTW: The take home message from all the insights above is that you should employ the wisdom of 'sleeping on something' to give your heart and gut a chance to digest, integrate and communicate via dreams their deep knowledge about any decision, problem or situation. Doing this will help you make better and wiser decisions. Your intuitions will be stronger. Also, make sure you track for the symbolism and signals that the gut and heart communicate to you in any subsequent dreams. And don't distract your gut's neural network during the night by eating 'hard to digest' meals just before going to bed.*]

Case Study - Navin R: Dreams, messages from the heart and gut

Navin R contacted us for advice about a recurring dream that was troubling and disturbing him. He launched straight in with, "I woke up today in the middle of the same terrifying dream. Basically, I was driving home and as I was getting off the freeway, and coming up to the exit, I could see a fairly large tornado across the road. As I entered the estate through a dirt road I could see two more tornados. Anyway, my girlfriend was in the car behind me, but next thing I know is that I am in the office at work and a colleague of mine is making dumplings. I tell him and my boss that there are tornados, but they say not to be concerned. I've been very spooked by this damn dream!"

Navin continued with, "So I did a bit of research on the web about what tornados symbolize, and came up with they symbolize inner turmoil and confusion. They say it's about being caught in an emotional storm or about large changes in your life that disturb you. And seeing several tornados is supposed to symbolize volatile situations with the people around you. But I don't know. The only thing I can think of at the moment is that a lot of what I am going through is based on the fact that no one in my family approves of my relationship with my girl friend, and this is eating into me, as I have been under stress to choose between the woman who has been so good to me, and who is so special to me, and my family whom I also love and respect very much. Then there is also the fact that I'm building my house, and my working life has a lot of stress at the moment.

The other thing is that I am at a stage of my life where I am having a massive personal growth spurt, and I'm having really strong feelings to follow my dreams and goals of helping people through a personal development career, like personal training, counseling or psychology. This is the first time in a very, very long time that I've been truly freaked out by a dream. What do you think this dream is about? I really need some help to get clear about what it's saying and resolve it."

As we explained to Navin, it's vitally important to note that dreams and nightmares are often ways in which the heart and gut brains symbolically communicate to the head brain. And in this case, notice the accuracy of the Tornado symbol from standard dream symbolism. In Navin's life there is inner turmoil and confusion over conflicting values, emotions and expectations — family loving versus deep, heart felt romantic loving. All core competencies of heart intelligence. Added to this there are stress issues around work and building a new home. Especially, notice his languaging of "this is eating into me" which is clear neuro-linguistics representing gut brain processing. And this is further highlighted by the food in the dream, the symbolism of someone in the office (external authorization, father/parental figure) cooking dumplings.

Navin's gut brain is in turmoil around the clash of deeply important values as he begins to shift his identity. He is starting a new life with his beloved, building a new home for them to live in, and this is not supported by his family. In order to resolve his situation, Navin needs the courage to get clear in his heart about what is truly most valued for him in his life at this time and to then motivate himself into creative action to follow his heart and gut wisdom. This is what we guided him to do, to tune into his heart and gut intuitions and to engender alignment to the Highest Expressions of these using the mBIT framework that we'll cover in the coming chapters.

Messages from the heart

"The best and most beautiful things in the world
cannot be seen nor touched but are felt in the heart."

Helen Keller

The heart communicates in similar ways to the enteric brain, however as well as the vagus nerve channels and biochemical/hormonal methods of the gut, it has other physical and electrical channels it can use. The following list summarizes a mix of neuroscientific research findings, esoteric wisdom traditions and our behavioral modeling work.

Heart communication mechanisms:

- Emotions and feelings
- Interest, attention and salience

- Symbolic images, dreams and visions
- Kinesthetic sensations e.g. pain, tightness, etc.
- Beats, rhythm
- Speed, timing of movements
- Breathing
- Tones (music, song)
- Quiet/small voice and simple words
- Heart-based language
- Smells
- Heart-related health issues
- *'Felt-sense'* and body/chest sensations
- Electrical signals

The beat of the drums

Deep in the jungles of Africa, tribes use the deep rhythmic booming sound of drums to communicate across distances. It's hard to physically move through the dense packed vegetation of the jungle, but sound travels easily and quickly providing a great way to send signals. The same is true of the heart. The pressure pulse of its beat travels throughout your body and communicates messages in the process. The research evidence described in the last chapter supports this. Remember the experiment on intuitive decision-making by Dr. Barnaby Dunn from the Brain Sciences Unit in Cambridge? He found that people who were more aware of their own heartbeat were able to make quicker and more accurate intuitive decisions. So the better you're able to sense your heart beat and the feelings from your heart, the more accurately you'll tune in to the messages it is sending you.

</== Discovery Exercise: Awareness ==/>

In this discovery exercise you will learn to become aware of and tune into the beat of your heart. Note that as in all the exercise in this book, you can download an audio file for this exercise from www.mbraining.com.

Awareness (Basic)

1. Sit comfortably in a quiet space, take a moment to settle and breathe gently and evenly. As you continue to settle and relax, allow any thoughts and internal dialogue to arise naturally and just observe them as they come and go. Be a detached observer of your own internal processes, just let them arise then let them go.

2. As you are sitting, breathing gently, and continuing to relax, allow yourself to become more aware of your chest area. Breathe into your chest area and become aware of the sensations you can feel with each breath. Now begin to listen for, feel and track your heart beat in your upper chest.

3. Once you can get a sense of your heart beat, begin also to notice any other sensations and feelings in your heart and chest region.

4. Practice this exercise as often as you can, whenever you have a spare moment, the better you are at tuning in to your heart beat, the better you'll be at receiving the messages and intuitions from your heart brain.

Awareness (Contrast)

5. Sit comfortably and once again breathe gently as you become aware of your heart beat. Notice its rate, rhythm, and strength/intensity.

6. As you maintain this awareness, begin to recall or imagine a stressful situation. Notice any changes to your heart beat (rate, rhythm, strength/intensity) and any other sensations in your body.

7. Now let go of those stressful thoughts, internal images, and internal sounds/dialogue. Allow them to just float away while you focus on breathing gently. Notice any changes to your heart beat as you re-settle and re-center yourself.

8. As you maintain your awareness of your heartbeat, now recall or imagine a pleasant, happy memory or situation. Notice any changes to your heart beat (rate, rhythm, strength/intensity) and any other sensations in your body.

9. Once again, allow those thoughts, internal images, and internal sounds/dialogue to naturally float away. Focus on your gentle breathing and notice any changes to your heart beat as you become present to the here and now.

10. Practice becoming more aware of your heartbeat throughout the day during times of stress, enjoyment, and relaxation. This will develop your heart-based intuition and overall self-awareness.

The heart electric

Notice the last dot-point in the list of heart communication mechanisms on the previous pages — *'Electrical signals'*. The electromagnetic signal of the heart is sixty times higher in amplitude than the signal of the brain. It emits an energy field five thousand times stronger than the head brain's, one that can be measured more than ten feet from the body. So your heart communicates not just throughout your own body via these intensely strong electric fields, but also across space and into or onto the people (and animals) around you. Research by the HeartMath Institute has found that electrical signals of a person's heart are easily measurable on another person's skin at distances of several feet. They've also shown that a person whose heart beat is strongly coherent (a measure of how balanced the sympathetic and parasympathetic systems are), can entrain another person's heartbeat into the same coherence. We'll discuss coherence and neural network entrainment in much more detail later in this chapter.

Communicating with the head

As we've said before, the head is a complex place. With its approximately 100 billion neurons, it has incredible complexity and can perform a myriad of amazing competencies. Communication in the head takes many forms, but for pragmatic behavioral modeling purposes, we know that consciously we can communicate with and in our heads using:

- Internal dialogue
- Internal sounds
- Internal images
- Internal Kinesthesia

While science and philosophy continues to argue about consciousness and whether the sense of conscious self really exists or is some sort of hallucinated epiphenomenon, we personally have a pragmatic orientation that is informed by behavioral modeling. When you model how someone communicates with themselves, and motivates and manages their mind, they describe talking to themselves, making internal pictures, sounds and attending to internal feelings. As a pragmatic way of speaking we consider this to be the person communicating with their head brain, and will use this terminology throughout the book.

The key distinction is that we have a conscious mind and it is able to communicate with and somehow influence the unconscious mind (the other than conscious mind). The idea behind mBIT is that through the conscious use of appropriate techniques and skills, you can learn to communicate with, align and influence your three brains to achieve greater wisdom and success in life, and as we say in the header of this book: *'Use your multiple brains to do cool stuff'*.

Gateways and bridges to the unconscious: communicating and facilitating via conscious intention

The first step in working and communicating with your multiple brains is to put them into a state in which the sympathetic and parasympathetic modes are calmly balanced and even. This is known as a *'coherent'* state. To achieve this, you need to control your Autonomic Nervous System (ANS) and this can be quite challenging to do through conscious thought alone.

Fortunately, there is a powerful key you can use to unlock the door to the control of your ANS, and it involves consciously working with gateways or bridges between the Somatic Nervous System (SNS) and the ANS. The somatic system is the nervous system that innervates the skin, sensory organs and all skeletal muscles. Unlike the ANS, the SNS is largely under voluntary conscious control. So these gateways are points in the body, key muscle groups, co-innervated by both the SNS and the ANS. As you consciously direct them, through voluntary control via the somatic system, you send powerful signals to the ANS and bring it into resonance with your conscious patterns of communication and control.

Stephen Elliot first introduced the idea of bridges back in 2004 in his work on heart rate variability and what he has called *'coherent breathing'*. Stephen's excellent work can be accessed at his website (coherence.com) and is well worth reading for in-depth discussions of the science behind both coherent breathing and the bridges.

According to Stephen there are 6 main bridges:

1. The face

2. The tongue and throat

3. The hands

4. The diaphragm and intercostals

5. The pelvic floor

6. The feet

Each of these points possesses musculature that can open and close, involves neural input and output, and has explicit unconscious and conscious control; three attributes that are apparently required for operation of the bridging function.

In our work, and because as you'll see below they are co-innervated by not just the SNS and ANS, but also co-innervated by the enteric brain, we have found that two key gateways are the most useful and powerful for ANS control and balance:

- The diaphragm (breathing)
- The tongue and throat (swallowing)

And we will concentrate on these and utilize them in the mBIT techniques that follow throughout the book.

Co-innervation of the diaphragm and esophagus

From an evolutionary perspective, the diaphragm can be viewed as two distinct muscles, the crural and costal, one a gastrointestinal muscle and one a respiratory muscle. These two muscles typically act in synchrony during normal respiration, but diverge during swallowing and the reverse process of emesis (a fancy term for throwing up). It appears that the crural muscle developed originally as an enterically controlled muscle for clamping the esophagus to stop gastric contents from refluxing upwards.

Vertebrates such as the African clawed frog for example, possess a muscular band around the esophagus that doesn't interact directly with respiratory organs in any way. However, in humans the two muscles generally work as one under both conscious (somatic) control and unconscious (autonomic/enteric) control.

The value in knowing this is that the diaphragm, being effectively two muscles in one, and therefore co-innervated by both the head and gut brains, is a powerful gateway between them. You'll shortly see how this links to breathing and its ability to bring all your brains into autonomic coherence through balanced breathing.

The esophagus has also been found to be co-innervated by both the enteric nervous system and the somatic nervous system. Proof of

142

this has only been scientifically validated over the last ten years, so it's a relatively recent discovery. There is remarkable variability of the co-innervation with some parts sharing almost 50 percent co-innervation and other parts more or less.

The significance of this finding of co-innervation is that swallowing is controlled by both the head brain and gut brain. This also explains the embodied cognitive metaphors in common expressions such as "I just couldn't swallow that idea" and "It brought a lump to my throat." In our modeling work we have often come across situations where a person is not able to communicate a message to the gut brain because of psycho-somatic constriction in the throat region. And as you'll explore in the discovery exercises later in this chapter, there are ancient Taoist exercises that use swallowing as a basis to send soothing, healing messages from the head to the gut brain.

Balancing the ANS: heart rate variability and coherence

When a nurse or medical practitioner measures your heart rate, they typically count the number of pulses over a period of 15 seconds and then multiply by 4 to get the average number of beats per minute. They might then write on your chart that your heart is beating at say 76 beats per minute (bpm). But in reality it's almost never exactly at that average rate. Your heart is constantly speeding its rate up and slowing its rate down.

This is because, when your autonomic system has sympathetic dominance, your heart rate speeds up, and then as your parasympathetic kicks in to bring the ANS back to homeostasis, your hear rate slows back down.

Heart Rate Variability (HRV) is the measure of the beat-to-beat changes that occur in your heart rate. Because of the links to the

ANS and the effects that thoughts, feelings and impacts from the environment have on your *mBrains,* your pulse rate and HRV are affected by all of these.

Researchers have found that HRV is a very useful measure of how you and your heart are coping with stress and what sort of state your ANS and *mBrains* are in. The graph below shows the heart rate of a person who is under stress.

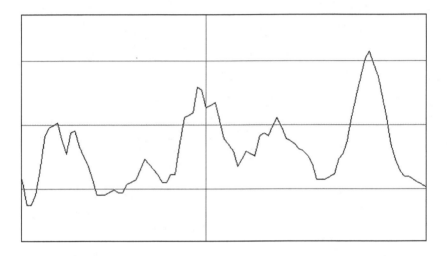

Contrast this with the one below from someone who is meditating and in a calm state, where they are focusing on feelings and thoughts of compassion and loving-kindness.

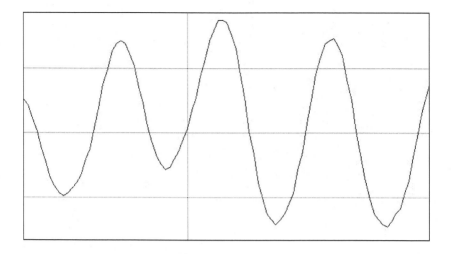

Notice how smooth and even the changes in the heart rate are for the calm state. The graph almost looks like a sine wave. This sine shaped graph is one that has *'high coherence'*. Coherence is a mathematical measure that describes how evenly repeatable from moment to moment a wave-form is. A chaotic, sharply changing wave has low coherence, it is not evenly repeatable. In high coherence however, the sympathetic and parasympathetic systems are working nicely together, in balance, gently keeping your mind and body in an optimal state, and this shows in the smoothly changing wave.

Numerous scientific studies have found that low HRV is one of the leading indicators of heart disease. They have also shown that high heart coherence is protective of the heart. Coherence acts to balance the heart, mind and emotions. It brings all the brains into resonance. When you are in a state of coherence you'll find you feel incredibly relaxed, your mind calms down and any stress levels markedly decrease. It's a powerful state and one we'll use for *mBrain* integration.

Sound good? Ok, so how do you do it?

Resonant breathing, balanced breathing

Breathing is primal and as we've intimated above, it's the bridge between mind and body; the gateway between consciousness and the unconscious. In many languages the words for spirit and breath are identical. For example in Sanskrit the word is *'prana'*, in Hebrew *'ruach'*, Greek *'pneuma'*, and Latin *'spiritus'*. Numerous ancient traditions such as those of the Native American Indians, also believe life enters the body with the first breath, not at the moment of birth or conception.

Breathing has direct and intimate connections to emotional states and moods. Take a look at someone who is angry, afraid or upset and you'll see a pattern of breathing that is shallow, rapid and irregular. Conversely, think about how you breathe when you are feeling happy, calm and contented. In fact, it's almost impossible to be upset if your breathing is slow, deep, gentle and regular. And there's a reason for this...

As you now know, it's in part because your breathing is connected via the bridge of the diaphragm which is co-innervated by both somatic and enteric/autonomic nervous systems. So calm *mBraining* states lead to and are connected with autonomic balance and therefore calm body states and calm, even breathing processes. But there's also another powerful physiological mechanism at work here. This mechanism involves what is known as the *'baroreceptor reflex'* found in receptors in the carotid arteries.

Deep in the sinuses of the large carotid arteries in your chest and neck, lay specialized neurons called baroreceptors. These cells are stretch-sensitive mechanoreceptors and are optimized for monitoring changes in blood pressure which they relay to the brainstem and ultimately, via the autonomic nervous system, back to the heart. The result of this is that as you breathe in, your blood pressure drops and the baroreceptors detect this and cause your heart rate to speed up. As you breathe out, your blood pressure increases and your heart rate slows down accordingly. In other words, through a complex process of information coding in the ANS, this baroreflex acts to speed up your heart as you breathe in and slow down your heart as you breathe out.

Why is this important? Well... it gives you a powerful gateway for controlling your autonomic nervous system and bringing your sympathetic and parasympathetic into balance and coherence. Via controlled, balanced breathing you can control the sympathetic and parasympathetic arms of the ANS through the baroreflex, and put your heart into high coherence.

Simply put, by breathing for an in-breath of approximately six seconds and an out-breath of exactly the same duration, the baroreflex, along with the co-innervation of the diaphragm, leads to coherence and balance in your ANS, and in your multi-brains. It all starts through conscious control of breathing, leads to the heart coming into resonance with the calm balanced breathing and this communicates and spreads to the gut and head brains all coming together into calm, balanced resonance with the heart.

Such a simple process, yet so powerful. And now you can see why breathing is linked to thoughts and emotions. When you alter your breathing, you profoundly alter the state and mode of processing of your multiple brains.

Note also the importance of having a balance between the in-breath and out-breath. If you breathe longer on the in-breath, you'll cause a gradual speed up of your heart and shift into sympathetic dominance. On the other hand, if you do lots of long sighs, that is, breathe longer on the out-breath compared to the in-breath, you'll end up slowing your heart down, and putting yourself into parasympathetic over dominance; another way of saying, you'll depress yourself.

These insights are obvious when you think about them. We've all had experiences of seeing someone panic and watching how they breathe when in that state. Similarly, you know when someone is depressed, they do lots of slow out-breath sighing. Start to notice this in yourself and others, and make sure you do balanced breathing to keep yourself in an optimal psychological and physiological state.

</== Discovery Exercise: Balanced Breathing ==/>

In this discovery exercise you will learn to do coherent *'balanced breathing'* to put your heart and autonomic nervous system into a balanced, coherent state.

Preparation

1. Sit in a comfortable and relaxed position. (Note: do this in a sitting position rather than lying down).

2. Make sure your spine is straight and your shoulders are relaxed. Avoid having your tailbone tucked under you and your shoulders hunched forward as it will restrict your ability to breathe into your chest area. Instead, sit upright (without tension or effort), lengthen your spine, allow your shoulder blades to gently flatten against your back, and keep your head positioned over your shoulders (not protruding in front of them) to make sure your neck stays loose and relaxed.

3. Your eyes may be open or closed. Begin to breathe in deeply yet gently through the nose, and breathe out through either

the nose or mouth, whichever is most comfortable. Do not use effort or force. Do this easily, naturally and in a relaxed manner.

4. While maintaining your relaxed and upright posture, breathe into and from your diaphragm. Feel your diaphragm naturally lower on the inhalation and naturally rise on the exhalation. Allow your deep yet gentle breath to also naturally expand your chest and ribcage area.

5. Combine the physical sensations of exhalation with feelings of deep relaxation. Do not force the exhalation. Exhale deeply without creating any tension in the torso. Maintain a relaxed and upright posture.

Balancing Your Breath

6. Now imagine an image of a sine wave in your mind. Imagine the sine wave spans a 12 second cycle, with approximately 6 seconds for the ascending part of the wave and 6 seconds for the descending part of the wave.

7. Imagine a ball moving along the sine wave and begin to breathe in sync with it. As it moves up the wave, gently inhale from your diaphragm for 6 seconds. As the ball moves down the wave, gently exhale from your diaphragm for 6 seconds. Try to make smooth transitions between inhalations and exhalations (and vice versa) as the ball moves around the top and bottom of this imaginary sine wave.

8. Remember to keep breathing from your diaphragm into your chest area. Keep your posture and spine upright and your shoulders and neck relaxed.

9. Continue balanced breathing in a deep yet relaxed manner for several minutes. The longer you can stay in a coherent state, the better. However even a couple of minutes in a coherent state has significant benefits. The mental, emotional and health benefits generated from this practice have been scientifically validated to be pervasive and long lasting.

Learning

10. Upon completion of this exercise, take some time to be aware of the changes in your mental, emotional and physical states as well as your overall state of being. Notice what is different in how you are experiencing your world and your ability to respond differently to whatever is presenting itself in the now.

Note: to help you we have created some breathing-pacer audio mp3 files, freely available at our website (www.mbraining.com) for you to download and use to pace your in-breaths and out-breaths.

Amplifying coherence through core heart-felt emotions

In the field of NLP there is a model called the Cybernetic Loop that encapsulates the deep understanding that the mind and body are connected in a powerful control loop — that your brains and body interact and affect each other, they are not distinct and separate and what affects one, affects the other. The Cybernetic Loop is summarized in the following diagram.

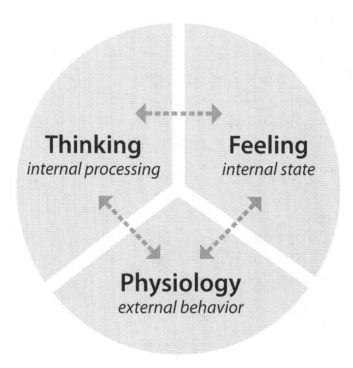

What this model shows is that your thinking (your Internal Processing — thoughts, images, ideas) connects to and both influences and is influenced by your feelings (your Internal State — your emotions). Your feelings in turn are connected to and influence and are influenced by your physiology (your External Behavior — your body, breathing, physical state), which in turn is influenced by and influences your thinking, in a loop. The process of control runs both ways, each of the three components influencing the other.

So for example, whenever you think of something sad or picture something that makes you unhappy or depressed, you'll begin to feel the emotions and feelings of sadness and depression, this in turn causes you to hunch over, to breathe slower and lower in your chest, to tense your muscles. These changes in your physiology lead to even more negative thinking and feeling which amplify the negative physiological state and cause a spiral into more and more negative experiences or attitudes. You can see this in people who are severely depressed, they carry their depression in their stance and posture, they rarely look up, are unlikely to smile or breathe fully and deeply. They will be slow and lethargic, lacking energy and zest. They also tend to think negatively and have higher levels of pessimism.

Alternately, this success spiral can also function in a positive direction. If something positive happens to you, or you access a memory of a positive time or experience in your life, you'll start to feel positive feelings and emotions. Your posture will change to being more upright, open and comfortable. Your muscles will relax. Breathing will be much more full and easy, bringing more oxygen to your brains and body. You'll smile. This in turn will support even more positive thoughts and feelings and the spiral will continue, generating positive changes in your mind and body.

The Cybernetic Loop is also deeply at work in the relationship between your three brains and in particular the connection between emotions and Autonomic Nervous System balance. When you focus on positive emotions you powerfully increase the level of balance and coherence in your heart and gut brains.

Since the prime functions of the heart are around relational affect, love, connection and values, by focusing on these emotions and experiences as you perform balanced breathing, you'll amplify the cybernetic control effects between all your systems. Indeed, research by the HeartMath Institute has shown that focusing on positive heart-felt emotions in the region of the heart as you perform balanced breathing strongly amplifies coherence in your heart and ANS.

</== Discovery Exercise: Amplifying With Emotions ==/>

In this discovery exercise you will learn to amplify your balanced breathing by breathing and communicating positive core emotions into your heart and communicating those messages to your head and gut brains.

1. Sit comfortably and begin the Balanced Breathing exercise described previously.

2. Once you have balanced your breathing for a few minutes along the *'sine wave pattern'* (breathing in for 6 seconds and out for 6 seconds), begin to think of a memory or imagine a scenario that produces strong positive emotions and feelings within you. This could be memories from your childhood, family, great achievements and celebrations, doing something you love or are passionate about, etc. Or they could be imagined scenarios of achieving future goals and aspirations, creative visualizations, *'what if'* and *'as if'* imaginings, etc.

3. Option: you may wish to also identify a language label for the positive emotion(s) and feeling(s) you are experiencing (e.g. love, happiness, peace, joy, etc). Some people find it useful to have a word label to use for the next steps in this exercise.

4. As you fully experience the positive emotions and feelings associated with your memory/imagined scenario, breathe

into your heart area and feel your positive emotion filling your chest and heart area with each breath. Feel any tensions and non-complementary emotions leaving your body with each exhalation.

5. Still maintaining your balanced breathing, imagine and feel your positive emotion expanding upwards to your head brain. You may find it easier to start sending the signals upward with an in-breath.

6. As you continue to breathe from your heart up into your head, notice how your thoughts and perceptions change when they are connected to your heart and its positive emotion.

7. While maintaining this connection between your head and heart, breathe back down into your heart area.

8. Now continue to breathe the positive emotion from your heart down into your gut area. Feel your lower abdomen naturally expand as you inhale (you'll find that it helps greatly to keep a straight spine and to allow your pelvis to also move gently and naturally). Imagine and feel your positive emotion filling your lower abdomen/gut area.

9. Become aware of the changes to your sense of '*self*', e.g. changes in body sensations the releasing of muscular tensions, increased feelings of self-confidence and safety/security, and an upgrading of how you can '*be*' in this present moment.

10. As you fully experience the changes in your gut intelligence, breathe those changes back up into your heart. Allow each balanced breath to send the signals upwards from your gut to your heart, and feel the connection between these two brains.

11. Now breathe once again mainly into your heart area. With each balanced breath, experience your positive emotion flowing through the connections between your heart, head and gut brains. Expand that flow throughout your entire body and notice the changes in your overall wellbeing with an enhanced/expanded sense of who you are in the world.

</== Discovery Exercise: Swallowing a Smile ==/>

In this discovery exercise you'll learn to use swallowing to send a powerful message from your head to your gut brain. This exercise is derived from the powerful and insightful work of Grand Master Mantak Chia. It's based on ancient Taoist teachings and works through co-innervation of the esophagus with the head, heart and enteric nervous systems. You can find more detailed information on this technique and many others at Master Chia's excellent '*Universal Healing Tao*' web site: www.universal-tao.com.

1. Sit comfortably and begin to focus on balanced breathing until you are breathing gently, smoothly, deeply, evenly, calmly and softly. Relax your forehead, let your eyes, ears and tongue soften. Allow your face to become relaxed and calm.

2. Imagine yourself in one of your favorite, most beautiful places in the world surrounded by the beauty and vitality of nature. Begin to smile, and as you experience the joy and happiness of your favorite place, amplify your smile, feel it in your face, your mouth, your eyes.

3. Let your relaxed smiling awareness flow down through your cheeks, down through your jaw muscles and tongue, and down through your neck and throat, soothing and calming as it goes.

4. Smile down to your chest and into your heart. Sense them opening like a flower with love, joy and happiness bubbling out of them. Do balanced breathing of the love and joy from your heart into your smile and into the saliva in your mouth.

5. Roll your tongue around your mouth until you have gathered a nice amount of saliva. Smile to the saliva and draw the smiling energy and golden light into the saliva transforming it into delicious healing nectar. Really feel this. Really taste the golden sweet smile into your saliva.

6. Swallow the saliva in two or three easy positive swallows. Follow it with awareness down your esophagus, smiling as it goes, feeling the healing nectar soothing and refreshing your esophagus.

7. Continue smiling through the rest of your digestive tract: your stomach, small intestine, gall bladder, large intestine, rectum, bladder and urethra. Thank these organs for their work in giving you energy through the processes they do.

8. Return your awareness once more to your smile and your eyes and recharge your smiling energy, directing it all around you here in one of your favorite, most beautiful places in your world.

9. Return to the here and now, filled in heart, mind, body and soul with your inner smile — filled with the joy of life deep within you now.

Using biofeedback tools

Your skills and ability to bring your heart into autonomic coherence can be powerfully augmented through the use of biofeedback technology. There are a number of inexpensive tools available in the marketplace that we have used and researched extensively and can certainly recommend. New models and manufacturers are appearing all the time, so check out our website (www.mbraining.com) for details about the tools and systems we are currently suggesting as the best of breed and best value for money.

The benefits of using these biofeedback tools is that they provide immediate, graphical and objective measures about what your heart rate is doing, how much Heart Rate Variability you're generating and how much coherence you have from moment to moment. The tools have sensors you hook to either your earlobes or fingers and then use your computer screen to display real time information about HRV, coherence and other important measures. Some tools also provide information about stress levels through tracking galvanic skin resistance at the same time as measuring heartbeat and heart coherence metrics.

If you are truly serious about learning to control your *mBrains*, your mind and your life, then for the small investment they represent, these biofeedback tools are an absolute must to purchase now. We like to think of them as life enhancing devices and use them regularly to hone our skills.

mBraining

"Using your multiple brains to do cool stuff"

Chapter 5

Aligning your
mBrains

"A house divided against itself cannot stand."

Abraham Lincoln

Congruence and Neural Integrative Engagement

What happens when your heart passionately tells you one thing, but your gut violently disagrees? Or when your head is at odds with the messages from either your heart or gut? Have you ever found yourself fighting amongst these parts of your mind? If you have, you aren't alone. Our behavioral modeling research suggests this is an all too common experience.

Incongruence or mismatch between the multiple brains undermines resolve, causes confusion and ultimately leads to incongruent behaviors and outcomes. You literally sabotage your own success. We've all had experiences of this, either in our own lives, or in the people around us. Think of times when you've felt torn on a decision, where one part of you has agreed but another part has not. How did that work out? Probably not as well as it could…

159

Yes, for success in life you need all parts of your self, all of your brains, congruently aligned and supporting your success.

The world reflects your processes back to you

You know, it's not just about what's happening in your own *mBrains* either. Incongruence within and between your brains is usually embodied and expressed (typically outside of conscious awareness) in your physical stance, your micro-muscle movements, your facial expressions and your non-verbal communication. Through methodologies such as NLP, you can learn to notice and track these signals and detect when someone is not fully supportive of the outcomes they're communicating or working towards.

Equally, any incongruence you're feeling is non-verbally expressed to other people's unconscious minds and undermines your chances of success with them. This is how self-fulfilling prophecies work within human relationships. We literally express and communicate all the messages from our multiple brains, and get responses from others that recapitulate our expectations.

As an example, if someone is sending out mixed messages, you'll feel it in your gut or heart as an instinct not to trust the person. This in turn influences your own decisions and behaviors and you'll end up reflecting back that lack of trust. This can amplify in a loop of mutual distrust and cause problems in how you work or relate together.

So congruence is vital for both working with your self and with others. Success and ultimately wisdom in all your outcomes and behaviors requires alignment and congruence at every level.

This is why one of the early steps in the mBIT Roadmap is *'congruence'*.

Wisdom

Highest Expression
Creativity (cephalic brain)
Compassion (heart brain)
Courage (enteric brain)

Congruence

Communication

How the roadmap works

As you saw in the last chapter, the way the roadmap works is that first you need to communicate with your multiple brains and bring them into balanced coherence. This then allows you to perform the next step and align them together into congruence — into matching states of flow and generative response.

In this chapter we'll explore how to perform this next step of congruence and alignment. And once you've mastered that, you'll learn in the following chapters how to utilize your brains' '*Highest Expressions*' to make amazing changes and create more wisdom and success in life.

mBIT Principle: The heart leads

"Your heart is your guide and compass.

It whispers softly, so listen closely."

According to ancient Taoist principles underpinning Traditional Chinese Medicine, the heart is the Emperor while the gut is the General. In other words, the heart is the leader and sets directions that the gut as General motivates to action (note the link to the concept of motility and motion). Sure you can fight your heart, but it takes energy and wears you down. The heart provides passion, desire and direction as it links to values. The gut intelligence provides courageous action, motivation and movement.

The mBIT principle that derives from these insights, and is backed up by behavioral modeling and neuro-physiological evidence on heart-lead coherence (described in the previous chapter), is that: *'the heart leads'*.

This is a powerful principle and it informs the mBIT Foundational Sequence you're about to learn for integrating and aligning your three brains.

The mBIT foundational sequence

"That which cometh from the heart goes to the heart."

Jeremia Burroughs

We discovered that whenever you are attempting to align your three brains, the order in which you work with them can make a significant difference to your results. The ease or difficulty of your efforts along with the quality of the end outcome can often be simply a matter of accessing each of your brains in a different sequence.

So is there a particular sequence that works better than others? As a general rule, yes. We've found from our action research that there's a '*neurologically-friendly*' sequence that works best for the majority of people. We call this the mBIT Foundational Sequence.

While specific individuals and specific issues may require a uniquely tailored sequence, as a general rule we've found the mBIT Foundational Sequence to best facilitate alignment, integration and congruence between the three brains.

Starting with the heart

Because the heart leads, the mBIT Foundational Sequence involves starting with the heart. Once the heart is engaged and in a generative flow state with both sympathetic and parasympathetic systems balanced and coherent, the next step is to communicate this experience or message to the head.

With the Autonomic Nervous System in a synchronized coherent state, this means that both the left and right hemispheres of the head brain will be equally engaged. From the head, the communication then returns to the heart on the way to the gut, gathering momentum and creating alignment throughout the *mBrain* system.

So the foundational sequence is:

Heart >> Head >> Heart >> Gut >> Heart

There is logic to this sequence. The heart is amenable to change via consciously controlled breathing and a focus on passionate and positive emotions. The heart's prime functions are also around values, passion and connection, so starting the aligning process from the heart links it to values and importance.

Moving next to the head brings creativity and generative complexity to the experience, done in a passionate, com-passionate and connected way. Going back from the head through the heart reinforces the experience once again to heart felt connection. Finally the gut brings motivation, movement and a will to action that is now creatively and com-passionately aligned. Finishing at the heart completes the loop and layers onto it a final level of importance, purpose and positivity.

It's important to note it's not just about the logic behind the foundational sequence, while the sequence was informed by science and esoteric wisdom, more importantly it was developed through behavioral modeling of people inherently able to align their three brains. These are people who are exemplars of working with, communicating between and integrating their multiple brains. When we examined how they generated their incredible results, we found they followed the process of the Foundational Sequence.

</== Discovery Exercise: Congruence ==/>

Now it's time for you to put your learnings into action by facilitating congruence between your three brains with the mBIT Foundational Sequence. In this discovery exercise you'll first get into a coherent state via balanced breathing. You'll then explore integrating your three brains' different core competencies starting with your heart brain, then up to your head brain, back down through the heart and into your gut brain, finally ending back at the heart.

While this discovery exercise works with the core competencies of passion (heart), curiosity (head), and motivated action (gut), you can modify this exercise to integrate any of the balanced states listed in the mBIT Core Competencies Framework.

1. Think of an issue or situation in which you would like to embody more passion and take more motivated action.

2. Now sit or stand comfortably and begin the Balanced
    Breathing exercise described in Chapter 4.

3. Once you have balanced your breathing for a few minutes
    along the sine wave pattern (breathing in for 6 seconds and
    out for 6 seconds), begin to recall a memory or imagine a
    scenario that produces a strong feeling of passion within you.
    This could involve engaging in activities you love to do,
    loved to do in the past, or would love to do in the future or as
    an aspiration. Connect strongly with these feelings of passion
    that arise within you as you do this.

4. As you fully experience your feelings of passion, breathe into
    your heart area and feel the feelings of passion filling your
    chest and heart with each breath. Amplify these feelings at
    least ten times for a deep, rich, heart-full experience.

5. Now begin to imagine and feel your feelings of passion
    expanding upwards to your head brain. As you send the
    signals of passion upward, allow your head to become filled
    with curiosity. Become curious about this passion. Entertain
    curious thoughts and perceptions about the nature of your
    passionate feelings, discover different possibilities for
    expressing your feeling of passion, and explore new ways of
    seeing and understanding the world starting from intense
    feelings of passion. Be open to what is there to learn with all
    of this and amplify your curiosity by ten times more.

6. Now begin to breathe this passionate curiosity from your
    head back down into your heart. Feel the thoughts of

curiosity harmonize with and enhance your feelings of passion.

7. Now continue to balanced breathe the feelings of passion from your heart combined with the curiosity of your head down into your gut area. Feel the sensations and impulse signals of your gut intelligence instinctively moving toward taking some kind of positive action from your combination of passion and curiosity. Let this feeling of motivated action fill your entire lower abdomen, hips and legs. Amplify your feeling of motivated action by ten times or more.

8. Now breathe these feelings and sensations of motivated action back up into your heart. As you send these signals upwards, allow each balanced breath to help you feel more and more strongly the integration and growing congruence between the passionate feelings of your heart, the curious thoughts and perceptions of your head, and the impulse to take motivated actions from your gut. Expand that flow throughout your entire body and notice the changes in your overall wellbeing with your enhanced and expanded sense of who you are and what is truly possible for you now.

Amping up integration using Neural Integrative Engagements (NIE's)

What we're after when integrating our *mBrains* is to ensure they're in optimal states to both send and receive signals from each other and additionally they're in optimal states to respond and align with the messages received. To do this we use what are called '*Neural*

Integrative Engagements' (NIE's). These are processes that amp-up the signals and states of the three brains and increase the integrative engagement between the neural networks. Developing your ability to work with NIE's dramatically increases your results when working with your three brains.

There are a number of key principles involved in how we can best work with our neural networks and how to amplify or increase the neural integrative engagement between the brains. These principles include:

- Utilize anything that puts a neural network into a receptive state to send or receive the signal (e.g. the need to be in a coherent state, congruence, trust etc.)
- Utilize anything that facilitates communication between neural networks
  - Optimize the signal to noise ratio
    - Anything that amplifies the communication signal (clearer, louder, more frequent, etc.)
    - Anything that reduces noise and distraction
  - Anything that removes blocks and allows the signal to get through (we'll cover Neural Integration Blocks (NIB's) in the next chapter)
- Utilize anything that removes a dysfunctional state within a neural network (e.g. indigestion, fighting illness or disease, etc.)

To apply these principles when working with ourselves and with others, we have found the following NIE's to be highly practical and effective:

- Visualization and imagery
- Sounds
- Physical movement and touch
- Smells
- Tastes
- Submodalities
  - Location and distance
  - Size
  - Brightness
  - Temperature
  - Colors, etc.
- Swallowing
- Symbols and metaphors
- Language and hypnosis
- Minimize neurological distractions

In the remainder of this chapter we'll explore details of these various NIE's that our modeling work has uncovered.

Key mBIT Principle: Use multiple sensory modalities

An underlying mBIT principle to be aware of when working with the various NIE's is that the predominant sensory mode of both heart and gut brains is kinesthesia (an NLP term for feelings). As we discussed in the previous chapter, the heart and gut brains communicate via a *'felt sense'* and a set of visceral kinesthetic experiences. Because of this the Foundational Sequence starts by getting you to engage with positive emotional and feeling states in your heart and chest. However, as you know from practical experience each of our sensory modalities can produce its own form of kinesthesia. We can generate a range of different feelings from what we see, hear, feel, smell and taste. The neural networks and communication channels within and between head and heart are amplified when we add in more sensory modalities such as sight, sound, smell and taste. Using both the visual modality along with the kinesthetic for example produces far greater integrative engagement.

Visualization and imagery

It's long been known that visualization and imagery can produce powerful and impactful effects. For some people, adding a visual representation to a feeling amplifies it massively. While one of the simplest ways to add visualization is to add a colored light to the feeling, there are many creative ways you can use visualization and imagery. For example, you might use a remembered experience or scene that matches the feeling. Or you can use creative visualization and imagine a symbol or image that supports or is evocative of the feeling you are working with. Alternately, you might trust and allow your unconscious mind to bring an appropriate image spontaneously into your awareness.

Using colors

As indicated, adding visualization through the use of colors can be a very powerful and effective way to increase neural engagement. Instead of just building a feeling in your heart region, imagine your heart filling with a colored light that matches the feeling. Give this a go right now. Most people notice that adding in visualization of colored light to match the feelings building in the heart, really adds an extra dimension and intensity to the experience.

Whilst there are some minor disagreements across the various esoteric traditions, the overall consensus is that the following colors are associated with and support the specified intelligence and core competency:

- Heart – Green or Pink for compassion
- Head – Blue or Violet for creativity
- Gut – Red/Crimson or Orange for courage
- Note: be flexible and adjust according to individual preferences

However, you should always be flexible and allow everyone to naturally use the color that works best for them with each brain and competency. We tend to only suggest the above colors if the person we are coaching is unable to naturally come up with their own color choice.

Case Study - Carla T

We were working with Carla T, helping to '*mBIT coach*' her through severe anxiety issues. We started off with mBIT Balanced Breathing and as she moved into coherence, we then asked her to breathe in positive feelings of compassion into her heart. Once this was solidly established and she could feel and build heart-felt feelings of compassion with every breath, we asked her to move the feelings from her heart up to her head. Nothing happened. Carla stopped and told us that the feelings weren't moving and she really couldn't get them up to her head. It was time to amp up the exercise with the addition of some NIE's.

So we went back to the beginning and this time, along with the feelings of compassion, we asked her to breathe the color of compassion into her heart with every breath, whatever that color was for her. Carla said that compassion was a clear mint green. And this time with both strong feelings of compassion and her heart filled and surrounded by vibrant green light, she was easily able to move both the light and feelings up to her head. There we asked her to add in the sense of creativity and the color she associated with that. Then with both colors swirling together, she moved them back to her heart and down to her gut where she added in a deep red for courage. You could see the change immediately in Carla. Integration had occurred and alignment of her three brains was obvious throughout her neurology.

Carla was amazed at how powerful and simple the exercise was and how the old anxiety had just dissolved and disappeared. She was excited to now have a new tool to use in situations that had previously caused her issues. Twelve months after that single mBIT coaching session she reported the technique continued to work for her and she'd generalized its use into many aspects of her life.

Using Sounds

For some people sounds really enhance the experience and increase neural engagement. Internally (or externally) linking a sound to each part of the Foundational Sequence adds a whole new dimension. Again, while not all esoteric traditions agree about the particular sounds associated with each intelligence, the following are in broad agreement:

- Heart – 'Ah' for compassion
- Head – 'Oh', 'Om' or 'Eee' for creativity
- Gut – 'Ki' or 'Ai' or 'Ha' for courage
- Note: be flexible and adjust according to individual preferences

In general, sounds and tones carry large amounts of emotional meaning in human communication. Changing the tone of words and sentences changes their meaning completely. An utterance can be altered from a command to a question by simply changing the end of the sentence to a rising tone.

We also know that music easily and powerfully evokes emotional response. Listening to heavy metal produces a very different emotional experience compared to listening to a melodic love song.

Within your own internal dialogue, notice the massive difference between using a comforting and soothing voice versus an angry, belligerent voice. Or try talking to yourself with a voice that sounds like a Disney character. It produces a very different emotional response, doesn't it?

As a NIE, you want to use sounds that are both congruent with and amplify the neural states you're activating. For a lot of people, simply adding in sounds produces a fundamental shift in state.

Physical movement and touch

While touch and movement are important senses for us all, some people in particular process the world primarily through kinesthetic filters. These people need to represent their experiences through movement, touch and feelings in order to get in contact with and make sense and meaning of the experience. In other cases, people get stuck in a particular state and are only able to shift by literally moving their bodies to get out of that stuck state. Additionally, many people find that simply by touching and or deliberately moving the physical areas of the lower torso/pelvic region, the chest/ribcage area, and the head/neck/shoulders area they are able to more easily and effectively breathe into and engage the related brains.

In any case, movement and touch add strongly to the engagement of our neural networks and the communication processes between them. This is especially true of the gateway points in our bodies we described in Chapter 4 — the key muscle groups that are co-innervated by both the Sympathetic Nervous System and the Autonomic Nervous System. Consciously moving or touching these areas sends incredibly strong signals between the brains.

As discussed in Chapter 3, we also know that massage of the gut region can release strong emotional responses. Touching, stroking and massaging the regions connected to a neural network evokes responses in that network. Similarly, stroking and moving from one region to another facilitates integration between the two regions and their connected neural networks.

As a behavioral experience and example, try breathing a heartfelt emotion like love into your heart and chest right now. Notice the ease or difficulty in doing this. Now, place both hands on your chest above your heart region, and imagine breathing love into your heart. Do you find it easier to feel and evoke the sensations of love when you are touching your heart? Now move the feelings of love from your heart to your head and as you do so, stroke your hands from your chest, up your throat and face to your head. Is it easier with the added sense of touch and movement? If you are like most people, you'll find that this adds to and enhances the experience.

(Note, the above examples apply to working specifically with yourself, however when coaching others you need to be respectful of physical boundaries and trust and realize that touching is not usually appropriate or recommended.)

Smells and tastes

The heart and gut brains attend intensely to smells and tastes. These are primal experiences. There's a substantial body of research showing we are able to smell danger, fear, fertility and attraction. You might also remember the research we described in Chapter 3 on the influences of olfactory/gustatory disgust on moral disgust.

As we know from the fragrance industry, the sense of smell is strongly linked to romance, attraction and bonding, and huge amounts of money are spent on perfumes across the world for this reason. So if you want to massively amplify kinesthetic states, use smells and tastes that match the feelings you want to evoke.

In our action research workshops we have used the fragrance and taste of chocolate for example to evoke and amplify feelings of motivation and hunger for completion of goals and outcomes. Check out our website for further detailed information about the links between smells, tastes and emotions.

Amplifying with submodalities

Submodalities are a discovery from the field of NLP. They're the building blocks of the senses and as such they structure the meaningfulness of our experiences. For each of our sensory modalities (sights, sounds, feelings, tastes and smells) the sub-components of each modality are its *'submodalities'*. So for sight for example, the pictures in your mind have submodalities like size, focus, distance, position, color/black-and-white etc.

Probably the easiest way to understand this is by exploring a mental image right now. Remember the last time you went on holiday and picture it in your mind now. As you look at this picture *'in your minds-eye'* begin to notice how far away the picture is. Is it really close or several feet away? What size is it? What about color and focus? Where is it positioned, high or low in your visual field?

Research in Neuropsychology has shown that internal imagery or visualization utilizes much of the same neural circuitry as used for external imagery or vision. For this reason, pictures in your mind use the same sort of submodalities as external vision. Just as objects you see in the real world have distance, focus, position, etc. so do images in your mind when you recall memories or you create imagery during fantasy.

Now the most interesting and useful aspect of this is that the submodalities of the image structure the meaningfulness of the image. And when you deliberately change the submodalities it changes your subjective experience of the image. As a graphic example, picture something you value very highly. Something that is really, really important to you. Notice where in space and how highly the image is positioned. Notice also how bright and close it is.

Now, picture something that disgusts you, that you hate or have a strong 'move-away' value about. Notice where in space that image is positioned. For the great majority of people, the image is lower than the highly valued image. It is often less bright and further away. As a generalization, the more valuable and salient an experience is, the higher it will be positioned in your mind-space, the closer the image will be, and the brighter it will be.

Just for a moment, try this experiment. Recall the image of the thing you value highly. Now push the image way off into the distance, making it really tiny, and dim it right down, maybe even give it a sense of black-and-white. Now, as you look at this distant, small, dim image, how does it subjectively feel? For almost all people, this process makes the experience seem much less important, much less meaningful.

Now zoom the image back in close, brighten it right up, and make it large with bold and vibrant colors. Just the way you like to have it. (You can feel that in your heart, can't you!)

This is the power of submodalities for enhancing and changing your experience and shifting the meaningfulness you make of memories and thoughts. And this process works not just for the visual modality of your experience. It works for the auditory, kinesthetic (feelings), olfactory and gustatory senses too. Auditory submodalities include volume, pitch/tone, location, mono or stereo, etc. Kinesthetic submodalities include temperature, movement, location, duration, etc. Olfactory submodalities consist of the various types of smells such as pungent, sharp, etc. along with the location of the smell, strength of the smell, etc. Gustatory submodalities on the other hand, include the types of tastes (sweet, bitter, sour, salty, savory, hot, watery, fatty, metallic, etc.) along with the location of the taste in the mouth, tongue and throat, its duration, texture, etc. (For a more detailed list of the various submodalities relating to each sensory modality visit our website: www.mbraining.com)

Linking this to neural engagement in your *mBrains*, can you see how the more impactful you make the sensory experience of the integration process, the stronger and more powerful it will be? Submodalities are like amplifiers. You can use them to make feelings larger, stronger and warmer, with more movement and intensity. You can use them to make imagery brighter, more saturated, the images closer, larger, moving. Sounds, smells, tastes all have submodalities. Use them to intensify the mBIT processes and you'll find neural integration is much more impactful and effective.

Swallowing

As described in Chapter 4, the esophagus is co-innervated by both the enteric nervous system and the somatic system. So swallowing is controlled by both the head and gut brains and thereby amplifies connection between the two. The tongue and throat are gateways to autonomic system control and can be used to amplify neural integration.

Whilst this can seem surprising, the use of swallowing can produce profound alignment and congruence. That this is true is evidenced in the reverse. When people are overwhelmed by emotion they get all choked up as an unconscious way of limiting and controlling the emotional response. When people are confronted by something they have to do and are afraid of, but finally accept they're going to do it, they gulp. To overcome fright and take action, people find they have to swallow their fear. These and many other gustatory behavioral experiences show how universal and powerful swallowing can be.

Using symbols and metaphor

In one of our Action Research Workshops a participant reported that he'd found using colors with his feelings had not really worked for him. But, as soon as he changed the colors to jewels and imagined large beautiful jewels in each of his brains, ones that resonated with and represented each feeling state, he immediately experienced a powerful and profound shift and amplification of his neural engagement. Using emeralds, diamonds and rubies in his heart, head and gut respectively, provided both powerful symbols along with deeply engaging colors and meaning. This really worked for him.

The key is that symbols and metaphor are one of the ways our neural networks communicate. The heart and gut do not use complex abstract verbal language. So integrating instead through symbol and metaphor can bring profound neural engagement. However, this doesn't work for everyone and can sometimes add an extra layer of cognitive processing that overloads or distracts from the core process. Symbols and metaphors also tend to be unique and specific to the individual. So listen for them in the expressions communicated to you and use them carefully and with sensitivity for each person's subjective world.

Using language and hypnosis

In Chapter 3 we described how the ACC (Anterior Cingulate Cortex) in the head brain is a key point of communication between the frontal lobes of the head and the heart and gut brains. As we pointed out, the ACC is strongly involved in motivation, conflict monitoring, error detection, reward anticipation, decision-making, empathy and emotion. It's also involved in regulating blood pressure and heart rate. In addition, the ACC is critically involved in processing the emotional component of visceral pain sensation.

All this is interesting, and provides back up for the core competencies of the heart and gut brains, but what's more fascinating is the research on hypnosis and its effect on the ACC. Studies show that hypnosis can be used to control the ACC's response to noxious and painful stimuli. In one experiment, hypnotic suggestions were used to selectively alter the unpleasantness of noxious stimuli, without changing the perceived intensity. Positron emission tomography revealed significant changes in pain-evoked activity within the ACC consistent with the encoding of perceived unpleasantness. These findings indicate that the ACC is strongly amenable to hypnotic commands and communication and therefore use of hypnotic language can be a powerful way to augment neural integrative engagement.

This idea is also backed up by research using hypnosis on the motility and perception of the gastrointestinal tract. Results clearly show that hypnotic commands are significantly able to affect visceral perception of rectal distension and increase and decrease colonic motility. The gut and heart brains respond to hypnotic commands and processes.

The work in Cognitive Linguistics described in Chapter 3 also supports the power of language and metaphor to affect perceptions and responses within our neural networks. Language and metaphor are largely embodied. This means when you use language that presupposes gustatory or heart-based effects, you increase the neural responses that are congruent with those presuppositions. For example, if you want someone to align their gut brain with a suggested outcome or change, you'll enhance the effect through language such as, "you can easily digest this new idea and absorb it deeply within you now".

Whilst the scope of this book precludes comprehensive exploration of hypnotic language processes or the use of advanced predicate patterns, we will be writing much more about this and making it available, along with videos and mp3's, on our website (www.mbraining.com). So check there regularly.

One really useful distinction to be aware of is that the heart responds powerfully to olfactory experiences and therefore also responds strongly to olfactory predicates (think about how perfumes are so important to romantic effect, and how we use fragrant flowers to show our heart-felt love). On the other hand, the gut responds more strongly to tastes and gustatory predicates.

Minimize neurological distractions

"Hold your council before dinner;

the full belly hates thinking as well as acting."

Benjamin Franklin

179

As Ben Franklin so astutely noted many years ago, the gut does NOT do its best thinking or processing when it's busy trying to digest a rich meal. Don't expect to engage massive amounts of wisdom, courage or motivation after filling your belly with food. We all know this intuitively and from experience. Esoteric and spiritual traditions also understand this, which is why they utilize fasting before undergoing important rituals or attempting to connect with deep intuitive processes. These are all great examples of the effects of neurological distraction and the importance of overcoming it.

In order to maximize the communication within and between our brains, we really do need them to be in optimal states for communicating and processing information. To do that we need to minimize neurological distractions such as:

- Beware of interference — strong emotions, a full belly, etc.
- Silence is necessary to hear/feel messages
- Fasting to amplify messages i.e. remove interference

So don't try to do mBIT processes when you are massively tired, in the middle of a noisy environment or swamped by external stressors. Give yourself the time and space to quiesce your neural networks and provide them with the best chance of communicating and processing the integrative changes you are facilitating.

</== Discovery Exercise: Utilizing NIE's ==/>

Ok, once again it's time for you to put your new learnings about NIE's into action. In this exercise you'll perform the mBIT Foundational Sequence adding in various NIE's to facilitate increased levels of engagement with each neural network.

There are many ways to work with NIE's and the following is just a starting point to begin exploring and experimenting with them. You'll want to play with a range of variations and combinations to find the specific NIE's that work best for you in particular situations.

(Note: You may wish to get someone to read this exercise to you so you are free to deeply focus on the experience. Alternatively, you may want to go to our website www.mbraining.com to download the audio of this process.)

1. Think of an issue or situation in which you'd like to experience a deeper connection with a core value and being able to express it congruently in your behaviors. Identify a specific issue or situation, and identify the specific core value. Examples of core values include joy, peace, happiness, love, integrity, respect, gratitude, honesty, etc.

2. Sit or stand comfortably and begin the Balanced Breathing exercise described in Chapter 4.

3. Once you have balanced your breathing for a few minutes along the wave pattern (breathing in for 6 seconds and out for 6 seconds), begin to visualize an image that best represents your core value to you. Allow your unconscious mind to '*intuitively*' arrive at an appropriate image for you.

4. Explore making the image in your mind bigger, brighter and more colorful. Bring it closer toward you and notice how your feelings and sensations change. Make refined adjustments to your image until it produces a strong feeling within you.

5. Now imagine a color for your core value. Imagine that color totally surrounding you like a comforting blanket. Breathe in that color. Breathe it into your lungs and allow the color to fill your heart area. Feel your value coming more and more alive in your heart as you breathe its color into you.

6. Feel the sensations associated with your core value moving through you and expanding your chest area with each breath. Feel its temperature and allow its movement to begin to rise up toward your head. You may even hear some sounds or tones as the sensations of your core value rises up and reaches your head.

7. See and feel your head fill with the color of your core value and allow it to color all of your thoughts, perceptions and internal dialogue. Hear how your own internal voice changes when speaking from the essence of your core value. Notice the new ways of thinking and new perceptions available to you now about your situation or issue.

8. Now imagine your core value flowing down from your head back down to your heart as easily as water flows downward along the natural contours of a terrain. Feel your heart fill with new ways of relating to others and to your specific situation or issue based on living and breathing your core value.

9. Now continue to allow the enhanced feelings and new perceptions from your core value to flow down to your gut area. Feel it gather there like a pool of living energy. Feel the

pulse of life and your own aliveness. Feel yourself awakening and moving with the pulse of your core value. Feel the impulse to move and act in accordance with the energy and truth of your core value. Be aware of the behavioral choices becoming available to you that embody, express and fulfill your core value into the physical world. Make a subtle or clear movement, gesture or stance that symbolizes to you the beginnings of a physical/behavioral manifestation of your core value.

10. Now take a deep breath and feel the energy of your core value begin to rise like an *'aliveness thermometer'* until it again reaches your heart. Breathe in the energy, colors, and sounds of your core value. Let it fill your heart as you gently sway and move to the pulse and rhythm of your core value. Imagine the fragrance your core value filling your nostrils and evoking new possibilities for experiencing your situation or issue. Imagine the taste of your core value as you gently swallow it into you, making it part of your very being.

11. Allow your core value to flow easily throughout your entire body and notice the changes in your overall wellbeing. Become aware of your enhanced and expanded sense of who you are and how you can now act in ways that express your authentic self.

Working with others

When coaching or working with others using mBIT, you should be ready to use any and all of the NIE's already described above as may be required. However, there are additional processes you can use to help facilitate another person's neural engagement:

- Voice tones
- Gestures
- Entrainment (getting into the desired states yourself to influence the unconscious processes of the other person)

Entrainment is the process that occurs when two or more oscillating systems (e.g. any rhythmic, patterned or pulsing energy wave such as your heartbeat, brainwave frequencies, etc.) influence each other and become synchronized over time. Applying the process of entrainment as a NIE means that to start with, you should ensure you're in a coherent state yourself before attempting to guide someone else into balance and coherence. As described in the previous chapter, the electric field of the heart extends out into the space around you and there's evidence it can entrain another person's heart into the same levels of coherence. Your unconscious non-verbal behaviors also send strong signals about the mind-body state you're in. When your sympathetic and parasympathetic systems are in balance, you send clear signals, picked up by mirror neurons in the other person's brain. So make sure you're experiencing all the states in your three brains that you want to entrain into the person you are working with.

In addition, make sure you use appropriately congruent voice tones and gestures with the messages you're sending. If you are talking to the person and guiding them into heart-felt states of compassion, talk in a peaceful and compassionate tone of voice. Use gestures that are open, even and flowingly point to the region of their heart. The same applies when facilitating states or experiences in a person's brains or guiding messages and movement between their brains. Make sure all your non-verbal messages are congruent with the content you're communicating. Ensure your communication processes match your content; it's crucial for gaining rapport, congruence and alignment.

In summary

To wrap it all up, the key points you need to remember are:

1. When working with your multiple brains along the mBIT Roadmap, make sure they're aligned and congruent with each other.

2. In order to facilitate your multiple brains to align and be congruent with each other, the sequence in which you work with them makes a difference. We have found the optimal sequence for most people starts with the heart, moves to the head, then moves back down through the heart to the gut, then back up to the heart. This is the mBIT Foundational Sequence.

3. When facilitating yourself or others, you need to engage each of the neural networks as strongly as possible. To help achieve this, the tools and techniques you can reach for are called NIE's (Neural Integrative Engagements).

NIE's for working with your self are:

*   Visualization and imagery
*   Sounds
*   Physical movement

- Smells
- Tastes
- Submodalities
    - Location and distance
    - Size
    - Brightness
    - Temperature
    - Colors, etc.
- Swallowing
- Symbols and metaphors
- Language and hypnosis
- Minimize neurological distractions

NIE's for working with others are:

- All of the above
- Voice tones
- Gestures
- Entrainment

Using your skills

Using the mBIT knowledge and skills you've learned in this book enables you to quickly align and integrate your three brains to attain deep levels of personal congruency. With continued practice and experience, you'll find however, not all states of congruency are desirable. For instance, you can be congruently angry, vengeful, uncaring or even depressed. These would be congruent states resulting from a sympathetic-parasympathetic imbalance. Obviously, we are not after such states but rather we're seeking coherent states that increase overall wellbeing and contribute to our personal evolution.

As outlined in the mBIT Roadmap, the next step is to ensure that when you align and integrate your three brains, you attain states of congruency that are based on your neural networks' highest levels of coherent functioning and expression. And this is the topic of upcoming chapters.

mBraining

"Using your multiple brains to do cool stuff"

Chapter 6

Neural Integration Blocks

Pattern interrupting Neural Integration Blocks (NIB's)

In a perfect world, your brains would always immediately integrate and align as you attempted communication between them. Of course, in a perfect world, your three brains would already be permanently in synch and aligned beautifully together. Unfortunately, it's not a perfect world…

So you'll find there are times while aligning *mBrains*, that one or more will block the process of integration. They just won't respond or allow the integration message through. We call these blocks Neural Integration Blocks (NIB's) and in our behavioral modeling work we've found six classes of NIB's each made up of a number of separate blocking processes.

In this chapter we'll examine each NIB and describe how it functions and what you can do to interrupt the blocking pattern and get integration to occur. Note up front that not all NIB's are amenable to mBIT coaching. Some are beyond the scope of this book and require medical or psychological intervention. We'll highlight these as we go through the list of the 15 NIB's we've delineated to date.

NIB's in overview

In summary, here are the top 15 reasons we've found why a person might get *'blocked'* while attempting to integrate using the mBIT Foundational Sequence:

Operating state issues

1. Dissociation (lack of neural engagement)

2. State of autonomic incoherence (when starting)

Alignment issues

3. Secondary gain

4. Ecology issues

5. Ill-formed/incompatible outcomes and intentions between the three brains

Emotive issues

6. Fear

7. Trust

8. Phobic responses (intense and pervasive negative associations/anchors)

Educational issues

9. No reference structure

10. Gut and/or heart brain needs upgrading/educating

Tailoring issues

11. Needs a personalized/tailored sequence

12. Needs tailored facilitation of the head brain's processing strategies

13. Needs personalized Neural Integrative Engagement facilitation

Medical/Psychological issues ***

14. Bio-chemical problems (medication, bad nutrition, endocrine problems, substance abuse, medical conditions-illnesses, etc.)

15. The person is mentally or emotionally unstable

*** Note: these last two require professional intervention prior to attempting any mBIT Coaching or mBIT processes.

Now let's explore each of the NIB's in detail and examine strategies for how to deal with them.

Operating state issues

With operating state issues, the person (or yourself) is not in an optimal state to fully engage or work with their neural networks — their brains — to allow the integration process to occur. This may be because they are totally dissociated from the experience; protecting themselves and distancing themselves emotionally or psychologically from the process. Or they may be in an exceptionally incoherent and abreacting state, one that doesn't allow them to think or act rationally and follow directions.

>> NIB: Dissociation

In the first case, you need to get the person associated and present in the experience. You may have to build strong rapport and trust and guide them to the here and now, associated to the place and experience that is unfolding. Once they are feeling safe and present, you can guide them to commence the mBIT Balanced Breathing process and then engage in the heart-felt feelings and experience that leads to integration.

>> NIB: State of autonomic incoherence

In the case of massive incoherence, you need to help and guide them to relax, to focus on balanced breathing, to let go of the emotional or cognitive processes they're going through that cause their abreactions.

For example if they're filled with anger and rage, you need to assist them to calm themselves, to let go temporarily of whatever it is they're using to build and maintain angering, and to associate instead into more optimally positive states. You may have to facilitate them in remembering times when they were feeling happier, calmer, more at peace. Once you calm them sufficiently to start balanced breathing, these actions will begin to shift the over-sympathetic dominance, and help an ongoing positive cycle of coherence to occur.

Alignment issues

Alignment issues are due to patterns of disagreement between the three brains. One or more of them just doesn't want to align with the messages or intentions from the others. Fundamentally this is about incongruent patterns of response between the neural networks. Let's look at each of the NIB's that make up this class.

>> NIB: Secondary gain

Secondary gain is where one of the brains has been achieving a secondary or veiled benefit through its actions. This is sometimes known as a hidden agenda. For example, the gut brain might be generating lustful states of over-eating leading to obesity. Whilst the person would like to stop this behavior, the gut brain may have a hidden agenda of keeping the person unattractive and thereby protecting them from close relationships and heart-break. The secondary gain is safety and protection.

If the alignment process doesn't account for and satisfy the secondary gains, the brain will block the integration. Fundamentally though, the three brains can best align and negotiate to satisfy all *mBrain* outcomes, gains and intentions when the process occurs in a frame of wisdom, creativity and heart-felt loving-kindness between the brains. Another way of saying this is that secondary gains are about unmet needs, and issues with this dissolve when alignment occurs through trust and positive intention. Facilitating this dynamic is one of the design elements underpinning the structure of the mBIT Roadmap.

>> NIB: Ecology issues

Ecology issues are about unintended consequences within the ecology of the whole system. If one of the brains thinks that the outcome being integrated is unecological (i.e. it anticipates undesirable side effects or consequences from the outcome) it is likely to block agreement and alignment. To overcome this you need to ensure all the brains understand they must find a compassionate and creative solution that is wise, ecological and satisfies all the needs of all the parts of the person within the problem context.

We'll discuss this process in far greater detail in Chapter's 7 and 8. It's really important to note however, that ecology is absolutely crucial and must be dealt with skillfully. You do NOT want to force integration between a person's *mBrains* unecologically. The heart and gut brains have their own wisdom and truly do know when something is not ecological and has negative unintended consequences. So respect this NIB and make sure you facilitate integration through a framework of wisdom, choice, creativity, flexibility and congruent ecology.

>> NIB: Ill-formed/incompatible outcomes and intentions

If your brains have incompatible outcomes or intentions they will definitely block communication and integration. An example of this would be if your head brain has planned out a detailed and intensive career path, your heart brain wants more family time and connection, and your gut brain wants you to relax and de-stress by withdrawing and having some downtime for yourself. As in any negotiation, the way forward is to get the parties to help each other satisfy their underlying values, needs and requirements. As with the two NIB's above, this can best be done through the framework of the *'Highest Expressions'* and *'Wisdom'* from the mBIT Roadmap that we'll cover in the following chapters. You can also use the mBIT Focus Reframe technique we'll describe later in this chapter.

Emotive issues

As you begin the Foundational Sequence process, you might find the head and heart will easily align. However, due to the core competencies of the gut around fear, protection, fight and flight, the person may experience abreactions or deeply visceral emotional responses such as fear, anxiety or phobia. This can be especially true if the gut brain has over-learned patterns of association that are triggered during the integration process. In NLP, these patterns of association are called *'anchors'*, and can be triggered by any part of the original pattern.

One way to help overcome fear and phobic responses is to go back to balanced breathing and regain a state of coherence.

Additionally, you can use the NLP processes of resource state anchoring; however the details of these skills are beyond the scope of this book and can be found in any good NLP training or book.

States of fear, anxiety or phobia can also be due to one of the brains communicating about issues of ecology. In this case you need to go back and sort out the ecology NIB first. If all ecology and secondary gain issues have been sorted, and the person is convinced alignment on the problem is wise and ecological, then you can use a kinesthetic pattern interrupt technique called a *'Kinesthetic Interrupt'* to interrupt the blocking process and allow the neural messages to go through. We'll describe this technique in the next section.

If the messages and intentions are truly ecological and generative, the brains will congruently align and integrate. If there are any residual issues, the brains will send intuitions and messages to alert that integration has been blocked at some deep level. You need to watch for and be aware of such incongruence signals, and we'll cover this in more detail later in this chapter.

>> NIB Tool: mBIT Kinesthetic Interrupt

In evolutionary terms, as the earliest simple celled organisms arose, the first sense that evolved was the ability to detect chemicals in the environment — the sense of taste. This was needed so organisms could detect *'food'*, the chemicals needed to survive, and additionally to allow them to detect and move away from harmful chemicals. The next sense to evolve was the ability to detect force — the sense of feeling, or what in NLP is called the kinesthetic sense. This sense allowed the evolving organisms to detect energy, force, movement and anything impacting upon them, and respond accordingly.

Overtime, as complex neural networks (brains) evolved in the growing complexity of life, organisms developed the ability to represent external sensory experiences as internal models of their environment. This internal sensory processing used the same neural circuitry as that originally evolved to track the external equivalent. This is why when you picture something in your *'mind's eye'* i.e. make an internal visual representation, you are actually predominantly using the same neural circuitry utilized when seeing the thing in the real world. This insight has been well proven and documented in the neuroscientific literature.

When it comes to internal feelings, to internal kinesthetic experiences, this means that every *'feeling'* is effectively a representation of some equivalent external force or impactor. You may not have noticed this before, but your internal feelings have vectors of movement. They aren't stationary. Feelings have an entry point, a trajectory and an exit point in your body. Emotions *'grip'* you, feelings *'bubble upwards'*, nothing is stationary.

Now the point of all this is... internal feelings use the same parts of the sensory-motor representational system as external feelings, and this means they are amenable to change and pattern interruption via external behavior. You can model or represent the internal feeling through its movement vectors or patterns and then interrupt those patterns, and it communicates amazing shifts within your brains. You can literally stop a dysfunctional feeling in its tracks.

The process to do this is called a *'kinesthetic interrupt'*, and it is easier to see than to describe verbally. So we suggest you check out the videos we've provided on our website (www.mbraining.com) to demonstrate it. But we'll do our best here to explain it in words. If you can't quite grasp what we're describing though, you'll need to go check the videos out and all will become clear.

Ok, imagine you have a 'stuck' feeling in your throat, some internal feeling of not being able to 'swallow an idea'. In other words (in mBIT language), your head is trying to tell your gut to assimilate an idea but your gut is trying to tell your head brain that it is not going to! (If you've never experienced this, then pick some other feeling such as dread in your chest, or nervous feelings in the gut and use those to get a sense of how to do the processes being described.)

Notice that such feelings are not stationary, but are moving and actually have a point of entry in the throat and a point of exit and a trajectory. Using your hands, you can 'model' the feeling outside your body so that your hand(s) physically describe the looping movement of entering in your throat from the front (say) moving up a couple of inches and then coming out the front again and looping around to start at the beginning. You'll know instinctually just how fast to move and how far outside the loop goes. Notice also that if you try to model the movement as slower or faster, in a bigger or smaller loop, it won't feel right. This tells you the processes we are dealing with are real. There actually is a vectored trajectory.

Now, here comes the kinesthetic interrupt. As you're modeling the kinesthetic pattern, in the middle of the loop, quickly swish your hands in a completely different pattern and direction. For example if the loop is going in a vertical up and down plane, then swish your hands left and right. Do it fast.

It also helps to add in swishing sounds out-loud as you do the hand movement interrupt. The addition of the auditory modality actually seems to augment the process and make a powerful difference by recruiting across sensory channels in the neural networks.

Repeat the process three times. Each time you'll find it more and more difficult to re-access the old feeling. Finally, you'll probably find it impossible to experience the old pattern in exactly the same way as before. Your neural networks will have now learned a new way to respond.

This technique works powerfully for dealing with kinesthetic blocks that can occur when *mBrains* are attempting to communicate, negotiate and integrate. By modeling the feeling of the blocking process and kinesthetically interrupting it, you allow the messages to go through and integration to occur.

So, in summary the *'Kinesthetic Interrupt'* technique is:

1. Determine the entry point, exit point and trajectory of the *'feeling'* that is blocking *mBrain* communication and model it outside yourself with your hands. Ask yourself, "Where in my body does the feeling start?", "Where does the feeling move to?", "Where does the feeling exit and loop?"

2. As your hands are looping around demonstrating the feeling pattern, quickly interrupt the pattern by swishing your hands across the line of the loop and making a loud auditory swish *'shhhh'* sound.

3. Repeat the procedure three times and notice how it's now impossible to do the old blocking pattern or feeling.

When working with or coaching another person, it works best for the coach to guide the person in determining and modeling the feeling pattern, and then while they are physically modeling the pattern, the coach does the movements and sound of the interrupt, close to the person, swishing the hands within the space of the original modeled loop. You'll see amazing changes in the person's neurology when you do this. Looks of momentary confusion are quite typical. We usually pace the experience as we do the technique by getting the person to model or demonstrate the feeling with their hands, and then while they are doing this, we say "so what happens for you when I do this?" just before doing the interrupt, and timing the interrupt just after the word 'this'.

The Kinesthetic Interrupt technique is incredibly simple yet powerful. You'll be amazed at the results it can generate.

Case Study - Alison E: Moving beyond fear

One of the best ways to get a sense of how emotive issue NIB's work and how to dissolve them using an mBIT Kinesthetic Interrupt is with a real-world case study.

Al is a young vivacious woman in her early 30's, who at the tender age of 16 was attacked, beaten and left with a permanently damaged spine and paraplegia. She was told she'd never walk again and would live her life in a wheel-chair. However, through sheer determination and an indomitable spirit, she learned to get out of that wheel-chair and walk again. Unfortunately though, the cowardly attack left her with continuous pain that she learned to armor against and transcend to live a normal life.

Recently, new evidence-based medical and scientific insights lead to an exercise regime that her doctors suggested might help restore function to her spine and potentially remove the pain she's experienced on a daily basis. The challenge for Al is that these new exercises are the opposite of everything she's done for the last 20 years and the opposite of what she was told long ago she must never do or she'd end up back in the wheel-chair.

Al came to us for mBIT coaching because she'd been attempting to do the new exercises but was experiencing massive fear whenever she undertook them. She'd tried everything she could, however she was unable to shift this uncontrollable fear and motivate herself to do the exercises. If she forced herself to start them, she'd freeze up and be unable to continue. She also found that if she did manage to do them even for a short while, she would begin gaining new found feeling in her spine, but would disturbingly relapse into states of spinal immobility. This had caused her anxiety and even more fear about doing the new exercise regime. She related how she'd been having very wild and amazing dreams since she'd started attempting the new exercises, and commented that all her intuitive processes were *'going overtime'*.

Listening to the neuro-linguistics around how she expressed her experience, we heard her say things like, "I want to get a taste of being able to be comfortable again", "I can't digest the fear of what might happen to my spine" and lots of related metaphors and issues around core identity.

We started by doing an ecology check around the nature of the exercises. Al was clearly able to articulate congruent intellectual belief in the efficacy and science of the changes she needed to make, she had done a lot of research to back up what the doctors were now telling her about the new processes, and she was cognitively congruent that the exercises were ecological and would do her no harm. With that assurance, we asked her to begin balanced breathing and moving into a state of coherence. We then asked her to think about her outcomes and to feel the desire for moving comfortably and being able to easily do the exercises, feeling deep appreciation and compassion in her heart for the successes she's achieved in her life to date, and to breath into those heart feelings, expand them and move them up to her head in order to align her thoughts with her heart-felt desires for generative change.

Once Al could breathe the experience of balanced appreciation and loving-kindness into her heart and then up to her head, we asked her to add creativity to the experience and then gently move this aligned set of feelings and messages down to her heart and on into her gut to add courage. When attempting to do this however, as she moved the experience down to her throat area, she immediately stopped and said her throat was blocking the feeling. Al related that the feeling was like nausea rising in her throat and that her throat was constricting the feeling from moving down to her gut. This was an obvious gut brain mediated communication and control response related to her gut brain fearing the change and attempting to keep Al's behavior patterns constant in her life.

We then got her to model the blocking feeling/pattern and did a kinesthetic interrupt to communicate kinesthetically with the gut brain and re-pattern its blocking response. As soon as we did the interrupt, immediately she burped loudly and started laughing a really deep belly-laugh. This was clearly a message that her gut had now released the old pattern and accepted the generative message from the head and heart brains and aligned with them. Al related that as soon as the kinesthetic interrupt had occurred, the feeling easily moved down to her gut where it felt strongly accepted and sat comfortably.

We got her to repeat the integration process and she was easily able to move the heart-felt feeling up to her head, add in creativity, move the experience back to her heart, then on to her gut and back to her heart. She said she felt much more aligned and comfortable and that inside her head, in her internal dialog, verbal blockage that she'd previously been doing around languaging her outcomes was now gone.

All in all, this was a quick, powerful and effective piece of personal coaching and change work. We completed the coaching session with some NLP future pacing and ecology checking, and all was *'sweet'* from Al's perspective.

An important thing to note from this case study is how the key issues were very much related to a mix of core identity, fear and lack of motivation — all gut brain linked core competencies and processes and clear indicators we needed to align the gut with the heart and head. In Al's case, she could clearly articulate cognitive acceptance of the new exercises and her heart was also happily aligned through values and a desire to be pain free and more flexible. However, the gut was holding on to old patterns that had been core to the identity of someone who had fought both the doctors and pain in order to get out of and stay out of a wheel-chair all those years ago.

At six month follow-up

Al reported that the mBIT change work had been and continued to be incredibly effective. The fear and lack of motivation dissolved completely during the single coaching session and she was able to start and continue the new exercises with ease and comfort. Her pain levels had now decreased substantially and with following the new regime she'd found increased levels of ease, flexibility and energy.

>> NIB: The structure of trust - Building trust between heart, head and gut brains

"Without trust there is nothing."

If there is no trust between each of your brains then you can forget true alignment and integration. If your head doesn't trust your heart, or your heart doesn't trust your gut, the lack of trust will undermine congruence and cause blocking of messages and integration between the brains. It's really no different from how you treat someone in your own life that you distrust completely. You'll ignore or discredit the things they tell you, thinking that it's just more lies.

There is a structure to the process of trust, and in order to build trust between the brains, you need to understand that structure and find the points of failure in the process and remedy them. As you rebuild trust, only then can you fully coach the three brains into congruence, agreement and alignment.

Trust between your brains involves four key components:

- Communication
- Caring
- Consistency
- Competency

Communication

Communication is all about listening to the feedback from *and* between the brains, and is a required component for building trust. If one brain refuses to communicate with another or stonewalls and ignores the communication it's receiving, this quickly destroys trust. Communication is about listening and sharing. Always listen with respect to every message that comes from each of your *mBrains*. The messages are important and provide valuable information you disregard at your peril. As a wise person once told us, "the facts are our friends."

From an *mBraining* perspective, it helps to remember that each neural network communicates its unique form of *'facts'* based on its prime functions and particular mode of communication. It's important that each brain works harmoniously with each other's *'facts'* and you are sensitive to each brain's unique language and method of communication.

Caring

Caring is concerned with intention and positive feelings of regard. It's about each brain recognizing the value of the other brains, and operating within a context of collaboration, harmony and integration. It's also about the strength of the relationship between the brains to work things through when things aren't working out.

This strength of relationship can be built over time the more you work with mBIT methods to keep your *mBrains* aligned and congruent with each other. Without caring and mutual respect, trust cannot be engendered between the brains and they will not negotiate or engage fully together. To facilitate this well, you yourself need to value and have positive regard for the role each of your brains play in your overall health, happiness and wellbeing.

Consistency

Building and maintaining trust requires congruence, reliability and consistency across time and contexts. Does each brain believe what the other says or promises to agree to? Will the gut brain be reliable in supporting the head or heart? Will the head allow the other brains to perform their core competencies and not interfere? Will the way your brains behave together be consistent and reliable?

If one of the brains delivers at some times, but not others, it destroys trust between them. If it acts erratically, the lack of consistency will render the relationship unreliable and damage the integrity and trust.

Once again, the more you use mBIT methods to facilitate the continual process of your *mBrains* communicating, aligning and integrating together, the more a track record of consistency and reliability will be built over time.

Competency

Lastly, the competency and skills of each brain can build or destroy trust. The *mBrains* need to be able to trust the skills, awareness and knowledge of each other to know they can consistently perform their prime functions. If one of the brains is incompetent the others will learn to block it or ignore it and find other ways to attempt to achieve the overall goals and outcomes. In these cases, you need to focus on what we'll be covering in the next section on Educational Issues.

One other important thing to note is that trust needs to be specifically built through the domains of expertise of the core competencies. For example, you wouldn't expect your accountant to successfully fix your teeth or your dentist to do a great job on your tax returns. Equally, your *mBrains* need to ensure they aren't expecting a brain to perform the core competencies or functions that are the rightful domain of another brain. In situations where this is occurring, the brains will learn not to trust each other, and this toxic and chronic pattern of behavior needs to be interrupted and the brains re-educated into the appropriate expectations, behaviors and patterns they're best responsible for and work optimally with.

>> NIB: Phobic Responses

A phobic response is an intense fear-based reaction to a certain type of stimulus or trigger (e.g. spiders, heights, enclosed spaces, etc.). The intensity of this reaction is often debilitating and can occur extremely rapidly upon experiencing the stimulus or trigger.

If you are working with someone who goes into a phobic abreaction, any attempts at aligning and integrating their *mBrains* will be futile. Your first goal is to get them out of their phobic abreaction. This is easier said than done and will require highly trained skills in techniques such as NLP's Phobia Cure, etc.

If you are not qualified to work with such techniques, we advise you to not work with people on phobia issues. If you want to work on any phobia issues of your own, we strongly suggest you find a Certified mBIT Coach to assist you in this process.

Educational Issues

Educating the neural networks may be required in two contexts. The first is if they don't have reference experiences anywhere in their personal history for the desired state to be integrated. For instance, one young adult who attended our workshops admitted that his heart brain had little to no experiential reference for states such as deep compassion or loyalty. We've also personally met people whose gut brains had minimal experiential references for highly focused will-power or high levels of true wellness and wellbeing.

In these situations, you'll need to help the person (or yourself) to either imagine and creatively construct what it would be like to experience the desired state, or to create a situation or condition where they can actually experience the desired state for the first time in their life.

The second context where education may be required is when a

206

neural network does actually have an experiential reference of the desired state or competency, however it was from a time period long ago. The neural network is operating from a limited knowledge/experience base that was formed at a level of mental, emotional and/or physical immaturity compared to the person's current age. The consequences of this can be immense.

Due to life experiences and intense early learnings, the neural networks of our brains can get conditioned into limiting and dysfunctional patterns. These learned behavioral patterns can become dominant strategies that filter all subsequent responses the brain makes and can easily generalize across contexts. For example, one person we examined in our behavioral modeling work had learned early in life not to trust their heart after having it badly broken by a best friend. Subsequently they'd decided never to use their heart intuitions again and not to get close to other people. Their heart had become 'hardened' towards emotional closeness. To compensate they had ramped up their focus and trust on gut intuitions.

The way to work with educational issue NIB's is to facilitate re-education of the brain(s) concerned. You need in effect to 'upgrade' their knowledge and skill base by either giving them new reference structure experiences or new learned ways of responding. Whilst we aren't able to cover these more advanced mBIT patterns in detail here, the following case study will provide you with an idea of what's involved, and if you're interested in learning more, please check out our website for information about mBIT Coaching Certification trainings and other advanced mBIT offerings.

Case Study - Beth D: Re-educating the gut brain

Beth D came for mBIT coaching due to severe issues with feelings of fear, panic and extreme anxiety. Beth's mother was a war survivor and had been quite psychologically impacted by those experiences. Because of this, Beth was raised in a constant mental-emotional context of fear and continuously reinforced to always be on-guard and vigilant about safety and protection issues. These were not just passing emotions but a psychological foundation deeply integrated into her identity and world model.

During the session, we realized that before integration of the three brains could occur, we first needed to do the reverse of integration and help Beth re-educate her gut brain into newer and more generative patterns. In essence, we needed to separate out what her gut brain was doing to keep her *'on-guard'* and vigilant 24/7. Then help her to cognitively understand what her head was doing with respect to thought patterns and generalizations she'd been making from the conditioning of her gut and the resultant emotional responses related to intense fear and overwhelm that subsequently occurred.

We started by separating out the contexts in which Beth operated. Within these contexts, and with a focus on her gut brain in a calm, coherent state, we re-educated and upgraded her gut intelligence using distinctions to sort out the many different levels of *'vigilance'* that are available. For example, being relaxed but aware in social situations with friends and family versus being alert and attentive when in unknown environments and situations such as walking down a dark street. Or being highly aware and on guard when in dangerous situations yet ready to do whatever it takes if physically attacked.

Once Beth's gut brain was educated and now '*wiser*' in its sorting abilities, we then future paced her through several scenarios related to each of the distinctions, and once she could do this easily, we facilitated her to engage in different strategies going from gut to head to heart related to those scenarios. In other words, we coached and tested her about, "What is the most appropriate gut response here?", "What thoughts and perceptions best support your gut in this context?" And, "What emotions now become available and arise when your gut is making a wise response and your head is supporting it with the appropriate thoughts, perceptions and beliefs?"

After this we did the normal mBIT integration process, which went smoothly. When we did a behavioral check, we were delighted at how nonchalant and matter of fact she had become about her previous issue. Asked to think of when she would next be in situations that in the past would have caused her to go into feelings of panic and extreme anxiety, she was calm, unfazed and totally at ease.

In Beth's case, she had previously lived with an uneducated/conditioned gut brain that did not make distinctions (everything and everyone, everywhere was always unsafe and dangerous) and this drove her head's thoughts and generalizations which ultimately evoked her heart's emotional response of panic and fear. By re-educating her gut brain into finer contextual distinctions, behaviors and decisions and then integrating these new learnings across all the *mBrains*, we were able to coach Beth into a new state of generative response and allow her to transcend the old strategy of self-traumatizing her life.

Tailoring Issues

Sometimes the generalized Foundational Sequence does not work for a specific individual. These people require coaching via a personalized or tailored sequence. They may need much more detailed Neural Integrative Engagement (NIE) facilitation in very specific ways. Or they may need particular strategy facilitation within one of their *mBrains*.

For example, there are people who have what in NLP is known as a *'meta-program'* or set of habitual perceptual filters that involves extreme *'mismatching'*. An extreme mismatcher is someone who habitually disagrees with or mismatches the things you say, no matter what you say! If you say something is black, they'll argue that it's white. They're also sometimes known as *'polarity responders'* and can flip from one polarized state to another. Attempting to facilitate neural integration with such people can be quite challenging and requires skills beyond the scope of this book. Tailoring is something that is taught in much more detail in mBIT Coaching Certification trainings and if you are interested in learning about these more advanced techniques you should consider checking out our website for information on upcoming mBIT trainings.

Medical/Psychological issues

Medical and psychological issues are not easily amenable to mBIT coaching processes by themselves. As we indicated at the start of this chapter, medical and psychological issues require professional intervention prior to attempting any mBIT Coaching or mBIT processes. You should always consult the appropriate health professional when dealing with either medical or psychological issues. This includes, but isn't limited to, situations where the person appears mentally or emotionally unstable, where bio-chemical problems are apparent, where the person requires or is on medication, has poor nutritional issues, has endocrine problems, medical conditions-illnesses, or where substance abuse is involved, etc.

One thing that can certainly help in a lot of these instances, and this is backed up by a huge and growing body of research, (covered in Chapter 3), involves the use of probiotics to bring the gut back to a healthy state. In almost all cases, it's worthwhile getting the person to see a health practitioner about commencing a course of probiotic supplements. Numerous psychological and health problems can be ameliorated through the use of probiotics, and it's a useful adjunct to explore.

Incongruence Signals

If the three brains are not in alignment or congruent with one another over an issue, any incongruence will show up as observable behavioral indicators, signs and signals. Since the brains, mind and body are connected in a Cybernetic Loop of control, what affects one, affects them all and this leads to observable signals. With sufficient sensory acuity you can see and detect these signals.

Some of the classic incongruence signals include:

- Facial expressions of distaste or grimacing
- Asymmetrical expressions or gestures
- Hunching over or closing up
- Pupil constriction and narrowing of the eyes
- Turning or leaning away
- Gut and heart reactions or feelings
- Shaking of the head as if saying 'no'

- Holding the breath, or short shallow breaths
- Quavering or hesitant voice tonalities
- Language indicators such as metaphors or expressions indicating non-alignment

Pay attention to these signals and watch for them during and after integration. If you see any sign of them make sure you check in with the person and explore what's going on for them. Incongruence signals are valuable messages that alignment is not complete and you need to do further mBIT coaching on the issue.

The mBIT NIB suite of tools

As you've seen in this chapter, there are a number of tools you can use to pattern interrupt NIB's. The base suite of tools that mBIT provides to pattern interrupt integration blocks includes:

- Balanced Breathing
- Kinesthetic Interrupt
- Focus Reframing
- Taste Blitz
- Smell Blast

The first two in the list have been covered in detail already in this and previous chapters, so let's examine the other three here now.

>> NIB Tool: mBIT Focus Reframing

There's strong evidence from fields as diverse as Clinical Hypnosis, NLP and Gendlin's Focusing methodology, indicating that the *mBrains* are amenable to guided visualization and focused reframing techniques. Whilst detailed exploration of these techniques are beyond the scope of this book and are covered in greater depth in mBIT Coaching Certification training, we'll share here a simple yet powerful technique called 'Focus Reframing' you can use to overcome some types of NIB's.

In this technique you literally talk to the brain that is NIB'ing and ask what its positive intention is. You get in touch with it, focus on it and all that it's trying to tell you, and you speak to it, asking what positive end-outcome it's trying to achieve for you.

There is a presupposition in NLP that all behavior has a positive intention. By exploring and finding this underlying positive purpose you can then negotiate within and between the brains to find a better, more creative and generative way of achieving and satisfying the positive intention or need that exists in your life.

The steps of the mBIT Focus Reframe technique are:

1. Get in touch with the full felt-sense of the blocking experience and the messages it represents. Calmly notice and attend to all the parts of it in your body. When you are ready, communicate with the brain responsible for the blocking behavior or message. Literally talk to it. Respectfully ask, "What is this message all about? What are you trying to tell me?" Then carefully notice the signals or response you get. It may be a word, a sound, a phrase or an image. Obviously the messages received in the head brain are a translation into words or images of the signals coming from the brain sending the message.

2. Determine the positive intention of the behavior. Thank the brain for communicating with you and ask it, "Please tell me what your positive intention is. What are you trying to do for me?" Notice the response you get. What intuitions or

messages does the brain respond with? What values, qualities or ideas come up for you?

3. Now ask the brain to work with the whole of your unconscious mind, including your head based creative parts, to generate new and more generative ways of accomplishing the outcome and achieving integration. Ask the brain to communicate internally with the other parts of your mind to find new behaviors and ways of achieving the positive purpose. For example, if the brain is signaling to you that the way you're living is doing you harm, then your unconscious mind can generate new patterns of behavior that are more healing and healthful. Your brains can then respect this process and support the new behaviors.

4. Ask the brain if it will agree to use the new behaviors and choices rather than the old behavior to achieve its outcome. If you don't get a yes signal from the brain, then return to step 2 until all values and positive intentions have been satisfied.

5. Do an ecology check of all of your brains and all parts of your mind by asking, "Does any part of me object to my new choices?" If you get a response that indicates there is an issue of ecology or potential negative consequence then return to step 2 and ask what positive intentions your brains are attempting to communicate and work with these until you are able to generate wise behaviors and choices that work for the whole of you.

This technique works very powerfully. You'll be surprised at just how clearly your brains can communicate. You need to trust your brains and your unconscious mind and work with them respectfully. They are trying to do the best they can with the knowledge and skills they have at this point in your life.

Remember to do this technique in a quiet place. Relax, calm your mind and then gently talk to the brains doing any blocking and find the purpose of the message they have for you. Be very positive and explicit in your communicating. With a bit of trust, you'll be surprised at how amazing this communication process can be. It's about getting in touch with your intuitions. It's about hearing the messages from your gut brain, your heart brain, your non-dominant hemisphere and other distributed intelligences around your brain and body and then working with them to overcome their unmet needs and valid objections.

>> NIB Tool: Taste Blitzes and Smell Blasts

Taste and smell are key sensory modalities that the gut and heart brains attend to and process. Intense tastes and smells can therefore be used to grab the attention of the heart and gut brains and shock or interrupt any blocking patterns they're engaged in. For example, if someone is abreacting you can use an intense aromatherapy essential oil, or even smelling salts, to quickly change their state. You can also evoke or change emotions by giving a food that has strong and delicious flavors.

Remember the research discussed in Chapter 3 about how momentarily savoring a sweet food increased participants' agreeableness and helping behavior? And how foods such as chocolate and apples elevate mood, induce joy, and can serve to temporarily repair negative mood? Also recall how smells affect disgust and moral behavior and are linked to experiences as diverse as risk taking and depression. And note the research evidence that showed how sweet drinks are able to modulate feelings of anger and aggression in subjects.

You can use this knowledge about these olfactory and gustatory responses to interrupt dysfunctional patterns in the heart and gut brains. You can also use these ideas to provide calm, sensory delightful experiences and help create states that are supportive of ANS balance and integration.

How each brain can do NIB'ing

Now that we've covered each of the NIB's in turn, it's also useful and instructive to look at how each of the brains can do NIB'ing by itself. Examining the blocking process in this way gives you specific tools and filters for determining when a brain is blocking and what to do in each instance.

How the gut can do NIB'ing

The gut brain predominantly blocks through the use of:

1. Armoring

2. Nausea, throwing up, pushing back, etc.

3. Scatological marking

4. Distraction (churning, dizziness, spinning, etc.)

>> NIB: Armoring

Armoring occurs when one of the brains blocks integration at the co-enervated muscles of one of the six bridges or gateways discussed in

Chapter 4. For example, when an integration message is blocked from the head to the gut, the gut brain can armor the muscles in the throat and stop the person from "swallowing and digesting a new idea." The way to overcome armoring is to use the Kinesthetic Interrupt technique we covered earlier in this chapter.

>> NIB: Nausea, throwing up, pushing back, etc.

One of the ways the gut brain blocks integration is through nausea and vomiting. These are very effective blocking processes since the person is rendered incapable of clear thinking and congruent action. The visceral feelings of sickness in the stomach and the physical actions of reverse peristalsis are often overwhelming.

The way to overcome this form of NIB'ing is to use balanced breathing to help calm the system and then the mBIT Kinesthetic Interrupt to powerfully pattern interrupt the physical feelings involved. By getting the person to model the feelings outside themselves with their hands, then quickly interrupting them, you open up the communication channels and allow the integration messages through. This works quickly and effectively and typically stops the blocking immediately.

>> NIB: Scatological marking

Another way the gut brain responds and blocks change is through 'scatological marking'. This is the process animals use to mark their spatial boundaries and protect themselves. With humans this extends to semantic boundaries; to the boundaries we use to define our deepest sense of self and the meaning we make in our world. This is why when someone upsets us we use expressions like "they're really giving me the shits, they're pissing me off."

So the gut brain often responds to things it perceives as a threat by generating a desire to go to the toilet. It's literally saying that the experience is *'giving it the shits'*. The easiest way to handle this form of NIB is to just get it over and done with, let the person go to the toilet, then come back and do balanced breathing, get into coherence, and continue the process. If the NIB happens repeatedly however, you'll need to use the same technique of Kinesthetic Interrupt described above.

>> NIB: Distraction (churning, dizziness, spinning, etc.)

Similar to the other gut brain NIB's above, the gut can generate strong states of churning and can, via its connection through the ACC and Insula in the head brain, trigger feelings of dizziness, spinning, etc. These experiences can be so strong they lead to nausea. As with the other gut brain NIB's described above, the solution to overcome this NIB is use a mix of balanced breathing and Kinesthetic Interrupt techniques.

How the heart can do NIB'ing

The heart brain can block integration through typical emotional and physical responses of:

1. Lethargy or apathy

2. Heart palpitations

3. Heart 'freak out'

4. Emotional shut down, emotional stonewalling

5. Anger

6. Emotional defensiveness and over-sensitivity

The heart typically blocks through heart-felt reactions; strong feelings that can be so intense they affect the physical beats and rhythms of the heart. While it may manifest as lethargy and apathy, it can also show up as palpitations, heart racing and even as a complete *'freak out'* of feelings and responses in the heart/chest region leading to a fight/flight reaction. In terms of emotions, the blocking can be via anger and emotional defensiveness. Any and all of these are indicators that the heart is blocking integration.

The way to work with these NIB's is to use the mBIT Focus Reframing technique described earlier in this chapter along with deep balanced breathing. In a sense, what you need in order to resolve heart blocking is to honor the value(s) in play, and find and align with the positive intent the heart brain is trying to express. You then expand the options so the heart becomes congruent with the creative response the head and gut want to put into action. If needed, you might also use the Kinesthetic Interrupt technique to get the heart brain to listen to the messages from the other brains.

How the head can do NIB'ing

The head brain has a huge array of blocking strategies it can use. These include:

1. Blaming

2. Justifying and rationalizing

3. Denying

4. Confusion

5. Smoke screening

6. Overwhelm

7. Going blank

8. Bolstering

9. Identification

10. Arguing for limitations

11. Insistence on not knowing ("I don't know, I don't know!")

12. Meta commenting (explain it away, or explaining yourself right back into your current situation)

13. Double binds

14. Quitting

The way to deal with all of these is to get the person to do Balanced Breathing and then bypass these head NIB's by having the person communicate with and from the heart and gut (especially from the Highest Expressions as we'll discuss in detail in the next chapter). From there you can help the person establish congruent goals.

In our experience, most head NIB's arise because the head is not integrated with the heart and gut and is in an incoherent state. We've also found that in complex and refractory situations, the head NIB's can require other interventions first before mBIT coaching is applied. For example, Cognitive Behavioral Therapy (CBT) or NLP therapeutic counseling may be needed before or in conjunction with mBIT coaching.

Cognitive Dissonance

In 1956, Stanford University psychologist Leon Festinger heard about a group of doomsday cultists who were predicting the Earth would be destroyed by aliens at midnight on December 21st of that year. Festinger and his students decided to infiltrate the group and covertly study what happens to people when their strongly held beliefs are disproved. What he discovered lead to the powerful and informative theory of Cognitive Dissonance.

So what did happen, in the minutes and hours after midnight, when the prophesied destruction and the predicted appearance of alien spacecraft to save the faithful didn't occur? Initially there was shock and disbelief by the members of the group; many had left jobs, colleges and spouses to prepare to escape on the flying saucer supposed to rescue them. Within hours however, people began to deny they'd ever believed in the doomsday prophecy. They were saying things like "I didn't really believe it, I was just going along for the adventure." Or, "Because of our strong faith, the aliens chose to save the planet." Basically, they said and thought anything other than the truth which was that they'd been duped all along.

Based on this research and thousands of subsequent laboratory and real-world studies, Festinger posited his theory that the unconscious mind does not like *'dissonance'* and will do anything to remove it. Dissonance is the disagreeable visceral feeling we get when faced with mismatching cognitions or beliefs. Our mind likes harmony and congruence between our thoughts and beliefs and will utilize a number of unconscious strategies to remove cognitive dissonance. The tension of cognitive dissonance leads people to change either their beliefs and attitudes or their behavior.

The importance of this is that it leads people to denying reality and deleting or distorting their cognitions and perceptions.

Cognitive dissonance can be incredibly damaging if it leads to denial of reality and bizarre distortions or behaviors. Of course, cognitive dissonance is like any tool or process; it can be used positively or negatively.

For example, you can use cognitive dissonance and your *mBrains'* response to it to motivate and assist you in creating generative change in your life by positively aligning your thoughts, values and actions. However, when cognitive dissonance occurs outside your conscious awareness it can minimize the quality of how you experience your life and lead you into ignorance.

We'll return to this subject in the coming chapters as we examine pivotal ways you can use mBIT to evolve your life and generate deep levels of wisdom in the world you are creating.

mBraining

"Using your multiple brains to do cool stuff"

Chapter 7

mBrain Highest Expressions

Wisdom

Highest Expression

Creativity (cephalic brain)
Compassion (heart brain)
Courage (enteric brain)

Congruence

Communication

The art and science of authentic self expression

What do we mean by *'Highest Expressions'*? There are two parts to this term that need unpacking to fully appreciate this step in the mBIT Roadmap. The first has to do with mBIT Principles explained throughout Chapters 2 and 3 that outline how your neural networks are able to function at different levels. As described in those chapters, imbalances between your sympathetic and parasympathetic systems can produce widely differing states within each neural network. And as mentioned at the end of Chapter 5, your neural networks can also be congruently aligned at low levels of functioning producing low-coherence states such as anger, depression, sadness, etc.

Naturally, these low-coherence states are not our preferred states of choice, nor are they how we'd want to continually experience life and living. If you had a choice, surely you'd opt for living in high-coherence states that produce high levels of health, wellbeing, and consciousness. Fortunately, with the mBIT methods you're learning in this book, you have that choice. And as shown in the mBIT Roadmap, you need to apply these high-coherence states in order to live with greater wisdom in your daily decision-making and actions.

The second part to the term *'Highest Expressions'* is the word *'Expression'*. We deliberately chose this word rather than the word *'function'*. The function of your neural networks is *'what'* they do in terms of their operational processes. As we've explained in Chapter 2, each of your neural networks has a set of prime functions specific to its form of intelligence. *'Expression'* however, is about taking what is occurring internally and manifesting or expressing it outwardly into the physical world. As your neural networks operate to fulfill their prime functions, how are these prime functions expressed in your behaviors, decisions, emotions, thoughts, and ways of being?

At this step in the mBIT Roadmap, the shift of focus from function to expression is a shift of focus from aligning yourself internally to applying yourself externally. It's about the quality of how you engage with the external world; your relationships, your situations and conditions, your activities and results, your life.

So what do we mean by the combined use of the words '*Highest Expression*'? To answer this, we need to first ask a more fundamental question; what is it that's being expressed? At a base level, it's the prime functions of your neural networks. However at the highest level, it's you! It's about who you are at the level of your truest, most authentic self.

Keep in mind that each neural network is only a part of the total '*You*'. The total '*You*' is much more than just a combined set of physical processes and functions. The total '*You*' is an emergent phenomena that cannot be understood just by looking at individual parts of your physical body. When we refer to your '*Highest Expressions*', we mean more than just the optimum functioning of your physical neural networks. We mean the quality of how your neural networks serve to express the authentic '*You*', as an emergent, conscious human being. This phase in the mBIT Roadmap is about harnessing the innate intelligences within you in ways that result in the Highest Expressions of your authentic self.

To illustrate this more concretely, imagine an artistically gifted musician playing a beautiful song on their guitar and keeping the audience spellbound, inspired and almost moved to tears. If we could see inside this musician's neurology, we would see the parts of their brain related to music, melody, rhythm, and refined finger muscle control all being activated. We would see the neuronal patterns in their heart continually shifting and changing as they went through a range of emotions related to the different parts of the song. We would also see the neuronal patterns in their gut brain continually shifting and changing as they experienced various states of identification and motivation throughout the song. All of this would be observations of how their neurology is functioning.

But these observations tell us nothing about the musician as a person. Who they are, why they chose this particular song, what it means to them, and how it is that they play this song so beautifully that their audience is deeply and emotionally moved. Their playing is an expression of who they are, which cannot be seen by focusing only on neurological functioning. Yet it's through neurological functioning, while playing their music, they're able to express their truest and deepest self.

The highest expressions: A powerful insight

Years ago, whilst researching esoteric wisdom practices, we came across a powerful insight from the Tibetan Bonpo tradition. It suggested that a person could be considered to have truly lived a wise and beneficial life if they'd mastered three core competencies: *Compassion, Creativity and Courage.* We were so intrigued by this insight we captured it in writing and set it aside, revisiting it periodically in our conversations and explorations.

After having factor analyzed the core competencies of the three brains, we were fascinated to notice that the Bon insight highlighted a key and generative competency from each brain:

- Heart brain – **Compassion**
- Gut brain – **Courage**
- Head brain – **Creativity**

As we continued our research we discovered very similar advice from other spiritual and philosophical disciplines. Although slightly different words were used (e.g. kindness instead of compassion, bravery instead of courage, etc.), they all conveyed core competencies that were similar in their qualitative nature.

We therefore became even more curious and intrigued by these three Tibetan Bonpo core competencies. We began to look for structures that could explain the consistency of these prescribed core competencies across so many different philosophies, practices and cultures. The question became: *"From an mBIT perspective, what is so special about these competencies?"*

We discovered three key qualities that make these competencies particularly generative. First, if you look them up in the Core Competencies Framework from Chapter 3, you'll notice they're all highly coherent states. Second, in actual practice, these *'virtues'* are neurologically integrative by their very nature. Each of these competencies requires the engagement of the other two neural networks in order for them to fully manifest in behavior. This is explained in more detail in the following sections of this chapter. And third, our behavioral modeling research found that the interdependent and integrative nature of these three competencies enables the emergence of a higher order level of consciousness and way of being. In other words, they collectively enable and facilitate the Highest Expression of an authentic self.

Subsequently, these three competencies became what we respectfully call the *mBrains'* '*Highest Expressions*', and we'd like to suggest that of all the competencies each brain evinces, these '*three C's*' (Creativity, Compassion and Courage) are the most generative and defining of them all. They're certainly the most integrative to work with for attaining greater levels of wisdom and personal evolution. Indeed, from our behavioral modeling and action research work, we've found these three competencies, when aligned together are able to produce a synergistic magic that is incredible to experience.

Heart brain - Compassion

"If you want others to be happy, practice compassion. If you want to be happy, practice compassion."

Dalai Lama

"Compassion is the basis of all morality."

Arthur Schopenhauer

"Love and compassion are necessities, not luxuries.

Without them, humanity cannot survive."

Dalai Lama

A compassionate heart is a heart that loves. It's also a heart that cares and connects, a heart that gives and forgives, and a heart that actively reaches out to help others in need. It is a heart that heals. We hope you'd agree that a person with a truly compassionate heart is worth admiring and emulating. And as you may come to realize from reading this chapter, such a person is you. You have these qualities and abilities because you have a heart. And your heart is highly intelligent and seeks to fulfill its prime functions. When you use mBIT methods to bring your heart into a state of high coherence, your true nature is free to emerge and starts expressing itself naturally from a way of *'being'* whose essence is love and compassion.

228

In our live workshops we are often asked why we didn't use the word *'love'* as the Highest Expression of the heart brain. To be honest, we could have. It certainly would fit better with most people's beliefs about the legendary powers of love. However in our behavioral modeling research we found that something more was needed within the context of a *'Highest Expression'*.

We found that sometimes people can use mBIT to bring their hearts into a coherent state of love, experience sublime internal feelings of love and being loved, and then *'do'* nothing more than enjoy the endorphin ride! While there's nothing wrong with bliss'ing yourself out every now and then, people were sometimes more focused on having an internal experience rather than expressing an authentic self into the external world.

Compassion, on the other hand, starts with love and includes kind-action. This aspect of kind-action is important as it engages your gut brain with its prime functions of core identity and mobilization. Without the heart including and integrating with the gut brain, it's not really compassion. This is where many people confuse or mistake compassion with sympathy, empathy, pity, and just feeling sorry for the other person. Merely feeling these internal states doesn't really help anyone in any tangible way. True compassion is more than just an internal feeling. True compassion has intention, it seeks to help by either alleviating suffering or contributing to the happiness of others. It requires the gut to take kind-action to express into the external world the heart's internal valuing of love, care and connection. True compassion results in compassionate acts.

Smart versus dumb compassion

Keep in mind that not all compassionate acts are intelligent. There is what Buddhists call '*dumb compassion*'. This can occur when the head brain is not included or integrated with the heart and gut for intelligent kind-action.

For example, many years ago on a trip to India our group was told by our guide that if approached on the street by child beggars or invalids we should not give them money, and if we did then certainly not to give a lot. Sure enough, we were constantly approached by children and invalids wherever we went. The guide's advice was difficult to follow as the children looked extremely destitute and their sad eyes could soften the heart of a statue. It was even more difficult to refuse the begging of the many invalids with no legs, no arms, who were blind, or had some other severe disability or deformity. Our hearts felt their suffering and our guts wanted to act by giving them money. But this would have been '*dumb compassion*'.

Our guide's advice served as the role of the head brain being integrated for '*smart compassion*'. As our guide explained to us, giving money to the beggars does not alleviate their situation in any way. The beggars have made begging their daily job and they're good at it. They know how to tug at our heart strings to get money out of us. Giving them money only reinforces their routines as '*successful*'. And once other beggars see you give money, you become bombarded with even more beggars. You'll go broke. And if you give a lot of money to a beggar, you've now made them a target for other beggars to beat and rob them for it. In other words, your dumb compassion either does nothing at all to improve the situation or make things even worse.

Smart compassion requires integration between the heart, gut and head.

Compassionate acts and '*You*'

As a Highest Expression of your heart intelligence, compassion is obviously not just an emotional state that comes and goes depending on how you're feeling at the time. True compassion involves doing good in the world because you act to relieve suffering or enhance happiness in others.

As a Highest Expression it's a way of being that embodies a consciousness of connection. While this may at first sound lofty to your head brain, it is in fact a natural state for your heart brain when functioning at levels of high coherence. Within the experiential world of the highly coherent heart, this is '*You*'. When your heart is in a state of highly coherent compassion, '*You*' are compassionate.

Numerous studies have shown that people who practice meditation on loving-kindness for as little as three months actually show more pre-frontal lobe activity than before. The functioning of the head brain literally changes and new neuronal connections and patterns are created by engaging in highly coherent states of loving-kindness. In other words, you literally change into a more compassionate '*You*' through the practice of compassion.

And compassionate acts are not totally selfless in their benefits. When you simply feel sorry for someone, you end up just feeling sorry. But when you act on your care and concern, when you actually do something to help a person or make a situation better, you feel good about yourself and your worth. Compassionate acts not only connect you with others, they connect you with yourself. They connect you to a truer, more generative self that is deeper than your ego-personality self. You get more in touch with your authentic self, the one that recognizes, experiences and acts from a consciousness of connection. This is why deep in our heart of hearts, we all appreciate and value acts of loving-kindness whenever we see or experience them.

Self-compassion

Perhaps one of the most important applications of compassion is with your self. Your relationship with yourself is the platform from which you relate to others. If you find it difficult to be kind to yourself when you make certain types of mistakes, you'll probably find it difficult to be understanding and compassionate with others when they make similar mistakes. If there are certain things you don't like about yourself, the odds are high you'll have little tolerance for others who demonstrate the same characteristics.

Many people wrestle with themselves on issues related to poor self image and low levels of self esteem. This happens if they continually judge, criticize and condemn themselves based on their perceptions of past *'failures'* or *'mistakes'*. This becomes a breeding ground for chronic feelings of insecurity, anxiety, guilt, worthlessness and even hopelessness. Without compassion for your self, it's difficult if not impossible to forgive your self. Without self-forgiveness, it's difficult to experience self-love, self-acceptance and self-belief. With compassion, however, all this becomes possible in an instant.

Compassion for self requires that you recognize that deep within you are a good person with good intentions trying to do good things. And that you are human. As humans, we all make mistakes and that's OK. We live, we do, we experience, and ideally we learn. With a compassionate heart, no matter what happens, you can affirm yourself as a good person doing the best you can. You can speak to yourself with internal dialogue in a kind voice rather than a critical one. You say affirming things to yourself that support you in growing and developing as a human being. You encourage yourself to fully express who you are based on your own authentic truth as you currently know it, at this stage of your personal growth.

Without compassion for yourself, you become your own prosecutor. Your critical internal dialogue conditions and keeps you small, constrained and fearful of taking further action in case you make another mistake. With compassion, however, you become your own best friend and mentor. You seek to understand yourself and your conditioning through self-awareness. You value and appreciate your intentions, efforts and the positive aspects of yourself in light of your personal history. You affirm and encourage yourself to learn from whatever happens, and to keep taking action with new knowledge and awareness. You relate to yourself from a place of love, kindness, appreciation and a generosity of spirit. With compassion for yourself, you give yourself the foundation for joyful living and full authentic self-expression.

</== Discovery Exercise: Compassionate Self Connection ==/>

You cannot truly understand compassion by intellectualizing it from your head brain. You won't *'get it'* since its main home is in the heart. It's more than just an emotional feeling state, it's a state of being. While compassion is expressed through the heart intelligence it arises from a state of highly coherent integration between all three brains. Compassion is a natural expression of the fully integrated *'You'* as a conscious human being, aware of your inter-connectedness with all other living beings.

In the following exercise, you'll learn to experience compassion as a Highest Expression of your self.

Connecting to how you currently relate to yourself

1. Sit comfortably and allow yourself to settle into your body. Breathe deeply, slowly, gently and comfortably. Calm and settle your mind enough that you can tune into yourself and be aware of your internal experience. You may wish to close your eyes if that helps you focus inward.

2. Begin to become aware of your relationship with yourself. As you think about yourself, who you are as a person, your strengths and weaknesses, what you've done and not done in life, start to scan each of your brains for their responses. Become aware of how you feel about yourself and the emotional quality of how you relate to yourself. Notice your head brain's internal dialogue and what it's saying about yourself. Notice the language and tone of voice it uses. Be aware of your own gut response to yourself. How is your gut reacting and relating to who you are?

3. Now stand up and shake your body a little to shift out of this state. Sit back down in readiness to enter a state of compassion.

Connecting to Compassion

4. Sitting comfortably, do Balanced Breathing for a few minutes until you are in a balanced coherent state.

5. Begin to breathe compassion and loving-kindness into your heart and chest area. Feel the feelings of compassion flow in and out of your heart and chest area with each breath. See the color of compassion (whatever that is for you) flowing in and out of you with each breath. Surround yourself with this color until you are bathed in it. Hear the sound(s) of compassion (whatever they may be for you) at just the right volume so that you experience it vibrantly in and throughout your body.

6. Now expand the feelings of compassion from your heart area until they fill your entire body. Intensify and expand these feelings even further until you are being compassion itself. Notice the changes in your gut brain as you become compassion. Notice how the thoughts, perceptions and internal dialogue change as you become the very essence of compassion and loving-kindness. Continue to be aware of the changes in your gut brain as you become the embodiment of compassion itself. Start to exude compassion outwards from yourself so that you feel a strong desire to reach out, connect, and to help.

Extending Compassion to Yourself

7. While '*being*' and exuding strong feelings of compassion, begin to think of yourself. Relate to yourself from a consciousness of compassion and loving-kindness. See yourself as someone who is intrinsically good, doing the best they can with what they know and don't know. Appreciate yourself as someone who has come this far given your

personal history, upbringing and life conditions. Have compassion for how you've had to deal with your challenges, struggles and conditioning. Appreciate and celebrate your strengths, abilities, passions, joyful moments and personal victories in life. Give yourself the gift of understanding, the grace of acceptance and non-judgment, and the freedom to be who you are.

8. From this state of appreciating and affirming yourself, become aware of how your sense of self — who you truly are at a deep level and your intrinsic worth — is expanding and evolving. As you feel more positively connected with yourself, notice what new possibilities become available for you in how you can authentically express your truest self in your daily life.

</== Discovery Exercise: Compassion for Others ==/>

In this exercise, you'll learn to experience compassion for others as a Highest Expression.

1. Identity someone with whom you would like to show more compassion. Often, your indicators are in the form of incongruency signals; tensions or conflicts within you because there's a part of you thinking, feeling and behaving in a non-compassionate way toward that person. Or there's some part of you that says you should be more understanding, kinder, or gracious. These feelings of incongruency are signals of in-authenticity, where your ego

is reacting in one way and a deeper, more authentic self knows those reactions are not representative of who you truly are at your Highest Expression of self.

Connecting to how you currently relate to other person

2. Sit comfortably and allow yourself to settle into your body. Breathe deeply, slowly, gently and comfortably. Settle your mind enough that you can tune into yourself and be aware of your internal experience. You may wish to close your eyes if that helps you focus inward.

3. Begin to become aware of your relationship with this other person. As you think about this person and whatever it is they may have done or didn't do, notice your reactions in your gut, heart and head.

4. As you notice your reactions, become aware of how you feel about yourself when you react this way. Do you like yourself when you react this way? Do you respect yourself when you react this way? Notice the differences between what your ego defenses come up with versus what a truer, deeper, and more authentic '*you*' says and feels.

5. Now stand up and shake your body a little to shift out of this state. Sit back down in readiness to enter a state of compassion.

Connecting to Compassion

6. Sitting comfortably, do Balanced Breathing for a few minutes until you are in a deeply balanced and coherent state.

7. Begin to breathe compassion and loving-kindness into your heart and chest area. Feel the feelings of compassion flow in and out of your heart and chest area with each breath. See the color of compassion (whatever that is for you) flowing in and out of your heart region with each breath. Surround yourself with your color until you are bathed in it. Hear the sound(s) of compassion (whatever they may be for you) at just the right volume so that you experience it vibrantly in and throughout your body.

8. Now expand your feelings of compassion from your heart area up into your head and then down into your gut until they fill your entire body. Intensify and expand the feelings even further until you are being compassion itself. Notice the changes in your gut brain as YOU become compassion. Notice how the thoughts, perceptions and internal dialogue change as YOU become the very essence of compassion. Continue to be aware of the changes in your gut brain as YOU become the embodiment of compassion itself. Start to exude compassion outwards from yourself so that you feel a strong desire to reach out, connect, and to help.

Extending Compassion to the Other Person

9. While experiencing, being and exuding strong feelings of deep compassion, forgiveness and loving-kindness, begin to think of the other person. Relate to the other person from a consciousness of compassion. See them not as their behaviors but as a person, a human being, someone who is intrinsically good, doing the best they can with what they know and

don't know. Appreciate them as someone who has a come through a personal history and upbringing, much of which you probably don't know about. Even if you do, you haven't lived their life through their struggles, insecurities, fears, challenges and triumphs. Can you honestly judge them from inside your skin, not being them? Have compassion for how they've had to deal with their challenges, struggles and conditioning. Recognize, acknowledge and appreciate the strengths they must have in order to have made it to where they've gotten to so far. Give them the gift of your understanding, the grace of your acceptance and non-judgment, and the freedom to be who they are, not as you want them to be. Be open to how you can relate to them differently now in your attitude, behaviors, and speech.

10. From this state of appreciating and affirming their innate worth as a human being, become aware of how your sense of self — who you truly are at a deep level and your own intrinsic worth — is expanding and evolving. Notice how, as you connect compassionately with others, you feel more positively connected with yourself, a more authentic '*you*'. Notice what new possibilities become available for how you can authentically express your truest self in your daily life.

The strength of compassion

Yes, when you look at the competencies and prime functions of the heart, it can be argued that of them all, the one that's the most generative and beneficial is compassion. Whether it's compassion for self, or for others, the emotion and act of compassion provides understanding, support, loving-kindness and care. Compassion builds trust. Compassion connects. Compassion encourages. Without compassion, our acts are heart-less and can end up selfish or even cruel. Compassion on the other hand is an active expression of love that affirms, values, relates to and appreciates the oneness in us all.

Almost all religions and spiritual traditions hold compassion as one of the highest virtues. Compassion is the fuel that drives deep bonding and allows us to flow, connect and change together. As the Buddha said, "In separateness lies the world's great misery, in compassion lays the world's true strength."

Gut brain - Courage

"Courage is the first of the human qualities because it is the quality which guarantees all the others."

Winston Churchill

"Courage is the ladder on which all other virtues mount."

Clare Boothe Luce

"Life shrinks or expands in proportion to one's courage."

Anaïs Nin

Without gutsy courage, you would not be able to act upon your dreams and goals. You wouldn't be able to live an authentic life as you'd be too afraid to do anything unknown, uncertain, or unfamiliar. Any action outside of what you already know would be too scary or too risky. Without courage, change from the status quo would either be impossible or by accident. If you're not able to courageously confront your own fears, you'll never be able to get beyond your conditioning for authentic and generative living. With courage, however, your gut brain is able to express your deepest sense of self by empowering you to act in ways that are true to the world you want to create.

When we refer to courage as a Highest Expression, we don't mean it as simply an emotional state or qualitative attribute. If that were the case then courage belongs in the domain of the heart. Many people typically view courage in this way. The etymology of *'courage'* is from the Middle English usage (c.1300) *corage*, from the Old French equivalent of *cuer* or *coer*, and from Latin *cor*, all of which mean *'heart'*.

From an mBIT perspective, we are using the word *'courage'* as a Highest Expression and as such it is expressed into the external world via gutsy courageous acts, and this is the domain of your gut intelligence. True courage is your ability to act in the face of fear, adversity, danger, and challenge. Put simply, if there are no courageous acts, it's not courage. Courageous acts are gutsy acts. The emotional aspects of courage may be integrated with the heart, but the physical expression of courage is from the gut.

Both intelligences are required for true courage. In our behavioral modeling research we discovered a fascinating insight that resolves the seeming contradiction between the etymology of courage referencing the heart and the fact that courageous acts come from the gut.

During times when courage is required, the gut brain is initially experiencing some form of fear, anxiety, danger, adversity or challenge. The gut intelligence, with its prime functions of core identity, self preservation and mobilization, is able to differentiate the fear response as separate from one's core identity. It recognizes that it needs to respond to the threatening situation in some way in order to preserve self. As the nerve signals flow up to the heart, the heart intelligence begins to process the relevant core values, and does so at such highly amplified levels of signal strength strong enough to over-ride the physical fear sensations in the gut. The heart intelligence is, in essence, telling the gut that the core values in play are more important to act upon than the flight or freeze reaction of the fear signals. As we mentioned earlier in Chapter 3, the heart is the emperor and the gut is the general. The gut intelligence responds to the signals from the heart and takes action based on the salience of the values in play rather than succumbing to the fear-based sensations. Guided by the heart, the gut acts in spite of the fear.

While the above gut-heart-gut neural sequence is the basic structure for doing courage, the head does have a role to play in all of this. In short, the head can either hinder or accelerate the process. Let's take an example of someone who's facing a challenging situation and needs to *'muster up some courage'* to confront the situation directly. What does it mean to *'muster up courage'*? How do people do it?

If you've ever needed to muster or build up courage, you might recall that, like most people, the internal dialogue of your head brain takes over in an attempt to talk yourself into it. Doing this, you're gathering up your internal resources by telling yourself how important it is for you to act, why you need to act, that you're not the kind of person who runs from a situation like this, and the other similar themes.

By telling yourself how important it is for you to act and why you need to act, your head brain is attempting to engage your heart intelligence and its values-based prime function. By telling yourself that you're not the kind of person that cowardly runs away, your head brain is trying to engage your gut intelligence and remind it that you are better than that, that your identity is that of someone who can and does face up to challenges. In this case, your head brain is serving as an amplifier and accelerator for the process of courage.

In contrast, perhaps you've seen other people who may have backed down and capitulated in a situation that challenged their values and integrity. In common parlance, this is called cowardice or *'gutless'*. In this case, the internal dialogue of the head brain probably gave a range of head-based *'reasons'* why it would be either better to not say or do anything, or described the situation as hopeless and so just gave up. Either way, the head brain *'dis-heartened'* the heart, which then disempowered the gut for any courageous action. And by not having taken courageous action to defend a sense of identity, the gut learns to have a smaller, weaker identity, leading it to take less action in the future. This is a recipe for diminishing one's self image, self confidence, and self esteem. In this example the head brain acted as a hindrance to the gutsy courageous expression of the truest self. It sacrificed a sense of self to the fear sensations and fed the fear and made it stronger.

Integrated courage

Once again, what makes a highest expression a Highest Expression is not that it's the idealized functioning of a specific neural network. Rather it's the role that your specific neural networks play in expressing your deepest and most generative sense of self through highly coherent levels of integration across all your brains.

This is a vital distinction to remember, as our goal with mBIT is to apply these Highest Expressions together for greater wisdom in decision-making and subsequent actions. Otherwise, all you're doing is engaging in the function without it necessarily evolving your levels of consciousness and wisdom.

For example, there are numerous case studies of people reporting how anger played a significant role in their courageous acts. In situations such as battles of war, being taken hostage in a crime, being subjected to street violence, or from someone breaking and entering into their homes, states of deep anger have been aroused due to the violation of personal boundaries and core values. With personalized intensity, their anger fueled the impulse to act courageously in the face of physical threat and danger.

Sometimes these anger-motivated courageous acts were highly appropriate and beneficial. Lives were saved and criminals were thwarted. Other times, one or more people ended up dead, hurt or maimed, even if they were the attackers or the perpetrators. The crisis situation may have been resolved, however we might ask, is anyone (much less society) any wiser? Often violence leads to more violence, anger leads to revenge, and the vicious cycle continues to spiral.

Courage takes on a different quality, however, when combined and integrated with the consciousness of compassion and creativity. What does courage look like when it is not just about taking action in the face of fear, but also includes compassion for both yourself and for those threatening you? And what do courageous acts look like when they are creative and wise expressions of your highest self? Instead of coming from a reactive state that tries to compensate for fear, what is the experience of courageous action when you are in a highly coherent, balanced state of integration between all three of your brains? What is the quality of your being and your response to a challenging situation when you are fully expressing your highest and most generative self through compassion, courage and creativity?

The courage to create

For many people living the majority of their daily lives in an incoherent state of autonomic imbalance, trying to imagine what a state of integrated courage might be like is difficult to do. And that's the point. Full authentic self expression is difficult if not impossible to relate to from a conditioned way of being. Courage as a Highest Expression is about the courage to connect with your highest sense of self and live accordingly. It's about the guts to look deeply within and to compassionately confront your conditioning and reactive ego patterns that prevent wise living. Supported by your heart and head brains, integrated courage enables you to create yourself anew, beyond your conditioned self. It enables you to live a creative life, one that is not defined by fear-based conditioning but one that is an authentic, generative and creative expression of you who are at both the deepest and highest levels.

</== Discovery Exercise: Embodying Courage ==/>

Preparation

1. Sit comfortably and allow yourself to settle into your body. Breathe deeply, slowly, gently and comfortably. Settle your mind enough that you can tune into yourself and be aware of your internal experience. You may wish to close your eyes if that helps you focus inward.

2. Think of a situation where you'd like to embody more gutsy courage in order to more fully express who you truly are at a

deep level. There may be situations in which fear, anxiety, insecurity, worry, self-doubt, or a lack of self-belief prevents you from taking action on your dreams, passions, goals, aspirations, beliefs and convictions, or living your values.

3. Now stand up and shake your body a little to shift out of this state. Sit back down in readiness to enter a state of courageous expression.

Connecting to Courage (starting with the heart, then engaging the gut)

4. Sitting comfortably, do Balanced Breathing for a few minutes until you are in a deeply balanced and coherent state.

5. Begin to connect with the values that are important to you and you want to express in this situation. Imagine having the courage to act on these values, and breathe that courage into your heart and chest area. Feel the feelings of courage flow in and out of your heart and chest area with each breath. It can help to imagine images of courageous people doing gutsy, brave and courageous acts from movies, books or real life. Or you may wish to hear in your mind some music or soundtracks that inspires you to strongly courageous action. See the color of courage (whatever that is for you) flowing in and out of you with each breath. Hear the sound(s) of courage (whatever that may be for you) at just the right volume so that your heart is filled with courage.

6. Notice what values and deep feelings arise within you that remind you of the personal importance of acting in this

situation despite your fears and insecurities. Connect deeply with these values and powerful feelings, and expand them so that you experience them as BIG, bold, strong, deep, and powerful.

7. Now breathe these powerful feelings down into your gut. Feel the feelings connect with your gut to produce the sensations of courage for action. Feel the strength and power of your values overriding the sensations of fear, insecurity, and anxiety. Feel your courage build within you, expanding into and filling your gut, your entire lower abdomen, your pelvis and hips, and extending down into your legs. Feel yourself want to physically move and take action.

8. Breathe the color(s) and sound(s) of courage (whatever that is for you) into your gut area and lower torso. Surround yourself with these colors and sounds until you are bathed in them and so that you experience them intensely in and throughout your body. Intensify and expand the feelings even further until you are being courage itself. Notice the changes in your gut brain as YOU become courage. En-couraged by your heart, notice how your thoughts, perceptions and internal dialogue change as YOU become the very essence of courage.

Acting from Courage

9. While feeling and being courageous, think of the situation you want to act on. See yourself in your mind's eye taking courageous action, expressing your deepest values of who

you are as a person. Imagine the feelings of taking action, encouraged and motivated by your heart, mobilized by your gut. Allow your head brain to create several options for how you might be able to take a range of different actions so that whatever you do fully expresses who you are as well as optimizes the impacts you generate and create for positive results.

10. From this state of *'being'* courage, become aware of how your sense of self — who you truly are at the deepest levels and your intrinsic worth — is expanding and evolving. As you feel more positively connected within yourself, notice what new possibilities become available for you in how you can authentically express your truest self in your daily life.

Courageously creating your world

Yes, if you look at what the gut does, when it's at its best, it is surely *'gutsy courage'*. Without courage we wouldn't take action, we'd be frozen and stuck in fear or apathy. Courage is the engine that drives the will to act. Courage gets us moving. Courage gives us strength and determination.

Courage is also your ability to act in the face of fear. It's about you (identity) taking action (mobilization), despite being afraid (conditions of perceived danger, lack of safety, risk, threat of harm). It's about being able to confront that which limits you from being all you can and want to be.

Without courage, we would not be able to act upon our dreams and goals. We would not be able to live an authentic life as we'd be too afraid to do anything unknown, uncertain, or unfamiliar.

Without courage, change from the status quo would either be impossible or be by accident.

With gutsy, motivated and integrated courage, however, your gut brain is able to express your deepest sense of self by empowering you to act in ways that are true to who you really can be.

Head brain - Creativity

"Creativity is the defeat of habit by originality."

Arthur Koestler

"Creativity is the greatest expression of liberty."

Bryant H. McGill

The head brain does many amazing (and stupid) things, but what truly sets humans apart from other primates and animals is our head brain's ability to create, to envision new things, to invent and develop new ideas, new ways, new knowledge and new understandings. Through the creative process we bring forth abstractions, language, communication, art, science, technology and ultimately the amazing society and world in which we live. Where would we be without creativity? Doing the same things over and over, swinging from the same trees, repeating each day more or less the same. Boring!

Fortunately, humans are inherently creative beings. And in the context of a Highest Expression, creativity is not just about lateral thinking. It's not simply about being artistic or innovative in what you do. It's about how you create and experience your world and yourself. It's about how you build and construct your own subjective reality through your thoughts, perceptions and interpretations.

While creativity is a natural gift for all of us as humans, *'what'* we create for ourselves in experience is a choice. Life happens, however things and events outside ourselves are open to our own interpretation. The meaning they have is the meaning we give them. And the meaning we generate creates the experience we have, along with our subsequent responses and actions. Creativity involves being conscious of how you choose to make sense and meaning of whatever happens in your life as a generative expression of who you truly are as a person.

Creativity is also about intention. What do you really want to create for yourself in both your subjective experience and ultimately in your actions and results in the external world? Given your natural, innate abilities as a creative, conscious being, what thoughts do you want to have? How do you want to interpret whatever happens in your life? How do you want to experience and respond to whatever is happening? You can choose, so what thoughts do you want?

We have met many people whose experience of themselves, and of life is constrained and shall we say, less than wonderful. They feel that their life should be more than it is, and that deep down there's more to them as a person than how they're acting and living on a daily basis. They feel unfulfilled, not because of what happens to them in life, but because of how they create the meaning and experience of it.

These people often tell us, "But it's not my fault, that's what happened!" Yes, that may have indeed been *'what happened'*, and what follows next, your interpretation of it, is your *'choice'*. How you interpret it creates your experience of it. It also creates your deep experience of yourself in relation to it. Your choices are creative.

For example, let's say you're desperately unhappy at work. Your boss or manager is offensively rude and unreasonably expects you to handle a ridiculous workload. You find your work tedious, boring and meaningless. You feel trapped because you need the income and it's difficult to find another job. Besides, you're not sure what you really want to do anyway. Put simply, life is miserable.

You'd have to agree that in this example you aren't living life at the Highest Expression of your truest and most generative sense of self. But that's what you've created. What? That's right, if you live this way then you've created it. You have created your work conditions and your *'trapped'* sense of a self who can do nothing about it.

How? By your head brain's thoughts and interpretations. Let's start with your boss. The facts are that this person may indeed speak in ways that are abrupt and without social graces, and they do delegate a large amount of work to you. Labeling those behaviors as *'offensively rude'*, *'unreasonable'* and *'ridiculous'* are your interpretations. Taking offense at their communication style is something you do, not them. Someone else might label the bosses communication as *'direct'* and *'no nonsense'*. Interpreting your workload as *'unreasonable'* and *'ridiculous'* is your own spin on it. All the boss did was give the work to you. Someone else might have labeled the workload as *'ambitious'* or *'high volume'*.

Each interpretation creates a different experience of work for you. Each interpretation also creates a different *'you'* — a stressed you, a motivated you, an offended you, a productive you, etc.

There are two lessons here. The first is that your thoughts are creative. They create your experience in any given moment and they create the way you are *'being'* given those thoughts. The second lesson is that you are the source of your thoughts in the first place. You created them as a natural consequence and expression of how you are being in that moment.

You are the author of your own thoughts and the creator of your own meaning, which in turn (re)creates you. If you think depressing thoughts, you get to feel and be depressed. If you think appreciative and happy thoughts, you get to feel appreciative and happy.

This is what we mean when we refer to *'Creativity'* as a Highest Expression of who you are. You cannot not create. You create your own thoughts. Your thoughts didn't come from nowhere, they came from you! You thought them. You are the source of your own thinking. And your thinking arises as a natural expression of how you are being, acting and experiencing your world. The great news is that as the creator and author of your own thoughts, you can choose the kind of thoughts you want to engage in. And since your thoughts then loop back and (re)create you, you can and do create yourself and your ongoing way of being. The question is, do you want to create yourself as a constrained, limited self or do you want to create yourself at the highest level of who you can be?

Creativity as a Highest Expression is about coming from the consciousness of being at choice. Creativity is freedom. It liberates you from ever having to be a victim of whatever happens or has happened to you because you can always create and choose your thoughts and your interpretations of them. You can also choose your responses so that you do not compromise yourself but instead expand how you *'are'* in relation to any situation. Creativity is what enables you to be the author of your life so that you are living authentically and generatively regardless of your circumstances.

Valuing your creative self

As humans, it's in our very nature to be creative. Just watch any child at play. And notice also the fabulously creative ways adults can either solve or generate problems for themselves. It still fascinates us, therefore, whenever we meet someone who doesn't think they're creative. How can this be?

Usually we find such people have a stereotyped view of creativity. They associate creativity with artists, musicians, inventors, designers, marketers, fashion designers, movie makers, choreographers, performing artists and other similar professions. They also think of creative acts as activities such as drawing, painting, sculpting, fiction writing, photography, etc.

Because of this stereotyping, they often say that they're not the *'creative type'*. When we refer to *'Creativity'* as a Highest Expression, we are not talking about it in relation to any of these stereotyped forms. We are referring to it as *'the quality of consciousness from which you author your life'*. It's about you choosing to realize your highest and most generative sense of self, and to experience and live life accordingly.

While being and living anything less is still choice, why would you? If someone truly understands that they are creative by nature and that they can create themselves at their highest level of being by choosing the quality of their thoughts, why wouldn't they do it? The short answer is that their head brain is not integrated with their heart intelligence.

As a Highest Expression, Creativity requires integration with your heart intelligence to appreciate and value yourself as a creative being. As we already discussed, the heart leads. When your heart fully values creativity, you will naturally start choosing your thoughts so as to express your creative nature.

Creating action

The ultimate test of creativity is creation. Did your creative process produce anything? If not, it wasn't creative, it was just imagination. As you think the quality of thoughts that are representative of your highest sense of self, your identity needs to expand and evolve to *'be'* this better *'you'*. And you need to behaviorally respond to the real world from this more generative sense of self. As you know by now, both the identity upgrade and the action-taking functions are the domains of your gut brain.

As a Highest Expression, your gut brain needs to be integrated into the creative process in order to achieve real, tangible results that are more than just a good feeling. It's not enough to fulfill your highest sense of a creative self by just thinking about it in the head brain. If your highest sense of self includes being peaceful and forgiving, then you must act in peaceful and forgiving ways. Until then, peacefulness and forgiveness are not really created in yourself and your world, they're only imagined and fantasized.

Once again, the lesson here is that the Highest Expressions on the mBIT Roadmap are not just the optimal functioning of each individual neural network. Rather, they're the highest *'expressions'* of who you are, as enabled through the *'integration'* of your three intelligences in highly coherent states.

</== Discovery Exercise: Integrating Creativity ==/>

Preparation

1. Sit comfortably and allow yourself to settle into your body. Breathe deeply, slowly, gently and comfortably. Settle your mind enough that you can tune into yourself and be aware of

your internal experience. You may wish to close your eyes if that helps you focus inward.

2. Think of a situation in which you feel stuck, limited, or would like more choices in how to respond.

3. Sitting comfortably, do Balanced Breathing for a few minutes until you are in a deeply balanced and coherent state.

Connecting to Creativity

4. Become aware of what values are important for you to express in this situation. Allow those values to come alive and experience them deeply in your heart. Breathe those values into your heart.

5. Now imagine yourself having the creativity to be able to express those values through a wide range of behaviors and responses. You don't have to know what those behaviors and responses actually are yet, you only need to connect with the idea of being creative enough to generate them. You may find it helpful to imagine images of creative people from movies, books or real life as role models. Or you might find it helpful to imagine creative works that inspire you and fill you with a sense of creativity. Allow your heart to value this creativity and fully appreciate its importance and worth in expressing your truest self.

6. Begin to breathe creativity into your heart and chest area. Feel the feelings of creativity flow in and out of your heart and chest area with each breath. See the color of creativity (whatever that is for you) flowing in and out of you with

each breath. Surround yourself with this color until you are bathed deeply in it. Hear the sound(s) of creativity (whatever that may be for you) at just the right volume so that you experience it vibrantly in and throughout your body.

Generating Creative Options

7. Now breathe your creativity up into your head brain. Feel your head become filled with creativity. Feel it expand and extend to your face, your neck, and your shoulders. Notice the free-form flow of thoughts, images, and sounds that arise within your head brain. Notice and appreciate how easily your head brain creates and comes up with whatever it does without you even having to try.

8. While continuing your Balanced Breathing, ask your head brain to imagine at least three new options for how you might respond to your situation in ways that fulfill the value(s) you want to express here. Don't try to analyze or consciously figure out these options. Simply keep focusing on your balanced breathing, feel the desired value(s) in your heart and allow those feelings to flow up into your head, hold your intention to create new options, and allow your head brain to freely generate these options for you. Just observe your thoughts, images, and internal narrative as they arise. Allow the new options to emerge and form on their own as you hold your intention to bring them forth into a clear creative and generative pattern.

9. As each new option emerges, do not judge it or evaluate it, especially not by the criteria of your current thinking. Simply thank all three of your brains for working together and generating new creative options, and just receive them. Each option may or may not be fully formed. You are purely after the creation of new options for thinking about the situation and how to approach it differently. Also, your head brain may generate more than just the three options originally requested. Be open to all creative possibilities.

Creative Alignment and Integration

10. Once an option has emerged that you resonate with, bring that option down into your heart. Allow your heart to value it and bring emotional significance to it. The specifics of the new options may start to modify in accordance with the heart's 'e-value-ation'.

11. Now breathe that 're-e-value-ated' option down into your gut area. Allow your gut intelligence to assimilate and modify that option even further so that you feel you can and want to congruently and intuitively act on that option. Feel how the option is transformed by your wise and intuitive gut intelligence so that taking action is now a natural expression of who you are and a natural expression of you manifesting your highest intention into your world.

12. Now breathe your transformed option back up into your heart, re-value that option in its new form, and from this state of appreciating the value of creativity and yourself as an

inherently creative person, become aware of how your sense of self is expanding and evolving. As you feel more positively connected with yourself, notice what new possibilities become available for you in how you can authentically express your truest self in your daily life.

Aligning and integrating through the three C's

As you may recall from Chapter 1, in many American Indian and Northern Asian tribal spiritual traditions there is a belief that we have three independent souls. In many of these wisdom traditions, healing is performed to bring the souls into alignment, as it's thought that psychological and physical issues are manifest when the three souls are not integrated together. This is also the thesis of this book. When the three brains, the three *'souls'* or intelligences, are out of alignment or are fighting with each other, they cause psychological and emotional problems. Incongruence between the three brains leads to undermining success and creates aberrant behaviors and outcomes.

Both the Buddhist and Bon traditions suggest that compassion, courage and creativity are powerful competencies that can be used together to generate wisdom and healing in life. As we've seen above, these *'three C's'* can be considered to be the Highest Expressions of the three intelligences. By aligning your three brains through these optimal expressions, you produce a powerful synergy for transformational change and personal evolution and create incredible results.

Through loving-kindness and compassion, your brains feel nurtured, trusted and supported. With creativity added to this, your brains find the most generative and flexible choice for moving forward. Then through a deeply gut-felt courage you motivate yourself to an incredible will to action that moves heart-felt generative change into your world.

She yields only to love

> *"You change your life by changing your heart."*

> Max Lucado

During our behavioral modeling research on communicating with and influencing the unconscious aspects of our *mBrains*, we investigated a wide range of diverse and unusual fields. We also interviewed an eclectic group of remarkable people, including a practitioner of Wiccan magic, a *'white witch'* who practices what is known as *'the craft of the wise'*, and who told us that, "She yields only to love!"

What this means is that *'she'*, the unconscious mind made up of the totality of all your mind/body intelligences, responds best and most easily to love and compassion. You cannot force or brow-beat the unconscious mind into long-lasting, sustainable change; doing so eventually rebounds. You might manage it for a short while, but ultimately it's only through a relationship of love, trust and respect that the conscious mind can work with and influence the unconscious aspects of your intelligence — your *mBrains*.

This supports the mBIT principle that the Highest Expression Foundational Sequence best starts with compassion and love in the heart brain. From this base, the process can then flow through to the other brains, as they truly only *'yield'* or respond best to compassion, caring, trust and love.

Integration and sequence counts

As mentioned at the start of this chapter, one of the characteristics of the '*three C's*' is that they are interdependent and integrative in their workings as Highest Expressions. Working with only some of the '*three C's*' independently from the others risks negating their ability to serve as Highest Expressions of an integrated authentic self.

For example, courage without compassion can quickly turn to cruelty, belligerence or domination. And as we mentioned earlier, compassion without generative creativity is what the Buddhists call '*dumb compassion*'; it can quickly lead to '*shared misery*' and do more harm than good.

Creativity not connected to courageous action is mere mental masturbation; it generates great ideas but changes nothing in the world due to inaction or ineffective action. On the other hand, courage without creativity can become bull-headedness and inflexibility, leading to courageous stupidity. Finally, compassion not channeled through a gutsy will-to-action helps nobody in any tangible way.

As you can see, by themselves each Highest Expression can lead to potential problems and issues. It's only by combining all of them together that you give yourself the best chance to produce wise and generative action in the world. Action that fully expresses the deepest nature of your integrated and authentic self.

Additionally, the sequence of how you use these Highest Expressions counts. As you learned in Chapters 2 through 5, the syntax, or sequence, in which the neural networks are accessed can make the difference between success and struggle when *mBraining*. When working with your Highest Expressions, the mBIT Foundational Sequence is your best starting platform.

By starting with compassion you put yourself into a caring, positive state of loving-kindness that then guides your head brain to produce generative and ecological creativity for everyone involved. Once you have a balanced and compassionate creative solution, your gut brain kicks in and provides gutsy courageous motivation and a will-to-action. Now you have a finely tuned and aligned process that is positive, loving, creative, generative and empowered. Now things really start happening in your world.

Sounds fantastic doesn't it! So let's put your learnings into action with the following discovery exercise.

</== Discovery Exercise: Highest Expressions ==/>

As in previous exercises in this book, you may wish to have someone read the steps to you so you can fully engage in the experience, or you can download the audio files for this exercise from www.mbraining.com

1. Think of an issue or situation in which you would like to embody a way of being that is more connected and congruent with your sense of whom you truly are; your authentic self. This may be an issue or situation where you are or have been behaving in a way that's reactive, ego-driven, defensive, or fearful. You can recognize it because your experience is of some form of suffering. Deep down you know you shouldn't or don't really want to behave in the way you have been. Deep down, you know that your behaviors are reactive and they don't really represent who you really are.

2. Now sit or stand comfortably and begin the Balanced Breathing exercise described in Chapter 4.

3. Once you have balanced your breathing for a few minutes along the wave pattern (breathing in for 6 seconds and out for 6 seconds), begin to recall a memory or imagine a scenario that produces strong feelings of compassion within you. Utilize NIE's such as visualizing the color of compassion and breathing it in, imagining the sound of compassion and letting it fill your heart, etc. Connect strongly with the feelings of compassion and loving-kindness that arise within you as you do this.

4. As you fully experience these feelings of compassion, breathe into your heart area and feel the feelings of compassion filling your chest and heart with each breath. Allow the feelings of compassion to resonate deeply with your sense of who you are at an authentic, essence level. Amplify the feelings at least ten times now for a deep, rich, heart-full experience of yourself with a consciousness of compassion.

5. Now begin to imagine and feel the feelings of '*you*' as a compassionate self, expanding upwards to your head brain. As you send the signals of compassion upward, allow your head brain to become filled with compassion and creativity. Connect with the realization that you are a creative being. Starting from a consciousness of compassion, experience your innate and natural creative abilities going to work and beginning to imagine new ways of being and responding to your issue/situation. Observe and enjoy how your head brain

easily produces more and more new ways to compassionately and creatively respond to your issue/situation.

6. Now begin to breathe these feelings of you being a compassionate and creative self, from your head back down into your heart. Allow your heart the freedom to appreciate and value the various options and new responses generated by your creative head brain. Let your compassionate heart prioritize the value of these new choices based on their resonance with the essence of who you truly are as a self-aware human being.

7. Now continue to breathe the feelings of creative compassion and these new choices down into your gut brain. Feel your gut brain assimilate the most congruent and resonant choices into your very being. Feel the naturally arising impulse to act courageously on the most resonant choices, as a natural expression of who you truly are as a compassionate, creative and courageous person. Feel the resonance of acting in accordance with who you truly are as a conscious, self aware human being. Amplify this feeling of courageous action by ten times or more!

8. Now breathe these compassionate, creative and courageous feelings back up into your heart. As these signals naturally and easily flow upwards, become more and more aware of your authentic sense of self, of who you truly are at a deep level of essence, resonating deeply with your expressive nature of compassion, creativity and courage. Be open to and

aware of the changes in your overall wellbeing and your expanded sense of who you really, truly are and how you can express your integrated authentic self into the world now.

mBraining

"Using your multiple brains to do cool stuff"

Chapter 8

mBraining Wisdom

In the 700 year old Soka Gakkai Buddhism teachings of Japan there is a mystic truth known as the *'Buddha state'* or *'Buddha wisdom'* that acts as a reservoir through which anyone can take control of their lives and fulfill their greatest dreams. According to these ancient spiritual beliefs, this state of wisdom involves a melding of creativity, compassion and courage.

The teachings indicate that enormous energy and power are generated when creative wisdom is enacted through boldness and courage, aligned with deep compassion to ensure that every action is both for the good of self and the good of all beings and the world at large. This last point is a vital key to the essence of *'wisdom'*. Wisdom comes not just by a narrow focus on serving self. Wisdom is embodied in a wider notion of choice, perspective and multiple distinctions; being able to flexibly embrace the right actions, at the right time, for the widest possible good.

Multiple perspectives

"Knowledge comes from but a single perspective; wisdom comes from multiple perspectives."

Gregory Bateson

According to Gregory Bateson, the great anthropologist, philosopher and systems theorist, wisdom requires multiple perspectives. In his typically thought-provoking style, Bateson was known to say "there is no inherent wisdom in only one point of reference." For instance, if someone is forty years of age, are they old? From a singular perspective there is only the number *'forty years'*. By and of itself, forty years has no meaning other than the fact of it being a quantity of forty years. However once we introduce a second reference point, that of a six year old child, then forty years takes on additional meaning. From the perspective of a six year old, yes, a person who is forty is indeed old! Now if we add in a third perspective, that of someone eighty years old, then forty years is not old at all, it's only mid-way to eighty.

Notice the difference in your understanding of what *'forty years old'* means when you hold all three perspectives at once — that of the 6 year old, the forty year old and the eighty year old. From three points of reference you can see the larger pattern not previously discernible from only one or two reference points. Because wisdom requires the ability to see the larger pattern of any situation or issue, the minimum number of reference points, or perspectives, for increasing wisdom is three. As Bateson points out in his incredibly insightful writings, it is only through multiple perspectives and multiple distinctions we are able to generate choice and can then examine which of those choices are ecological, wise and sound.

The mBIT model embraces these insights through its requirement for aligning and integrating all three brains. If you only use your head brain to make important life decisions you limit your choice and limit the neural network perspectives you are bringing to the situation. By using all three intelligences of your *mBrains* you provide a minimum of three perspectives for the decision process. In addition, as we saw in the previous chapter, when you align these perspectives through the Highest Expressions of compassion, creativity and courage you unlock a form of wisdom that is truly incredible.

Generative wisdom

It's often been said that wisdom comes with age. If you're like us, you probably noticed that this isn't necessarily true. Some people age without getting wiser, while at the same time there are young people who appear to demonstrate levels of wisdom well beyond their years. As behavioral modelers, we get curious when confronted with these types of seeming contradictions. How can this be, and what can we learn about how to better live our lives from this?

Obviously, age equates to the length of time you've lived on the planet and therefore the quantity of life experience you've had. But some people have more breadth and depth of life experience than others in the same amount of years. Even so, wisdom comes not just from chalking up quantity of experience (although that helps), but more from the quality of '*how*' you experience whatever life gives you. Is your experience of life's events something that happens '*to*' you and through which you act as a recipient coping just to keep on going, or do you experience life as an ongoing process of learning, growing and expressing yourself at your highest levels of being?

It's this latter orientation that enables you to develop wisdom rather than simply memories from whatever number of years you've experienced. This is what enables you to truly live and feel alive, rather than merely existing and surviving. And this is what enables you to continually evolve yourself and your levels of consciousness for generative wisdom.

However, generative wisdom is far more than just having wise insights from your life experiences; insight that goes nowhere other than around the inside of your head does nothing. Generative wisdom is wisdom that is enacted, it's wisdom that is inculcated and behaviorally practiced in the way you live life. And because it's applied in your daily life, it generates results in the real world which you get to personally experience and from which you then generate more wisdom. It's a virtuous cycle of wisdom begetting more wisdom through the practice of real world application.

And of course, to achieve this requires all three of your brains to be engaged at their highest levels of expression. Wisdom is not generative if it's not creative, compassionate and courageous. The perspective of a compassionate heart provides the emotional fuel and desire to make things better for others, for yourself and for the world. This directionalizes the creative perspective of the head brain to synthesize all available information into a larger pattern for a new way of seeing and understanding the situation or issue. These new insights and understanding are given high value and salience from the heart's perspective, and then they inform the gut brain's perspective on how to take wise action in the real world. Additionally, the gut brain's perspective on your identity, who you are as someone who lives wisely, is greatly expanded and evolved through this action-taking.

Generative wisdom is about wisdom applied for the good of all, and because of this it also plays a significant role in the process of your self-evolution. It is not an end state of *'being wise'*. Rather it's an ongoing process of learning, living and emerging your highest sense of self through highly coherent states of consciousness and being. It is a wisdom that is transformational. It continually transforms who you are, how you see the world and how you relate to it. In essence, generative wisdom is about continually emerging your highest sense of authentic self through the pragmatics of daily living.

Aligning wisdom

"You have to master not only the art of listening to your head, you must also master listening to your heart and listening to your gut."

Carly Fiorina

As suggested by numerous converging avenues of evidence, and described throughout this book, the mBIT model says that wisdom is generated through listening to and engaging all three brains through their Highest Expressions. The mBIT Roadmap operationalizes this and provides a structure that guides you to:

1. Engage your neural networks and communicate with them through conscious control of the autonomic gateways. Then enable them to communicate with each other.

2. Align your neural networks so you are congruent in your being and your responses.

3. Evolve your self/neural networks in order to function from levels of higher consciousness and the Highest Expressions of your authentic self.

4. Apply this higher level of consciousness and authentic self to practical life situations and thus have greater wisdom in your decisions and actions.

The key to this process is step 4 — in the application of multiple perspectives and Highest Expressions to pragmatic real-world situations. As the noted systems theorist, biologist and philosopher, Dr. Humberto Maturana highlights, "All knowing is doing." You only truly know something when you can use it with deep wisdom and insight to create real-world actions and results.

Wisdom in action

As indicated, wisdom involves action and expression into the world. Wisdom that is not embodied in pragmatic action is not wisdom at all, it's merely entertaining ideas. What's more, ideas that don't guide or generate change in the world are a waste of valuable time and effort. They're more like puerile fantasies than wise ideas.

Because wisdom only becomes true wisdom when it's pragmatically applied to practical life situations, the remainder of this chapter is taken up with the mBIT Toolkit — the application of the mBIT model, roadmap and principles to real world contexts.

The mBIT Toolkit

While there are certainly many significant skill domains important for life success, we've found from an mBIT perspective there are six vital areas of application most people experience some issue with at various times in their lives. Learning and applying mBIT processes to these domains can make a fundamental difference to the quality of your life and the results you're achieving. The mBIT Toolkit domains include:

1. Self-awareness & Evolving your intuition

2. State management & Self-control

3. Courage, Motivation & Action-taking

4. Decision-making & Problem-solving

5. Habit control & Overcoming compulsions

6. Health & Wellbeing

[BTW: *We are not implying in any way that there aren't other important skill domains that mBIT can add to or really amplify and enhance. For example, relationships, communication and conflict management are all significant life areas. However, we suggest that these skills require prerequisite expertise in the six mBIT Toolkit domains to do them well. Indeed, check out our website for applications of mBIT across a growing set of work and life contexts as we continue our modeling work and share it with all those who are interested.*]

Evolving your intuition

> *"Everyone has intuition. The more you acknowledge it,*
> *the stronger and more accurate it gets."*

Marla Mitchell

Intuition is deep inner knowing. It's defined as the ability to acquire knowledge without inference or the use of reason; in other words, it's a way of knowing that goes beyond conscious head-based processing.

According to Professor Gerard Hodgkinson from Leeds University, intuition is usually (but not always) experienced when people are under severe time pressure, in situations of acute danger or information overload, where conscious analysis can be difficult or impossible. (Paradoxically, intuition can also be experienced during times of deep relaxation, during '*alpha*' states when the ANS is in a balanced, coherent mode and all brains are connected with both head brain hemispheres in balance.)

In an article published in the British Journal of Psychology, Professor Hodgkinson cites the case of a Formula One driver whose life was saved when he slammed on his brakes at a hairpin bend and narrowly avoided hitting a pile-up of cars on the track ahead. During forensic analysis with psychologists after the event, the driver stated that at the time he had no conscious knowledge of why he suddenly braked, but had felt an intense urge that was stronger than his desire to win the race. Through video and memory analysis he was able to determine that the response of fans and spectators in his peripheral vision, as he neared the bend, had cued his unconscious mind something was wrong and triggered his intense unconscious urge to brake.

Messages from your multiple brains

In mBIT terms, intuition is the integration of messages, wisdom and information from all three brains. This matches common understandings that suggest intuition involves "gut feelings, heart messages, hunches or a sixth sense." Indeed, the root of the word intuition is *'tuere'* which means "to guard or protect," and this is exactly the prime function of the gut brain. We can see this clearly in operation in the example of the racing car driver above.

Behavioral modeling shows that intuition comes via gut and heart feelings, strong impulses, urges, dreams, visions, a *'quiet inner voice'*, smells, tastes and sounds. It's also been described as "the small quiet voice within" and has the following characteristics:

- Intuition is typically sensory, visceral and not overly verbal (i.e. not complex internal dialogue)
- Intuition is calm and not fearful
- Intuition is encouraged through respectful questioning within and cannot be forced
- Intuition is often revealed in dreams and is symbolic and metaphorical

Our multiple brains are continuously attempting to provide us with knowledge and insights about what's happening in our world. The key is to tune into these messages and make sense of them consciously; to refine and hone them. Aristotle said it best when he defined wisdom as "intuitive reason combined with scientific knowledge."

"Intuition favors the prepared mind."

Antonio Damasio

This is an important distinction. Wise intuition requires in-domain knowledge. You can't make wise insights in areas in which you have no knowledge or experience. No amount of integration of your three brains will help generate insightful intuitions about brain surgery for example, if you've never studied medicine. You need preparation. You certainly require conscious head-based attention and cognition involved in the process. But head based knowledge and experience alone won't produce wisdom.

Integrated intuition

Note we're not providing the ultimate discourse on intuition here. We're not drilling into an encyclopedic treatise on every aspect of intuition. Instead, we are looking at the kind of intuition that leads to practical and pragmatic wisdom.

We're also not suggesting that intuition is some magic, esoteric or mystical *'thing'*. The evidence from our research is that intuition has a neurological and physical process and structure. Our modeling work with mBIT has uncovered key distinctions on the process of intuition applied to wisdom. So leaving aside notions of intuition as some psychic phenomena or ability, let's explore intuition as a deep, insightful and integrated sense of knowing generated through the Highest Expressions of each of your brains.

The inner voice

Some researches make a distinction between a pure head or *'ego-based'* inner voice versus a *'heart/gut intuitive'* inner voice and say that the heart/gut voice comes through a focus on love, compassion, peace and courage. This is a really important insight. Each of your

274

brains can provide intuitive messages. There can be an '*inner voice*' or communication (via symbols, imagery, felt-sense etc.) from the head, heart or gut neural networks, and as suggested in Chapter 4, such an '*inner voice*' is likely to be the translation of non-verbal messages from the heart brain, gut brain or the right-hemisphere of the head brain into words you can attend to in conscious awareness. But listening to only one of your multiple brains' signals can lead to very un-wise decisions. Your heart, gut or head can swamp the intuitive messages from the other brains. So you need to be aware of and track for which inner voice is speaking to you. With practice you can become aware of the difference between ego-based messages, heart messages and gut messages.

The structure of intuitive wisdom

There is a structure to the process of wise intuition. As we've seen, each of your brains can and will provide intuitive information about your situation and your world. But there's a significant difference in the quality of the insights and information generated by the three brains when they're functioning in their Highest Expressions. Intuitions generated by neural networks that are in massively sympathetic or parasympathetic states can be distorted and unwise. For example, in a state of anger or fear your brains will definitely send you intuitions and messages. But these will be very different in quality and insightfulness to those provided when you are operating from a state of loving-kindness, balance and calmness.

To achieve intuitive wisdom you need to utilize the Highest Expressions of your brains, within a balanced coherent state, and within that framework communicate with your brains to respectfully ask for their intuitions and insights.

The mBIT model for tuning into your intuitive wisdom involves:

1. Communicate with and ask each of your brains to provide messages and deep intuitions about the context or situation you are exploring

2. Attend to and make refined discriminations of the messages and signals from each of your neural network intelligences as they respond to your request for information

3. Perform Balanced Breathing and bring each of your brains into a coherent state and Highest Expression

4. Now allow deeply intuitive insights to cohere into conscious awareness the meaning of the *'intuitive'* information that arises from the alignment/integration of your three brains

5. What comes out of this is deeply intuitive wisdom

</== Discovery Exercise: Intuition ==/>

In this exercise you'll learn to gain insights and deeply intuitive messages from your unconscious mind and multiple brains.

1. Think of an issue or situation in which you'd like to tap into your intuition and inner wisdom.

2. Now sit comfortably in a quiet room, free from interruptions or distractions and begin the Highest Expression Balanced Breathing exercises described in the previous chapters.

3. Inner stillness is a pre-requisite to tapping into intuition, so make sure you guide yourself into a deeply calm and peaceful state of coherence. Align your heart, head and gut

brains by breathing in peace, joy and compassion and moving these feelings and messages across your three brains.

4. Once you are calmly aligned, respectfully ask yourself questions about your situation and listen to the first answers that pop into your mind. They might be images, sounds, a felt-sense, feelings or some words. Whatever they are, just notice them. Pay attention. Thank your brains for the messages. Now begin to explore what they mean. Ask your unconscious mind to help you understand their insights. Don't force this, just allow the intuitions and ideas to flow naturally into your conscious awareness. You can ask each of your brains individually for their wisdom. Ask your heart what it means. Ask your gut. Ask your head. And keep Balanced Breathing as you do and continue calm Balanced Breathing as you wait for their responses.

5. Remember that intuition is calm and not fearful. So if you feel any strongly visceral fear or panic based response then note it and Balanced Breathe until you come back to autonomic coherence. Then ask your brains to tell you what is driving the response, what is the intuition or insight you need to learn in order to bring generative wisdom to your situation. This is all about unpacking the deeper messages that underlay the initial response.

6. With trust, respect and practice you'll find that your deep intuitions become more accurate, more insightful and come to conscious awareness more quickly and with greater ease.

Accuracy develops with practice and trust

Research shows that intuition can be developed with practice. The US Army for example, has developed a program that trains officers to increase and improve their intuition skills. The program is designed to assist combat officers in coping with what are called VUCA situations; Situations involving *'Volatility, Uncertainty, Complexity, and Ambiguity'*, all of which require full use of the insights from all three brains.

One of the main findings of intuition training is that accuracy increases with refined practice. This is not surprising given that intuition involves using and building patterns in and between the neural networks of the three brains. Indeed, this is how neural networks work. Patterns build through repetition. It's much the same as exercise and muscle building. If you're weight training you know that lifting a dumbbell once won't build muscle. It's all about reps. You build strength through repetition. The more reps, the stronger the muscle, the easier it gets. Building *'intuition muscle'* works exactly the same way.

Another key finding from recent research is that trust is an important factor for building accuracy. The more you trust your intuitions and feelings, the higher their accuracy. Across a series of eight studies, participants were asked to predict various future outcomes, including the 2008 U.S. Democratic presidential nominee, the box-office success of various movies, the winner of American Idol, movements of the Dow Jones Index, the winner of a college football championship game, and even the weather. The researchers discovered that intuitive predictions were strongly enhanced when subjects either naturally trusted their feelings and decisions, or were influenced into trusting their intuitions. Despite the range of events and prediction horizons, the results consistently revealed that people with higher trust in their feelings were more likely to correctly predict the final outcome than those with lower trust in their feelings. The take home message from this... trust your multiple brains and they'll respond to that trust. Practice tuning in to your intuitions, feelings and the messages from your multiple brains, and as you gain success, celebrate and amplify the trust you're building in your intuitive abilities.

Self-awareness: Deconstructing the messages

In a similar manner to intuition, self-awareness requires noticing and listening to the messages and responses from all your brains. For true self-awareness you need to explore what your head thinks about your situation, what your heart feels and what your gut senses. You need to deconstruct and examine what each neural network is perceiving and attempting to tell you. Separate out your feelings, thoughts, responses and reactions. Get multiple distinctions on your inner knowing. Until you've done this you're only getting part of the picture of your inner world.

Self-deception

But you also need to be aware of self-deception and overcome it. Brains are capable of obfuscation, deception and confusion. Much of this is state based. In highly sympathetic and stressed states, the heart and gut can send messages that are incredibly destructive. Brought back to a balanced coherent state their responses and messages become much more ecological.

You can also deceive yourself by attending to and only focusing on the messages from one of your brains. For example the use of head-based intelligence without involvement of the heart can be dangerous. There are many heartless but very smart people in the world who do a lot of damage to the people and systems around them.

By bringing your mind-body into balanced coherence and facilitating your brains into their Highest Expressions, you'll give yourself the best chance of getting open, honest information, intuitions and feedback from and between all of your brains.

Cognitive Dissonance

In Chapter 6 we introduced the important concept of cognitive dissonance. As you'll remember, based on years of research and thousands of subsequent laboratory and real-world studies, Professor Leon Festinger posited that the unconscious mind does not like mismatching cognitions, thoughts, beliefs or ideas and the visceral feelings of '*dissonance*' that such mismatch produces. As a result the unconscious mind will do anything it can to remove cognitive dissonance and will utilize a number of unconscious strategies to eliminate it. Typically, the tension of cognitive dissonance leads people to change either their beliefs and attitudes or their behavior through the processes of:

1. **Avoidance** — people avoid information that is likely to lead to dissonance

2. **Distortion** — people delete and distort facts and beliefs to reduce dissonance

3. **Confirmation** — people are attracted to or perform selective bias on information that confirms or bolsters their cognitions

4. **Reassurance** — people look for reassurance from others that their cognitions and beliefs are correct and ok

5. **Re-valuation** — people change the importance of existing and new ideas, facts and cognitions to reduce dissonance

Understanding and tracking this process is an important component of self-awareness. While cognitive dissonance often leads people into denying reality or deleting and distorting their cognitions and perceptions, it doesn't need to be that way. When you're aware that your brains don't like mismatching ideas, thoughts or beliefs, you can start to notice whenever dissonance occurs and accept it as a natural response. You can then treat it as a valid signal coming from your heart or gut brains alerting you about mismatch in your internal world.

The very act of valuing cognitive dissonance as an awareness tool is itself a cognition and via bolstering leads to your unconscious mind not having to automatically delete or distort the mismatching cognitions. This process allows you to gain choice and control over how you are creating your cognitive world — the world of your beliefs, values, ideas and identity. In this way you can use cognitive dissonance as a tool for positively aligning your thoughts, values and behavior.

Cognitive dissonance also relates to decision-making. Research has shown that the more effort and time invested in a decision or the forming of a belief, the larger the potential dissonance created if mismatching evidence is discovered. The more important the outcome you are working with, the more likely your unconscious mind is to perform the above dissonance removal strategies. For example, if you purchase a low cost item, you're unlikely to experience buyer's remorse. However, for an expensive item you spent a lot of time evaluating, you're more likely to experience buyer's remorse and therefore more likely to go seeking confirmation and reassurance after the purchase. Awareness of these natural and inbuilt processes puts you at choice and allows you to wisely decide how you respond to life.

Calm wisdom

"The wise are always at peace."

Arab Proverb

The year is 1974 and in British Colombia a fascinating social experiment is unfolding. In the middle of a long, sagging and immensely scary suspension bridge spanning Capilano Canyon, an attractive young woman is waiting. As men pass on the their way across, hovering more than 230 feet above the river far below, she is stopping them and asking if they'd be willing to fill in a questionnaire. Once they've completed the questions, with the bridge swaying and rocking in the wind, she shows them a picture of a woman with her face covered, and asks them to make up a back story for the image. She then tears off a piece of paper and writes her phone number on it, telling the unknowing subject of the experiment that he can call her later that night if he'd like to discuss the survey further.

With this strange and unusual psychology experiment, researchers Dr. Donald Dutton and Dr. Arthur Aron were attempting to study the effects of arousal and anxiety on false identification of emotional attraction. To compare the results from the scary bridge they replicated the same experiment but this time the bridge was wide, stable and only a couple of feet off the ground. What they found is that out of a total of 85 subjects, 50% of the men from the scary bridge called the woman's phone number later that night, compared to only 12% from the safe bridge. And analysis of

282

the back stories the men made up about the image, showed that the men on the scary bridge were twice as likely to generate a story with sexually suggestive themes.

So what is happening here? How come men on a scary bridge became flirtatious, sexually interested and eager to call the woman, but men on a safe bridge didn't? And how does this relate to mBIT and wisdom?

To make sense of this you have to think about Autonomic Nervous System (ANS) arousal and how sympathetic ANS arousal puts the head, heart and gut brains into a sympathetic dominant state. From this state of arousal and excitement, the core competencies of the aroused sympathetic state are more likely to be co-accessed. Thus arousal, anxiety and excitement from the suspension bridge lead to an unconscious linking of perceptions and experience of attraction and sexual arousal towards the female interviewer.

What this means from an mBIT perspective is that you need to be aware of the state of your ANS when you are deconstructing the messages from your *mBrains*. Wisdom is also best served by bringing your ANS back to calm coherence and quiescence before making decisions or gathering intuitive insights. Otherwise you run the risk of confusing the messages and linkages of your brains. By using Balanced Breathing and congruently aligning your brains via the Highest Expressions you can engender a calm wisdom, one that is not distorted by the current state of an aroused or depressed ANS.

State management & self-control

The ability to control and manage your state is crucial for success, happiness and wise action in the world. There is a famous series of experiments in psychology called the *'Stanford Marshmallow Studies'*.

In these experiments, preschool children were asked to choose between a smaller taste-treat they could have immediately versus a larger treat that required waiting. Professor Walter Mischel and his colleagues found that the number of seconds a child could exercise self-control and wait for their marshmallow treat predicted everything from future SAT scores, emotional coping skills in adolescence, levels of happiness and the ability to relax and cope with stress.

Numerous longitudinal studies have shown that self-control in childhood predicts a range of adult outcomes including life expectancy, career success, and education level. In adulthood, the ability for self-control has also been found to reduce the negative effects of interpersonal rejection. Overall, the ability to delay gratification and consciously control emotional and mind-body state predicts and supports a wide range of positive outcomes.

Research has also shown that the Anterior Cingulate Cortex (ACC) in the head brain, described in detail in Chapter 3 and 4, is strongly involved in self-control. This area of the head brain is intrinsically connected and related to the heart and gut brains, providing a linkage point between all three brains. The evidence that the ACC is involved in self-control bolsters results from our action research showing that self-control requires alignment and direction of all three brains.

In our modeling work we've found there are three key skills that support self-awareness and self-control. These are:

- The ability to do Calm-abiding
- The ability to do Forgiveness
- The ability to do Mindfulness

And in the following sections we'll explore these in some detail.

Calm-abiding

"A calm mind is key to happiness."

Dalai Lama

"If we were able to maintain a calm and peaceful mind all day long, we would never experience any problems or mental suffering."

Geshe Kelsang Gyatso

Your ability to calmly abide the vicissitudes of life can make the difference between living a life of heart-felt peace versus a tumultuous life of suffering and misery when things don't go your way. As the Buddhists point out so perspicaciously, the nature of the Universe is impermanence. Nothing lasts forever. So it's a certainty that you'll experience times when something you love and value breaks, dies or disappears. You can upset yourself to no avail over this, or you can learn to calmly abide with peace in your heart, mind and gut.

So what's the structure of calm-abiding? Notice the inherent neuro-linguistics of the term *'calm-abiding'*. Calmness is both a heart and gut predicate. The heart can beat frenetically, and usually does so during times of stress and sympathetic arousal. Alternately, it can beat calmly and evenly when in balance and coherence. The gut can also be calm and flowing or turmoiled and upset.

The word *'abiding'* on the other hand is a movement or motility predicate that links strongly to gut brain competencies and functions. So to calmly abide you need to calm your heart and quiesce your gut; to calmly abide and settle and allow the battering

285

waves of life's challenges to wash easily over you, knowing that everything changes and that *'this too shall pass'*.

The way to calmly abide therefore is to balanced-breathe calmness into your heart, move this up to your head and then breathe it back down through the heart and into the gut. It's such a simple process and so self-soothing. In times of anger, disappointment, emotional-pain and upset, it is an incredibly useful and generative response to utilize this calm abiding breathing technique. Once you have brought yourself back into positive, calm coherence you can then add in an extra component which we'll describe in the next section that sweetens up the experience.

Uplifting your heart, calming your gut: In-joy-in-yourself

Eckhart Tolle, in his intriguing book *'The Power of Now'* describes the importance of being truly present within yourself and the power that focusing on the heart-felt joy of the present moment brings. He describes how too often we get lost in habitual processes of waiting; waiting in lines at the bank, post-office or supermarket, waiting in traffic jams, waiting for the next holiday or break, waiting for things to start, to end, for success, for money, for happiness. Instead, Eckhart reminds us, when you are focused in the moment on the joy of your own aliveness, you can truly enjoy yourself — truly be *'In-joy-in yourself'* — all it takes is to focus on gratitude for the present moment, to connect within yourself and creatively *'in-joy'* feelings of love and peace.

In this enhanced version of the calm-abiding process, you will learn to embody *'in-joy-in yourself'*. With this technique you breathe light-hearted joy into your heart and up into your head on the in-breath, and then breathe peaceful calmness from your head to your heart and deeply down into your gut on the out-breath. It's a

286

powerful technique that with practice gets stronger and more impactful. And it's a delightful and easy method to control your state and shift it in ways that allow you to express a wiser and more generative you.

</== Discovery Exercise: Calm Abiding '*In joy in yourself*' ==/>
In this exercise you'll build a deep state of calm peaceful joy within your heart, head and gut.

1. Whenever you're feeling stressed or in need of some uplifting or calming, simply take a few minutes to sit and start Balanced Breathing. Breathe in and out calmly and evenly, taking approx. 6 seconds on the in-breath and 6 seconds on the out-breath. As you know, make sure your in and out breaths are of the same duration.

2. As you breathe in, imagine that each breath is uplifting your heart with light-hearted joy. Really feel that uplifting feeling. And smile as you do this. Smiling makes a key difference. Deeply feel your heart being uplifted as you breathe. You can imagine a color or sparkling light filling your heart with uplifting positive energy and love. And you can take that light, color and feeling and experience it going all the way from your heart to your head, taking your delightful, joyful and uplifting feelings and messages from your heart into your mind.

3. As you breathe out, imagine your breath going down from your head/heart to your gut, taking with it calming feelings

and messages. Really feel that letting go, relaxing, calming and peace-filled sense of joy fill your belly. Add a light or color that deeply enhances your gut-felt feelings of peace, joy and contentment.

4. Breathe in *'uplifting in-joy-in your heart'*, breath out and down *'deeply calming in-joy-in your gut'*. Continue doing this, as you smile, swallowing peaceful joy from your head to your gut and feeling so profoundly aligned, peacefully integrated and joyfully calmed.

Forgiveness

*"Forgiveness is the most powerful thing you can do for yourself.
If you can't learn to forgive,
you can forget about achieving true success in your life."*

Dr. Wayne Dyer

Forgiveness is a powerful emotion. When practiced it floods the body with soothing and healing neuro-hormones and stimulates positive emotions and positive states of being. The wisdom of forgiveness is highlighted in almost all spiritual traditions and more recently, research from a number of scientific fields is backing up the importance of practicing forgiveness. For example, both Buddhist philosophy and recent research from the new field of Positive Psychology have shown that compassion, forgiveness and loving-kindness are key components to happiness.

The research from Positive Psychology has demonstrated that people who forgive are healthier and happier than those who hold grudges. In one Stanford University experiment, people who learned and practiced forgiveness reported fewer backaches, headaches, muscle pains, stomach upsets and other common physical signs of stress compared to a control group. They also reported higher levels of optimism, hope and self-confidence. Showing forgiveness really is both good for you and good for happiness and peace of mind.

The converse is also true. People who focus on anger, injustice and who feel they've been treated unfairly suffer from a higher risk of heart disease. A study of 8,000 people by researchers at University College London found that those with a profound sense of injustice had a 55% higher chance of suffering serious heart disease. Researchers found that the focus on injustice and unfairness engendered negative emotions that lead to biochemical changes in the body. Anger, bitterness and vengeance are sympathetic dominant heart core competencies that do untold damage to your heart, health and life.

An inability or unwillingness to forgive has also been found to be associated with persistent rumination and dwelling on revenge, while forgiving allows you to move on. When you're angry, resentful and bitter you truly only hurt yourself. So it's important both for your mental and physical health that you forgive. Certainly, the evidence is that practicing forgiveness is an important daily activity for living a happy, fulfilled and wise life.

Integrating forgiveness

> *"Forgiveness is not an emotion, it's a decision."*
>
> Randall Worley

Most people forgive at only two levels; the level of head based logic and the level of the heart. But this is imperfect forgiveness and leads to ongoing issues. In order to truly let go and move on, you have to decide to fully and deeply forgive on three levels: intellectually, emotionally, and at the gut level. Notice the natural neuro-linguistics of that last statement. "In order to truly *'let go'* and *'move on'*..." These are motility predicates and indicate a gut brain based involvement. While your gut is holding on to the issue and maintaining it at the level of core identity, you will never *'let it go'*. And in gustatory and vernacular terms, "you'll continue to give yourself the *shits* over the perceived injustice."

By applying the mBIT Foundational Sequence using the filters of the Highest Expressions, you can align healing and forgiveness to all three brains. Through the competencies of compassion, creativity and courage you can generatively and authentically let go of any hurt and truly move on. This is the embodied act of perfect forgiving in which the injustice no longer has any power over you or your life and in fact is no longer experienced as an injustice.

Letting go

We all make mistakes. No one, and we mean no one is perfect! Indeed, *'perfection'* doesn't exist in the world. It's an ideal. From physics we know that we live in an *'entropic universe'*. What this means is that everything we do ultimately creates more entropy or disorder in the universe. Even the creation of order actually produces more disorder. For example, an air-conditioner cools the air in a room, thus reducing the entropy (disorder) of the air. However, the heat generated in operating the air-conditioner always makes a bigger contribution to the entropy of the environment than the decrease of the entropy of the cool air that is produced. So the overall total entropy in the universe increases from the operation of the air-conditioner.

So there can never be something that is perfect. Everything is in a constant state of change and everything is impermanent. That's the nature of the entropic universe we live in. By attempting to be perfect and blaming, disappointing or angering yourself when you or the people around you don't live up to some ideal is both un-sane and counterproductive.

It's time to let go of anger, of old regrets, of blame and recrimination. When you apply the Highest Expression of compassion, loving-kindness and forgiveness to yourself and your life you let go of these negative emotions — of negative emoting. Trust yourself. Support yourself. Forgive yourself. You deserve loving-kindness. Calmly abide the trials and vicissitudes of life. Nothing's perfect, no one's perfect, we all continue to learn and try to find our way in this wonderful but imperfect world. So relax, think *'calm-abiding'* and let go of any fearing, angering or blaming that you have been doing in the past now.

The courage to let go

Some people think forgiveness is a sign of weakness. Those who've studied it can tell you without qualification that forgiveness is a sign of strength. It takes guts, immense courage and strength of purpose to choose to practice forgiveness and let go, especially in the face of anger and bitterness.

Consider the example of Ken Marslew. In 1994, Ken's young son Michael was senselessly and violently murdered in a bungled robbery at the Pizza Hut in which he worked. The offenders who committed the crime went to prison, but Ken was still completely devastated by the loss of his son. Needless to say, he was angry and bitter. He demanded the return of the death penalty and was so emotionally outraged that he took out a contract on the people who committed the botched robbery.

But Ken realized doing this was just more of the same that had killed his son. So, amazingly, he dug deep within himself and despite the intensity of his feelings, and knowing that revenge and retaliation was not the answer, he cancelled the contract on the perpetrators and instead decided to do something positive with his anger and hate. This was no easy task and required Ken to stay connected with the Highest Expressions of his heart, gut and head to rise above his reactions. While no one could've blamed Ken if he'd remained angry and hateful toward those responsible for the death of his innocent son, now he's an inspiration to thousands of people for what's possible when we align our three brains and express our highest sense of who we truly are.

Ken founded the anti-violence organization "Enough is Enough" along with the "Michael Marslew Peace Foundation" and has made tremendous contributions in reducing the levels of violence in the communities he works with. No one can accuse Ken of simply espousing anti-violence messages. Truly, he is an exemplar and role model for *'walking your talk'*. He ultimately met face-to-face with his son's killer, mentored him during his incarceration, and when released from prison offered him a job in his own organization. To stop violence in society, Ken knows he had to begin with himself. It took and continues to take immense guts and strength for Ken Marslew to let go of all that anger and bitterness, and instead embrace life and make a positive difference based on the tragedy of what happened. And because of his wise decision and gutsy courage, he has created an incredible organization that continues to make ongoing and impactful changes that decrease violence in our world. [For more information about Ken and Enough Is Enough, visit www.enoughisenough.org.au]

Forgiving as *'for-giving'* to yourself!

"Hate hurts the person who does the hating the most. Why would I want to continue to hate myself?"

Ken Marslew

You know, forgiveness doesn't mean condoning wrongful behavior, excusing thoughtlessness, or forcing reconciliation with the offender. Forgiving is not the same as condoning. Forgiving is done for yourself; to heal and support yourself. It's a gift of happiness and peace of mind that you give yourself. It's about letting go of anger and resenting. It's about moving out from under the emotional burden of bitterness and liberating yourself from negative feelings of hurting or angering. It's for giving the gift of peace to yourself.

As described in the research from Positive Psychology, an inability or unwillingness to do forgiving has been found to be associated with persistent rumination and dwelling on revenge, whereas forgiving allows you to move on. When you are angry, resentful and bitter you are only hurting yourself. So it's important for your mental health and important for your physical health that you forgive.

Another important thing to note is the distinction between the inner experience of forgiving and the public expression of it. They need not both be performed to gain the health and happiness benefits of forgiving. The research suggests it can be sufficient to practice *'silent'* forgiving in the form of a softened and more sympathetic heart. This can be useful when the aggressor does not earn or merit the forgiveness.

Remember, forgiving is about healing yourself and letting go the negative responses and burden. In cases where the aggressor has apologized and made redress, a public expression of forgiveness can be appropriate and can support building better and more healthy relationships. It's up to you to decide what's appropriate for your own outcomes and happiness. The main thing to note is the inner process of multiple brain forgiving is vital for building positivity and healing in your own life.

Healing the heart, gut and mind

The key is that forgiveness is about healing yourself and letting go of any negative responses and burden. The main thing to note is that the process of forgiving is vital for building positivity and healing in your own life.

A useful strategy for practicing forgiveness is to use your heart-mind to focus on forgiveness and to hold the feelings of forgiveness in your heart and then spreading those to your head and gut. Your heart-brain learns from experience and from practice. So by concentrating on and holding feelings of forgiving in your heart you can gradually and gently build up your skills and unconscious competence at doing forgiving. As your heart gets stronger at forgiving it can lead that skill to both your head brain and deep within your enteric brain. It's an important process that will allow you to live more wisely, healthily, happily and with joy in your heart, mind and life.

How do you DO forgiving?

How do you do loving-kindness and forgiving? As indicated above, you start by creating and holding feelings of forgiving and loving in your heart and then apply them to the situation or context that you feel needs forgiving. You start by thinking of memories or experiences that fill your heart with loving-kindness, with compassion and forgiveness and then you expand them from your heart to your head and back through the heart down deeply to your gut. This sends important messages from your cardiac brain to your cranial and enteric brains; from your heart brain to your head and gut brains. This aligns your three brains together around deep and total forgiveness. In the following exercise you'll be guided through a process that facilitates multiple brain forgiving and allows you to let go of old hurts, grudges and residual anger, replacing them with deep inner peace.

</== Discovery Exercise: Deep Inner Forgiving ==/>

When doing forgiving, it's important to realize you cannot easily get to highly coherent states of loving-kindness and forgiveness when you are in overly sympathetic or parasympathetic modes of functioning. You must first get yourself into a state of coherence, generate pure states of love and forgiveness and then apply those states to whom or what you want to forgive.

1. Identify with whom or with what you want to do *'forgiving'*.

2. Sit comfortably and engage in Balanced Breathing for several minutes.

3. Set aside for now any and all of your current feelings of *'unforgiveness'* (e.g. anger, resentment, hurt, being offended, violation, betrayal, etc.). Regardless of what happened and your internal dialogue about it, focus on maintaining your Balanced Breathing. Create a clear mental and emotional *'space'* within you to access feelings of forgiveness and love as pure states, not associated (yet) with your memories of who or whatever happened.

4. With each breath, create and hold feelings of pure forgiving and loving in your heart. As you breathe in and out, amplify the feelings with each breath, feel them expand and grow, until your whole chest, your whole torso, your whole body is filled with deep feelings of loving-kindness. Make sure you expand them from your heart to your head and then back through the heart down deeply to your gut, deep inside your torso and stomach. This will send important messages from your heart brain to your head and gut brains. This will align your three brains together around deep and total forgiveness. Keep expanding these pure feelings of forgiving and loving until they fill your entire body and way of being.

5. Now start to think of who or what you want to forgive. Continue to breathe and amplify your heart, head and gut feelings of forgiveness and compassion as you think of who or what you are forgiving. Breathe forgiveness and compassion into your head brain and notice how your thoughts, perceptions and meaning of what happened begins to change and soften. Notice your openness to new ways of understanding the person or situation from a place of compassion, loving-kindness, and a generosity of spirit.

6. Breathe these new understandings and new awareness back down into your heart. Value these new perceptions highly. Notice how forgiving feels good, how it brings greater peace and wellness to you. Be aware of how your heart opens and lightens up.

7. Now breathe these enhanced and highly valued feelings and perceptions down into your gut. Swallow them down if that helps. Feel your gut take in and assimilate these new learnings. Feel your gut relax and *'let go'* of any tensions related to defensiveness, protection, or aggression. Feel how your gut welcomes and responds with a sense of ease, peace and security. As your gut lets go of the old way of being, feel how it and you are becoming increasingly ready to move on in life. Feel how letting go of this past *'baggage'* makes you feel lighter, freer, and makes it easier to focus on moving forward from now on in. Experience the sensations of your gut updating its learned responses, releasing what is no longer useful to hold onto, and mobilizing you toward acting from a new, freer identity.

8. If you experience any Neural Integration Blocks (NIB's) during any part of this process, use the skills and techniques from Chapter 6 to dissolve and pattern interrupt those NIB's and then return to Step 4 above and re-do the steps of the exercise till you can experience deep integrated forgiving.

9. Say to yourself:

   "I forgive. I do forgiving, I feel forgiving, I am forgiving. I forgive [*the name of who or what you have forgiven*] completely. I release any and all un-useful feelings and stories that do not serve me and that do not express my truest self. I forgive myself completely. I am a worthwhile person who deserves loving-kindness and support. I let go and am now ready to move on in my life."

Say these words several times, with warm, loving tonalities. Hug yourself both physically and in your imagination. And all the while keep breathing love and forgiveness into your heart, your head and your gut.

You may wish to repeat this process two or three times. Each time you practice the '*doing*' of forgiving and compassion you'll find it gets stronger, easier and more integrated into your evolving sense of self. Your heart and gut brains will learn and remember how to do this re-patterning process more easily and quickly with any other people or issues you need to or want to forgive.

Mindfulness

According to ancient Buddhist texts, the practice of mindfulness supports understanding and the arising of wisdom. Mindfulness involves bringing your complete attention to the present moment, non-judgmentally, so that each thought, feeling, or sensation that arises is acknowledged and accepted as it is. Mindfulness allows you to stay present and leads to an increased appreciation of each individual moment.

Mindfulness techniques, inherited from the Buddhist tradition, are increasingly being employed in modern psychology as an adjunct treatment for a variety of mental and physical conditions such as anxiety, depression, compulsive behavior, chronic pain and stress. Research has shown that in as little as two months the practice of mindfulness can produce positive changes in both brain function and immune response.

From an mBIT perspective, mindfulness involves *'Mind-full-ness'*. That is, being mind-full of the messages, feelings and sensations from all of your brains. All three brains working together make up the emergent process of the *'mind'*, so being totally *'mindful'* means bringing awareness to the states, messages and integration or lack of integration of all three brains on a moment by moment basis.

The opposite of this is mindlessness, and from an mBIT perspective this means ignoring information, messages and signals from your three brains. In our modern society, most people are relatively mindless about their heart and gut brains. We have tended to focus on and elevate the importance of head based experiences, thoughts and sensations. But this has caused our lives and world to get out of balance. Mindfulness means bringing back balanced, integrated awareness and attention to all three brains.

As we've pointed out throughout this book and in particular in the current chapter, much of our intelligence and cognition is *'embodied'*; a large and important proportion of our processing of our world is done through the brains in our hearts and guts. By practicing multiple brain mindfulness we are able to experience fully and viscerally the temporary, fleeting and ever changing nature of our sensations, feelings and thoughts that occur within and between our neural networks. The evidence from both Buddhist teachings and modern research is that when we practice mindfulness, more creative solutions emerge spontaneously and this leads to greater wisdom. By bringing a multiple brain approach to this we amplify the creativity and generative wisdom produced by mindfulness techniques.

</== Discovery Exercise: *mBrain* Mindfulness Meditation ==/>

In this exercise you'll learn to calmly direct your attention towards what's happening in your mind, body and multiple brains.

1. Start in a comfortable sitting position. This is an eyes-open exercise and is best done in a relatively quiet environment. Sit so that your posture is upright and not rigid. Allow your spine to gently straighten, keep your head nicely balanced, your feet flat on the floor and your hands resting comfortably in your lap. Set your gaze so that it softly and easily focuses on the floor somewhere in front of you.

2. Commence Balanced Breathing along the sine wave pattern so that you are breathing in for 6 seconds and out for 6 seconds, evenly and effortlessly. Do this for a couple of minutes till you can feel the calm experience of coherence envelop your heart, head and gut brains.

3. Put aside any thoughts of the past or future and stay focused in the present. Keep your attention on your Balanced Breathing, noticing the air moving in and out of your lungs, feeling the rise and fall of your belly and diaphragm. Focus on how each breath is new and fresh. Allow your breathing to continue naturally, without being controlled.

4. Start to watch and experience any thoughts, feelings or sensations as they arise. Notice where in your body they begin and move to and from. Are they from and in your heart? Are they from and in your gut? Are they head based? Don't ignore any thoughts or feelings and don't suppress

them either. Just simply observe them and remain calm as you continue to breathe in a balanced and coherent way.

5. Your goal with this exercise is to stay present and gain insight into your experience of reality. Your intention is to be mindful and aware of what's happening within your mind, body and multiple brains. Simply sitting, breathing and noticing your ongoing internal experience. Everything is welcomed. Nothing is ignored. Similarly nothing is analyzed. Just notice the patterns of your thoughts, feelings and messages that are flowing in your mind and body.

6. There is no failure with this exercise. If you notice your attention wandering, then gently and calmly bring it back to your breathing. If you find yourself lost in discursive thought, in confusion or in analysis, just calmly bring your focus back to your breathing. The act of noticing is itself part of mindfulness. Your role is to play the part of an impartial observer of your ongoing attention and experience.

7. When you have performed the exercise for the allotted period of 10 or more minutes, finish by breathing compassion into your heart, move that up to your head where you can add creativity and then breath both of them back through your heart to your gut, adding in gutsy courage to your experience. Cycle through your Highest Expressions across several breaths, building up the wonderful and generative experience that they bring. Finally, stand up slowly and gently stretch, feeling alive, energized and renewed.

The aim of mindfulness meditation is to achieve a mind that is stable, aware and calm. Through mindfulness practice you develop and strengthen your neural circuits in the skills of peace, calmness and emergent wisdom. The more often you practice the greater the results. Even 10 minutes a day can make a world of difference to how your brains calmly integrate and communicate together to produce generative awareness in your life.

Courage, motivation and grit

Nearly everyone's experienced times when they've lacked the courage to take gutsy motivated action in life. Whether it's compassionate caring or a great creative idea, unless you express it through motivated action you'll produce no real or lasting change in your world.

But as we discussed in the previous chapter, there's a crucial distinction between physical courage and moral courage. While having the guts and determination to push through fear and uncertainty are important and useful skills, physical courage alone can often as not create more trouble and risk than it solves. Moral courage is gutsy courage that's directed by deep, heartfelt and generative values. For truly wise outcomes in your life, you need to guide, link and temper gutsy courage with generative compassion and creativity.

An important aspect of courage and motivation is the tenacity to keep pushing and flourishing even in the face of adversity. In the field of Positive Psychology, this ability is known as 'grit' and has been studied extensively. As Dr. Angela Duckworth, one of the key researchers defines it, "Grit entails working strenuously toward challenges, maintaining effort and interest over years despite failure, adversity, and plateaus in progress. The gritty individual approaches achievement as a marathon; his or her advantage is stamina. Whereas disappointment or boredom signals to others that it is time to change trajectory and cut losses, the gritty individual stays the course."

Numerous studies have shown that grit significantly contributes to successful outcomes in life. Students who display higher levels of grit achieve higher grade point averages than their peers over and beyond IQ or conscientiousness. Grittier individuals also attain higher levels of education overall and in the workplace are more successful and make less career changes than those with less gutsy determination.

In our behavioral modeling work we've found that tenacity and perseverance are often experienced as a gut-felt hunger for heartfelt dreams and desires. This deep hunger is only satiated once the goal has been achieved and thereby acts as an ongoing motivator for action, even in the face of setbacks and roadblocks.

</== Discovery Exercise: Hungering for Success ==/>

In this exercise you'll build a deep visceral hunger in your gut for an intensely heart-felt goal or outcome. This exercise is about building intense motivation, a deep sense of encouragement and a passionate and congruent hunger for the success of your outcome. [Note: do NOT do this exercise immediately after a meal, it is better done when you are physically hungry.]

1. Think of an outcome, goal or dream that you want to have achieved. Make sure it is well-formed, achievable and ecological in your life. For example, there must be no

negative consequences for yourself or others. It should also be self-initiated and achievable within your control. And there must be specific steps and tasks that you can begin immediately so that you are moving towards your outcome in a relatively expedient timeframe.

2. Begin Balanced Breathing for a couple of minutes until you are in a deeply coherent and balanced state.

3. Start connecting to the values and intentions that underpin your outcome and feel these deeply in your heart. Breathe your passion and desire for your outcome into your heart. Expand these feelings throughout your chest region and breathe them up into your head and down into your gut. Add in colors, sparkle, sounds, images, whatever adds to and enhances your experience of your outcome and its connected values.

4. As you are breathing your values, desires and a passionate sense of your outcome down into your gut, begin to feel a real and growing hunger for your outcome. Imagine that you can almost taste your outcome and it's delicious. Savor it. Salivate for it. Massively desire it! Intensify your hunger for it. Really build an incredible taste and hunger in your gut for your outcome. And cycle with your breathing from feeling the passion and desire for your outcome in your heart, down to an incredible hunger for achieving your outcome in your gut. Intensely feel the motivation to start moving on making your outcome a reality now.

5.　Once you have cycled between your gut and heart a number of times, amplifying it with every pass, begin to add in your head-based creativity. Move the sense of your outcome up into your head and focus on allowing your unconscious mind to generate creative ways to help you get moving on your goals and ways to quickly and powerfully achieve the results you so hungrily desire.

6.　With each option that your head brain brings forth, cycle through steps 4 and 5 and feel yourself getting more and more motivated and excited to take action NOW!

Heart-lead courage

In our modeling work with incredibly brave and courageous individuals we've found some fascinating distinctions on how to trigger, support and generate courage. These gutsy individuals talk about the importance of intensely focusing on heartfelt values to help overcome fear. They also describe how fear is felt in the front of the gut, whereas courage is experienced as a gutsy push from the back of the gut that helps "push through the fear."

It is interesting that during development in the womb, the enteric brain is innervated in the foregut by cells from the truncal part of the neural crest, whereas the post-umbilical bowel and hindgut are innervated by cells from the sacral area of the crest. This may explain how one part of the gut brain is able to push gutsy courage through the fear response occurring in the front of the gut.

In his inspiring book, "Once a Pilgrim – A true story about courage and bravery under fire", Will Scully describes how he saved the lives of over 1000 people. It was May 1997, in Sierra Leone,

Africa and a military coup had plunged the country into chaos. Rebels were running amok, raping, robbing and killing innocent civilians. Caught in this maelstrom, a group of people had taken refuge in the Hotel Mammy Yoko, including Will Scully, an ex-SAS soldier working in the country to protect geologists prospecting for gold. With the hotel under siege, Scully single-handedly fought off over 200 rebels and eventually lead the hostages out of danger.

As Scully describes it, "I was shitting myself... The adrenaline and tension in my stomach made me feel sick. My arse tightened spasmodically as I flinched at each crescendo of gunfire around me. This was crisis... I hated it, and I heard myself swearing aloud, over and over and over. This was terror. Pure and simple. Hot waves of it washed over me, but my thoughts worked with astonishing clarity. Curled up, I fought each surge of panic rising from the depths of my stomach. I told myself I had to hold it together. I had a job to do. All the people down in the hotel depended on me. The logic was utterly clear. I had to do what I had to do. I could not, I would not stay where I was. I detected a slight pause in the rebels' firing... Abruptly, angry, I rolled back in front of the drain hole, rammed the gun into my shoulder, found a target in the hollow, behind a tree and shot them. Without waiting, I rolled back out of sight, wriggled to the next drain hole further along, and repeated the action." Ultimately, Scully was able to fight off the rebel attack and save the lives of the people trapped in the hotel.

Notice the strategy Will Scully utilized: he used his head and heart brains through heart-based emotions of hatred and anger at the attackers, and an intense desire to help others, coupled with the logic of what needed to be done, to overcome the gut brain mediated fear response. His courage to act kicked in through heart-lead drive and he overcame panic and terror to perform his incredibly heroic act.

This is something we found over and over in our modeling research. Anger at injustice is often used to motivate and overcome fear. Strongly felt heart-based emotions help overcome negative gut responses. We also discovered that in times of extreme terror, making guttural sounds and screams can focus the *'push through fear'*. Martial artists know this. In most martial arts you're trained to focus your force, energy and will through the center of your solar-plexus or gut, what the Japanese call the *'hara'*, via the use of guttural sounds.

</== Discovery Exercise: Pushing through Fear ==/>

In this exercise you'll practice creatively using your head and heart to motivate your gut to push through gut-felt feelings of fear. While it's best to practice this ahead of time in safe and comfortable situations, it can be used in acute situations where you need to overcome debilitating fear. The more you practice this, the more the process will become available to you in the heat of the moment in which it is needed.

[**Important Note:** This exercise is NOT to be used with phobias or other intense psychological or emotional abreactions. You should seek professional guidance when working with such issues. This exercise also doesn't address issues of chronic anxiety. It is designed for pushing through normal, situationally-based immediate fear where taking action is an appropriate response.]

1. Think of an issue or situation in which you experience fear that prevents you from taking appropriate and necessary action, and that you need to push through. Start remembering or thinking of the situation vividly enough that you feel the sensations related to the fear.

2. It is massively important in such situations that you immediately begin Balanced Breathing to control your autonomic balance. You'll find that in fear filled situations, your breathing will NOT be balanced, and so it's vital you control this consciously. Balanced breathe for a number of minutes until you are in a coherent and balanced state.

3. The next step begins in your head. Notice the fear sensations occurring in your gut and body. Talk to yourself and label these sensations. Become aware of how your true identity, who you are in your Highest Expression of self, is separate from these sensations. Notice that there is a '*you*' that can actually observe them. Notice also how you are bigger and better than these sensations and mere reactions, and in spite of these, you can choose to respond more generatively. Tell yourself what you want to and have to do in this situation that is truly representative of what's deeply important to you and who you know yourself to truly be.

4. Balanced Breathe your ideal sense of self and the values that truly define you from your head down to your heart. Feel them so very strongly and deeply in your heart. Brighten them up. Add in the color of your deepest and truest sense of self. Expand these in your heart. Amplify them with every

breath. Tell yourself as you breathe down into your heart what you must do, what you have to do, what you can't NOT do! Link this sense of truth deeply into your heart.

5.   And when you are ready, take a big breath in and send this deep conviction down to the back of your gut! Swallow hard. Zoom your conviction and determination into your gut. Really feel it pack a punch! Straighten up your entire spine all the way down from your lower back and pelvis. Really feel your gutsy determination slot powerfully in. And as it hits the back of your gut, make a deep guttural sound and move forward. Actually step forward. Fast! And grunt, growl, or yell a powerful sound out loud. Like a powerful martial artist in action! Physically move as you make these sounds and push through that fear. Push forward into the true embodied action of your highest self. You can do it! You cannot NOT do it! You are powerful, bold and filled with courage!

6.   Feel powerfully and massively emboldened with your new found courage to act in spite of the mere sensations of fear and TAKE ACTION NOW!

Overcoming fear through autonomic facilitation

When fear is present, wisdom cannot be."

Lactantius

There's a fascinating piece of psycho-therapeutic research from back in the early 1970's that shows how autonomic nervous system state can be facilitated to produce incredibly useful outcomes. In 1973, Researchers Shirley Bryntwick and Leslie Solyom used hunger and food provision to help cure elevator phobias. They got patients to voluntarily forgo eating and drinking for a whole day before getting them to eat a meal of their favorite food in an elevator.

As they reported in their published paper, "Mr. B. M., a 32-yr-old businessman, had suffered from an elevator phobia for about 5 years. He attributed his fear to two occasions within a 2-week period when he was trapped in an elevator for a few minutes. Since then he would climb 16 floors rather than take an elevator. Several times daily he climbed three flights of stairs to his office. On a 0-4 point scale, he rated his fear of elevators as 4, corresponding to 'terrifying panic attacks if avoidance impossible'. No other obvious psychopathology was apparent."

Mr. B. M. was instructed not to eat or drink for 24 hours prior to the treatment session. After that deprivation period, "the patient was led to an elevator where he found a table attractively arranged with his most preferred foods. For the next 35 minutes he sat eating his dinner while the elevator moved up and down. At the end of the session, the patient was encouraged to take self-service elevators in as many different buildings as possible." Mr. B. M. subsequently, "reported minimal anxiety and for the first time did not avoid taking elevators." At a two year follow up, there was no recurrence of the phobia.

The same method has been used to treat dog phobias. And it even works in animal models, where fear habits in laboratory animals have been diminished by first depriving the subjects of food and then rewarding them with it in the fear provoking situation.

So what's going on here? From an mBIT perspective we know that fear is a gut brain mediated response. It's a sympathetic dominant fight or flight process. But when you deprive someone of food for an extended period you put the gut brain into a strong focus on the prime function of self-preservation. And when you finally provide food, the gut brain moves into a massive parasympathetic mode. In this mode, the sympathetic process of fear cannot easily be supported. So the three brains now learn and associate the previously fearful situation or context with the new positive state. In the case of the elevator phobia above, the elevator has now become a place associated with food and self-preservation and is no longer an object of fear. This is a wonderful example of the mBIT principle of *'Autonomic Counterbalancing'*.

mBIT Principles: Autonomic Affinity, Autonomic Counterbalancing and Autonomic State Dependency

As described in Chapter 3, your brains can operate in autonomic states of sympathetic or parasympathetic dominance. The core competencies of each brain are grouped and controlled by autonomic state. Therefore you cannot easily access or trigger parasympathetic based competencies when your brains are in a sympathetic dominant state, or vice versa. The case study of Mary J in Chapter 3 is a great example of this. In her state of broken-heartedness she was unable to attend to values, dreams and purpose.

This is the principle of *'Autonomic State Dependency'*. You cannot easily operate a core competency unless the neural network is in a state that supports it. Competencies are dependent on ANS state.

A further mBIT principle that comes from this process of autonomic state dependency is that you can block core competencies by using *'Autonomic Counterbalancing'*. If you want to block a competency that occurs in a particular ANS state, then put the brains into the opposing or counterbalancing ANS state. For instance, you cannot express amped up excitement and depression at the same time. In the phobia example above we saw that satiated hunger and fear cannot easily co-occur. One counterbalances the other.

On the flip side, if you want to support a particular competency then you can facilitate your brains into a core competency that is allied or has an affinity with the desired ANS state. This is the mBIT principle of '*Autonomic Affinity*'. As an example, compassion, love and joy support the competencies of passion, dreams and values. And it's easier to experience joy if you're already in a general state of happiness or peace.

Decision-making and Problem-solving

Classical decision theory posits that optimal decision-making occurs through purely rational logic processes and that emotion and intuition have negative impacts on this process. Classical decision theory has been shown to be patently wrong by recent neuroscience! While decision-making certainly involves the head, a growing body of research is clearly showing that decision-making is predominantly an emotional business.

To begin with, there's a large amount of literature that suggests that under appropriate conditions, intuition may be as good as, or even superior to, classical decision-making approaches. But, there's an important caveat in this; accurate intuitive decision-making requires experienced domain knowledge and expertise. As we saw earlier in the section on intuition, wise intuition requires in-domain knowledge. You can't make wise intuitive decisions in areas in which you have no knowledge or experience.

Based on mBIT principles, it's blindingly obvious that decision-making and problem solving based on head-based logic alone will not be as effective or as wise as that generated using all three brains.

This is strongly validated by research from neuroscientist Prof. Antonio Damasio who has found that when emotion is left out of the reasoning process, logic alone can become incredibly flawed. In his fascinating book *'Descartes' Error'*, Damasio talks about the importance and validity of gut and heart based feelings as *'somatic markers'* and core components of the decision-making process.

Damasio studied subjects with brain injuries involving specific damage to parts of the brain where emotions are generated and processed. In all other respects these people were normal, however they'd completely lost the ability to utilize emotions. Their IQ and memory abilities were intact and they could logically describe all the facts needed to make decisions. Yet their abilities to actually make decisions and solve problems were seriously impaired. They suffered badly from *'analysis paralysis'* and were unable to make practical life decisions about the simplest of things such as what and where to eat, when to meet and where to live.

Damasio's work highlights the crucial role of visceral *'somatic'* feelings in navigating life's endless stream of personal decisions. These intuitive signals guide us via heart and gut messages so that listening to your heart and gut reactions, Damasio's *'somatic markers'*, helps you quickly reject negative courses of action and allows you to choose from among fewer and better alternatives.

What mBIT and Damasio's research indicate is that effective decision-making and problem solving require attending to and bringing to bare the intelligence and integrated wisdom of all your three brains. The importance of this for truly wise decisions is demonstrated in the famous and true story of the *'Wisdom of Solomon'*.

A wise decision

The biblical King Solomon, son of King David, was known for his deep and insightful wisdom. He became ruler around 967 B.C. of a kingdom that stretched from the Euphrates River in the north to Egypt in the south. One day, two women who lived in the same house, came to his court with a baby that both claimed as their own. They asked King Solomon to resolve the bitter quarrel over who was the true mother of the child.

After some thoughtful deliberation, King Solomon called for his sharpest sword to be brought to him and then perspicaciously suggested that the only fair solution would be to divide the living child in two so that each woman could have half. Hearing this terrible verdict, the true mother cried out, "Please, my King, give her the live child. Do not kill him!", and was thereby swiftly revealed as the true mother as she was willing to give up her child rather than see him killed. King Solomon wisely declared that by showing genuine compassion she had demonstrated she was the real mother, and he gave the baby to her.

What we see in this example of deep and insightful wisdom is a decision that goes way beyond simple head-based logic. Simple first-order logic dictates that splitting or sharing the baby, 'splitting the difference' is the only fair and logical solution. But both heart and gut wisdom balks at such a simplistic solution. The heart requires compassion, and King Solomon's wise solution was to call upon compassion as a defining heart-based characteristic of a true mother. By combining a gutsy and bold move of calling for his sword, to take action on a solution, and creatively integrating that action with heart required compassion, he created a deeply wise solution and quickly uncovered the real mother.

The fickle heart

Making a decision purely and only from the heart can be dangerous. The heart can be a *'fickle'* friend. The heart gets infatuated in people, places, things and ideas. What the heart desires today may not be what it desires a week, month or year from now. So decisions based solely from the heart brain are not wise or ecological in the system of your overall life. This is why you need to bring the wisdom of integration from the multiple distinctions and perspectives of all your brains. Your gut can and will provide intuitions telling you that what your heart wants is a mere fleeting infatuation. You need to ensure you ask for and listen to the information provided by your gut! Too often people ignore or denigrate the communication from their gut brains to their detriment.

The heart does core competencies of both values and desires. Values are about salience and importance. Values remain relatively stable over long time durations. Desires on the other hand are different. Desires almost have a gut linked hunger to them and typically only last for a finite amount of time. Infatuation is an intense form of desire. It can consume you. Research shows that the experience of infatuation is linked to the neuro-hormone oxytocin. Oxytocin is known as the love and bonding hormone. When you fall infatuatedly in love with someone or something you become intensely bonded and your bloodstream gets flooded with oxytocin. But oxytocin wears off. Infatuation doesn't last. You eventually either move to a deeper experience of valued love, or you move on to the next addictive infatuation.

The case study of Jason T from Chapter 2 eloquently highlights how your gut brain alerts you when it knows that your heart is lost in infatuation. Jason commented to us, "You know the saying *'love is blind'* — such a great saying, and I'm really beginning to see that maybe it's the truth. I meet a woman, fall in love and my heart tells me to trust her, to believe everything she tells me... and yet my head is there on the other side cautiously observing, and sometimes there's a small voice in my gut saying *'hey, watch out, there's something not quite right here'*. But what do you do?" And that's the key point of this section on problem solving and decision-making. What you do is listen to the communication, distinctions and intuitions of all three brains, and realizing each has valid and important messages, you wisely make a decision that creatively honors all of your intelligences.

Gut reactions from irrational fears and old patterns

There are times when the gut reacts to outmoded or irrational fears. The gut brain learns and has memory. It can *'over-learn'* patterns when young and these can carry on into later years when they're no longer appropriate or relevant. Being aware of this is important for the process of decision-making. You need to track for the difference between fear based gut reactions versus intuitive insights. Your gut provides insightful information, but not when it's operating from overly sympathetic or parasympathetic dominant states such as fear, anxiety or depression. As in all the mBIT techniques, the key is to bring your ANS back to balanced coherence and from this state communicate lovingly with your gut to get its intuitive insights.

Hungering for risk

There's some fascinating research published about the effects of hunger on decision-making. In one study, researchers analyzed more than 1000 decisions made over a period of 50 days by Judges ruling on prisoner parole. The results showed that shortly after a meal break Judges gave favorable verdicts up to 65% of the time, compared to nearly zero just before a meal break when physical hunger was at its greatest. So if you're a prisoner it's definitely in your interest to have your parole hearing at the start of the day, or just after lunch. But for the rest of us, from an mBIT perspective, it's equally important to realize that hunger strongly influences our decision-making processes. When your gut brain is distracted by its need for food, it does not partake in the decision process in the same way as when it is satiated.

In another important study, researchers examined how hunger and metabolic state affect economic decision-making and financial risk strategies. They discovered that as people get hungrier they become less risk averse and start to make riskier decisions. As described in the conclusion to their paper, the Researches from University College London stated, "human risk preferences are exquisitely sensitive to current metabolic state" and point out that this "has significant implications for both real-world economic transactions and for aberrant decision-making in eating disorders and obesity."

What this means is that when making important decisions you need to ensure you're attending to your hunger levels and are neither too hungry nor too satiated. Remember that the gut brain cannot do its wisest thinking when it's busy digesting a stomach full of complex food. Yet when it is overly hungry you'll make riskier decisions. Being aware of these processes allows greater self-awareness and helps you fine tune your decision-making strategies to match your outcomes and produce the wisest decisions.

Multiple brain decision-making

As described in earlier chapters, we know that sleep and dreaming are deeply integrative processes that allow your brains to communicate with one another. So when addressing important problems and decisions you are best served by *'sleeping on your ideas and decisions'*.

In addition, scientific research shows we have water taste receptors on our tongue and throughout the Gastro Intestinal Tract. That's right, a specific taste for water. Our gut brains can tell how much water is contained in what we are ingesting using these water taste buds. So in the process below, you'll drink a glass of water on arising, allowing the gut brain to immediately feel satiated by the water it requires and overcome hydration losses that occurred during sleep. In this way this distraction or pressure is immediately removed from its mind, allowing it to more easily focus on letting you know insights and intuitions about your situation and decision.

To tune into and garner the wisdom from all three of your brains when decision-making, the optimal mBIT based process is:

1. Consciously review and attend to all the facts before you go to sleep

2. Speak to your heart, head and gut brains asking them to digest, evaluate and sort through the facts and inform you in your dreams as you sleep on it

3. On waking, don't eat a meal first thing or drink coffee or tea or any other stimulant as this will swamp your gut brain

4. Drink a glass of clear (room temperature) fresh water to satiate hunger and balance any dehydration

5. Sit quietly, ask your heart, head and gut (in that order) for insights and wise intuitions about the situation and attend to their responses

6. Eat a small, light breakfast so that your brains aren't affected by low blood sugar and riskier modes of processing

7. Now, following the mBIT Roadmap begin Balanced Breathing and align your brains via their Highest Expressions and from this state, using all the intuitions provided at step 5, utilize your head brain to creatively find a way to compassionately honor all the messages, intuitions and needs expressed by your brains and make the most generatively wise and courageous decision you can. You'll know you've made the right decision when all three brains say '*Yes*' and can congruently agree i.e. when your heart is in it, your gut wants to move on it and your head agrees its totally logical and right

Habit control and overcoming compulsions

In her deeply insightful book '*The Gift of Compulsion*', Mary O'Malley claims that compulsions are unconscious patterns we have learned for managing our feelings and needs. They are ways of momentarily satiating the needs and hurts of our hearts; ways to satisfy a deep hunger and ways to numb ourselves from the struggles of our lives. But rather than fight compulsions and urges, O'Malley explains they can be embraced as guides and healed through compassion and acceptance.

Based both on personal experience and three decades of research and teaching, Mary O'Malley shows that heartfelt compassion can assist in overcoming compulsive behaviors. According to O'Malley, lasting healing comes from being curious and creative rather than controlling, and deep self-acceptance comes through forgiveness, not shame.

The idea behind Mary O'Malley's work, and backed up by our action research, is as Mary so eloquently puts it, "…whenever we are compulsive, what we are really longing for is to reconnect with ourselves. We are hungry for the experience of being grounded in our bodies again so we can live from the wellspring within that connects us to wisdom, to our hearts, and to our lives." It is this disconnect between gut (hunger), heart and head that's the message and outcome of a compulsion. The compulsion is a message, a *'gift'*, and a best attempt by your multiple brains to bring an out of balance system back to loving, congruent and integrated coherence. And isn't that what multiple Brain Integration Techniques (mBIT and *mBraining*) is all about? Aligning, connecting and integrating your three brains together through Highest Expressions to bring loving, compassionate, creative and courageous wisdom to your life!

The process for dissolving compulsions is to use the mBIT Roadmap to embody and embrace the needs and messages the compulsion is attempting to communicate and satisfy. When experiencing a compulsive urge, you start by coming back to a state of autonomic coherence via Balanced Breathing. You then bring heart-felt compassionate attention and acceptance to the compulsive urge. As Mary O'Malley explains, "All the desperate wanting behind your compulsive activities is really a longing for tender self-acceptance." Through filters of love, kindness and self-compassion, you then focus your head brain attention onto the compulsive urge to explore it with curiosity and creativity. You ask questions about the compulsion to truly understand it and the needs that drive it. You embrace the intuitive messages from your head, heart and gut about the compulsion. Next you motivate gut felt courage to accept and love yourself as you truly are. You embrace and enact a deeper sense of your authentic and true self. You integrate across all the parts of yourself. And finally you come back to a heartfelt spirit of joy; a heart filled with the blissful joy of being alive and in love with yourself and your life.

The following discovery exercise guides you through the steps of the process we have just described.

</== Discovery Exercise: Dissolving Compulsive Urges ==/>

In this exercise you'll practice using your heart, head and gut to align, forgive, accept and satiate compulsive urges.

1. Do this exercise when you're feeling any compulsive urges that you want to interrupt and dissolve. Begin by calmly accepting your situation, your feelings and the current experience of the compulsion.

2. If you can, sit in a comfortable balanced position. Allow your spine to gently straighten, keep your head nicely balanced, your feet flat on the floor and your hands resting comfortably in your lap. Set your gaze so that it softly and easily focuses on the floor somewhere in front of you.

3. Commence Balanced Breathing along the sine wave pattern so that you're breathing in for 6 seconds and out for 6 seconds, evenly and effortlessly. Do this for a couple of minutes till you can feel the calm experience of coherence deeply envelop your heart, head and gut brains.

4. With your right hand, gently touch your heart region and remind yourself that you are worthy of love. As you do this, begin to breathe love, compassion and a positive feeling of appreciation into your heart. With every breath expand and intensify your feelings of loving-kindness and compassion throughout your chest and up into your head, and then down deep into your gut. Enhance this with colors and sounds. As you move your feelings from your heart to your head, add in creativity, and then as you move those feelings back to your heart and then to your gut, add in deep feelings of gutsy courage. Flow these wonderful integrated feelings of love, kindness, compassion, creativity and courage up and down and throughout your mind and body.

5. As you think about those compulsive feelings you were having, become curious about them. See those old compulsive urges as a gift of information. Ask each of your multiple brains, "What do I really need?", "What message was the compulsive feeling giving me that I need to acknowledge?" and "What are the intentions of that compulsion?" Listen to your intuitive answers, responses and feelings from each of your brains. Thank the gift of your compulsion for bringing powerful insights to your life, so that you can now begin to creatively find ways to honor the intentions and needs that underlay those old compulsive urges. Thank the parts of your multiple brains that were doing the compulsing in their best efforts to support and protect you.

6. Continue your Balanced Breathing from your Highest Expressions, and ask your creative head brain to come up with at least three new ways to better honor those messages and intentions that underlay the old compulsive urges. Be sure your heart and gut brains are supporting the head brain by being involved in generating these new options.

7. Now take your sense of each creative and generative solution and breathe it from your head down deeply into your heart, really feel it merge with your love and compassion. Then when you are ready, swallow your creative positive new behavior and solution deeply into your gut. Feel it satiate the old compulsion. Feel your gut fill with love, forgiveness, support and calm, peaceful joy. Really taste those feelings and swallow them down into your gut. Let the experience of joy and appreciation for yourself and your life fill your stomach, fill your torso, fill your gut brain and fill your body all the way back up to your heart and beyond. Finish by feeling an incredible sense of value, appreciation and love in your heart, mind and soul for your wonderful life and your wonderful generative self as you move forward in life.

8. As you do this exercise, if you experience any major Neural Integration Blocks (NIB's), use the skills and techniques from Chapter 6 to dissolve and pattern interrupt those NIB's and then return to Step 4 above and re-do the steps of the exercise till you can experience deep integrated satiation of any compulsive feelings.

What you resist, persists... resistance is futile!

The more frequently and recently you resist a desire, the less successful you'll be at resisting subsequent desires. This is what the research shows. Wilhelm Hofmann of the University of Chicago, Roy Baumeister of Florida State University and Kathleen Vohs of the University of Minnesota found that what you resist keeps persisting. They also discovered that when willpower is low, everything is felt more intensely. According to Baumeister, "Low willpower seems to turn up the volume on life." In a series of experiments, Baumeister and his colleagues found that people experiencing low willpower reported more distress in response to an upsetting film and rated cold water as more painful during a cold-water immersion test. They also had stronger desires to open a gift and to keep eating cookies.

This is why resistance is futile. Resistance just leads to lower resistance and a greater focus on the things being resisted, until you finally give in. And once your will power has collapsed, you feel things so much more intensely and this leads to further indulgence; leading to a negative spiral of compulsion and addiction.

As we've seen above, the solution is not to resist, but to re-focus your attention and satiate your heart and gut-felt needs through flooding your three brains with coherent positive feelings of the Highest Expressions. Interestingly, research by Nicole Mead and her colleagues at the Catolica-Lisbon School of Business and Economics supports the concept that by refocusing and delaying or postponing giving in to the compulsion, you can more easily overcome it.

In one experiment, Mead's team gave subjects a bag of potato chips and instructions to either postpone, restrain, or consume the chips. Over the course of a week, participants who initially postponed eating the chips subsequently ate the least amount of chips. Subjects who were instructed to resist eating the chips ate even more than those who were instructed to eat them as desired. So a strategy of redirecting focus away from a compulsion and onto more coherent and generative responses, while at the same time postponing the action involved in the compulsion, gives you the most effective chance of generating the sorts of behaviors and results you truly desire.

Health and wellness

Health and wellness are both important in and of themselves and as indicators that all is not well in how you're living and creating your life. A healthy life is a core part of a wise life. It's hard to live well and wisely when you are in pain and suffering.

Your levels of health and wellness also act as '*self-awareness*' signs that all is not well in how you're doing the parts of your life described in this chapter. In other words, how congruently and wisely you're integrating and aligning in the domains of:

1. Self-awareness & Evolving your intuition

2. State management & Self-control

3. Courage, Motivation & Action-taking

4. Decision-making & Problem-solving

5. Habit control & Overcoming compulsions

6. Health & Wellbeing

Misalignment in any of these domains affects your life and the wellness of your body and connected bodily/brain systems. If for example, you aren't managing your emotional states effectively and are creating situations and times of massive stress and anger, while in addition ignoring the many intuitive messages from your heart and gut telling you that the way you're living is out of balance, then you'll end up with health issues and disease symptoms. All of which will be vital messages from your mind/body system and multiple brains that you need to refocus, realign and reintegrate into more wisdom.

As we described in Chapter 2, approximately 80% of your immune system is located in the gut. So the state of your gut brain and your Gastro-Intestinal (GI) system inherently impacts your overall health. Both your enteric brain and your immune system are deeply involved in maintaining core physical self. They determine what molecules and cells need to be absorbed, replicated, destroyed or eliminated. Your heart provides the blood and thereby the oxygen to assist your gut and other organs and systems to do their job. So it's incredibly obvious that when either of these intelligences is not functioning at their highest, your health and wellness are likely to be adversely impacted.

When your three brains are unaligned and in antagonism they produce states of stress which down-regulate immune response and ultimately lead to issues with disease and illness. By following the mBIT model for congruence, alignment and coherent Highest Expression of self you are supporting the most optimal states and processes you can for health and wellness.

We are what we eat

An important part of the process of wellness is what you eat. You need to ensure you're aiding your gut in its job of core-selfing by providing it with healthy food and water. Diet is fundamental to how well the gut can do its job. If you fill your stomach with rubbish and toxins, you push your gut brain into a stressed state and limit its ability to do optimal functioning. For this reason you need to eat nutritious healthy fresh foods. Obvious isn't it.

A healthy micro-biome

Maintaining healthy bacterial colonies in the gut — the micro-biome discussed in Chapter 2 — is also absolutely crucial for health and wellbeing. Within the Gastro-Intestinal (GI) tract, the microbiota that make up the micro-biome have a mutually beneficial relationship that maintains normal mucosal immune function, epithelial barrier integrity, motility, and nutrient absorption. Disruption of this relationship alters GI function and disease susceptibility.

Research shows that stress can negatively impact the composition of the microbiota in your gut and has been shown to be associated with increased vulnerability to inflammatory stimuli in the GI tract. The reverse is also true. Perturbation of the microbiota can alter behavior. The key message here is that you need to support your gut brain and your health by maintaining a good population of gut flora.

To keep your micro-biome healthy, it's definitely worth considering probiotic supplements. Probiotics have been demonstrated to be an effective treatment for anxiety, depression and other debilitating psychological conditions. Probiotics appear to support the gut brain in optimal functioning. But please note you must consult your health practitioner about these supplements to see if they are appropriate for your specific health and medical needs.

Sweet dreams

If you've ever suffered from insomnia you'll understand how vital good quality sleep is for wellbeing. When you're tired you can't think or function properly. And tiredness doesn't just affect your head brain. Your other brains also suffer from poor quality sleep. As we saw in Chapter 3 and 4, the gut brain goes through a nightly process of sleep and dreaming equivalent to what the head brain is doing. So when your gut brain doesn't get a good night's sleep, it can't function optimally and you can experience both digestive issues as well as the other core competencies can be negatively impacted. You become more defensive and more likely to react in a stressed way to the normal exigencies of daily life.

There's a reason we wish someone *'sweet dreams'* when we are suggesting to them that we hope they have a good night's sleep. The gustatory predicate *'sweet'* is indicating the gut's role in the quality of the sleeping process. We know this intuitively and now science is providing evidence for the validity of these age-old insights.

The gut brain is responsible for monitoring safety and threats, both external physical threats and internal *'semantic'* or psychological threats. So if before sleeping you put yourself into a hyped up vigilant state, if you ruminate over perceived injustices, or focus on upcoming fearful events, you'll find that your gut brain will kick into threat monitoring mode and your brains won't be able to do deep high quality sleeping.

You obviously also shouldn't eat rich and complex meals just before sleeping. Anything that disturbs or distracts the gut brain from calm sleeping can detract from how restful and *'sweet'* your sleep and dreams can be.

Instead, as you lay in bed, just before drifting off to sleep, do Balanced Breathing and fill you heart with peace, love and compassion. Then breathe these up into your head and down to your gut. Fill all your brains with calm, peaceful love. Talk kindly and lovingly to your brains and ask them to do high quality and integrative sleeping. Directionalize your brains respectfully and then filled with warm feelings of safety, love and peace, gently drift off into a refreshing night of health-filled sleep.

The power of touch

We all know the power of loving touch, human contact and physical massage and there's a huge body of research that backs up these insights. For example, a recently published study showed that massage turns off genes associated with inflammation and turns on genes that help muscles heal. Other studies have found that a number of important brain chemicals are released by touch that have healing and positive benefits. And these neuro-hormones aren't just expressed in the head, but also in all of your brains.

The gut brain in particular responds strongly and positively to stroking, touch and massage. Abdominal massage stimulates the Parasympathetic Nervous System and induces deep states of relaxation and release within the gut brain. Abdominal massage is therefore a wonderful method for soothing anxiety, stress and insomnia.

As indicated in Chapter 3, massage of the gut and visceral area can release strong emotional responses and reactions. The gut brain is closely linked to many of our deepest emotions to do with protection, fear, core identity and the memories from traumas related to this often get pushed down and hidden deep inside our gut. This makes abdominal massage a very powerful tool for releasing and unbinding old emotional damage from our past. As described in Chapter 3, people who have suffered abuse often experience gastro intestinal disorders. The unexpressed emotions, memories and response patterns held within the gut brain disrupt the natural flow of peristalsis and the digestive processes in the intestines. Abdominal massage can therefore improve digestion, release toxins and provide you with energy and wellness that has been restricted by old patterns and responses.

> *"Massaging the stomach enhances your powers of concentration; massaging the large intestine reduces emotional stress."*

> Pierre Pallardy

In his holistically perceptive book, "Gut Instinct: What Your Stomach is Trying to Tell You", Pierre Pallardy, the world-renowned osteopath, dietician and physical therapist, describes a number of important techniques for tapping into the healing power of the gut brain. As Pierre points out, massaging your gut is a natural and instinctive process and can relieve numerous issues and conditions. Pierre describes a series of specific massage techniques for self-massage of your abdominal area and your gut brain.

While you can certainly perform self massage on your gut, we recommend you initially seek the help of a qualified massage professional trained in gut work before undertaking intensive gut or visceral massage. There are many contraindications to gut massage, including hernias, obstructions of the bowel, acute inflammatory conditions, the presence of cancer, etc., and we therefore strongly suggest you seek the advice and assistance of both your Medical Health Practitioner and a qualified Massage Therapist.

Don't 'dishearten' your life

In terms of overall health and wellness, it's truly important you're aware that there are healthy versus unhealthy heart emotions. As discussed in Chapter 3, the emotions of despair, hopelessness, apathy and depression are all associated with a strikingly increased risk of coronary artery disease, heart attack and sudden cardiac death. There are numerous studies with huge cohorts that confirm this finding. A large number of studies have also shown that the negative emotions of anger and hostility can severely damage the heart. For example, a review of 25 clinical studies of coronary artery disease risk in healthy populations, found that people who scored highly in terms of anger and hostility were nearly 20 percent more likely to develop coronary artery disease or experience heart attacks, even when other preexisting risk factors were controlled for.

The flip side to this is that positive emotions are protective and an antidote to heart disease. They've also have been shown to increase immune function. In one study, researchers followed the health of 1,739 healthy adults over a period of 10 years, and found that positive emotions such as joy, happiness, excitement, enthusiasm and contentment were significantly protective of the heart. And people with high positive affect were significantly less likely to suffer from heart disease over the period.

The message to take to heart about this is that anger, bitterness, despair and other negative emotions eat away at your heart and impact your immune function and ultimately your health and overall levels of wellness. You need to engender and build positive emotions such as compassion, love and peace into every day and all the contexts of your life. This is the mBIT model and message. And we'd like to respectfully and lovingly suggest you do this as if your life depends on it, because guess what... it does!

Facilitating emergent wisdom

"Quality questions create a quality life."

Anthony Robbins

"We make our world significant by the courage of our questions."

Carl Sagan

There is an incredible power in questions. Questions directionalize your conscious and unconscious minds and open up pathways of connections within and between your neural networks. The quality of the questions you ask yourself on a daily basis can massively impact the quality of life you generate. For this reason, we'd like to finish this chapter, and the mBIT Toolkit, with a series of Generative mBIT Facilitation Questions.

These questions are designed to bring forth emergent wisdom in your life. Explore them while in a deeply integrated and coherent state of Highest Expression, and be sensitive to what each brain tells you (remember that each brain speaks to you in different ways). As you gain the insights and wisdom from each brain, continue your Highest Expression Balanced Breathing as you swallow each learning deeply into your gut and life.

Establishing Communication

- What is my real issue and/or goal?
    - What does my head say?
    - What does my heart say?
    - What does my gut say?

- Where is the conflict / doubt / uncertainty / confusion / hesitation / reluctance-resistance?
    - At the head? heart? gut?
    - Between my head and heart? head and gut? heart and gut? all three?

Facilitating Congruence

- Based on the nature of my issue and/or goal, which intelligence is most appropriate to take the lead given its prime functions?
- Which core competencies are currently being manifested by my head, heart and gut? Are they overly sympathetic or parasympathetic?
- Which core competencies of high coherence are required for each of my brains so that my lead intelligence is congruently supported by my other two intelligences?
  [Do Balanced Breathing to access those core competencies within each of your brains.]

Accessing Your Highest Expressions

While in a high coherence state:

- What does it mean to experience deep and full compassion in my heart regarding my issue and/or goal?
- How is my compassion creatively transforming my thoughts, perceptions and internal dialogue about my issue and/or goal?
- How do my transformed thoughts, perceptions and understanding support and enhance my feelings of compassion and loving-kindness?
- How does my enhanced state of compassion with my new thoughts and perceptions transform my sense of who I am and what I have the courage to do about my issue and/or goal?

Emerging Wisdom for Action

- As I experience the integration between my heart, head and gut in their Highest Expressions, what is emerging for me in my consciousness? What new possibilities are opening up for me in relation to my issue and/or goal?
  And in relation to:
  - Significant others?
  - Specific aspects of self?
  - Work?
  - Health?
  - Wealth?
  - Habits and routines?

- What insights and awakenings are arising within me about who I really am, what really matters to me, and what behaviors and actions fully express the essence of my deepest/highest self?
  - What does *'fully and authentically expressing myself'* smell and taste like?
  - What fragrances, aromas, flavors and taste sensations represent the truest essence of who I am? And in my relationships to others and the world?

- What actions can I take now to fully express my deepest/highest sense of who I am, and for the highest good of all in relation to my issue and/or goal?

Take those actions Now!

mBraining

"Using your multiple brains to do cool stuff"

Chapter 9

mBraining your World

"The intuitive mind is a sacred gift and the rational mind is a faithful servant. We have created a society that honors the servant and has forgotten the gift."

Albert Einstein

"Our science and our technology have posed us a profound question. Will we learn to use these tools with wisdom and foresight before it's too late?"

Carl Sagan

This chapter is personal. It's about you.

And it's also about us. All of us. It's about what mBIT makes possible in the world in which we all live, based on the choices *'you'* make. You are far more influential than you realize. The degree to which you live wisely from your Highest Expressions affects not only *'your'* experience of life but also that of your loved ones, your friends, your work associates, acquaintances, the strangers you interact with, and in many ways the extended network of people they're all connected with.

It doesn't take much to see we are all influencing each other in some way, directly or indirectly, by the way we choose to '*be*' in the world. And the wisdom of our choices, or lack of it, in how we express ourselves creates our personal world. On a societal and global scale, this collectively creates '*the*' world.

As indicated by Einstein's and Sagan's perceptive quotes above, and as detailed in Chapter 1, our world is out of balance. Over the centuries we've elevated and focused on head-based rational cognition over deeper heart-connected and intuitive gut-based ways of knowing. Our infatuation with the rational mind has led us to focus solely on logic to our detriment, so that if we can't explain something in head-based objective terms, we denigrate or ignore it.

Our purely head-based way of living and decision-making has created many of the modern global-social issues we now struggle with. As pointed out in Chapter 1, unfettered greed and a deep lack of awareness of systemic consequences has led to:

- Overpopulation and environmental degradation
- Unbridled consumerism
- Stress and health issues
- Accelerated change without meaningfulness; change for change sake
- Social fragmentation and work life imbalance; people are no longer connected in meaningful ways even though we have more ways to communicate than ever before
- Inflexibility, lack of acceptance and compassion leading to violence, wars, global conflict

- Unethical corporate behavior and collapse of financial systems due to either greed, lack of diligence or outright corruption

Even a rudimentary awareness of global events, environmental issues and social concerns is enough to highlight we now live in a world that is out of balance and out of alignment. We urgently need to find a way to bring integrated wisdom to how we're living on our fragile planet.

Now don't get us wrong. We are not doomsayers. There are definitely many things that are right, wonderful and beautiful in the world. It's great to be alive and there's so much to be appreciative about. What we're saying though, is we need to wake up and see the larger pattern and the systemic effects of the consciousness driving our daily choices. This requires seeing multiple perspectives and not denying one for the other. We need to integrate multiple perspectives to make wise choices that not only address critical issues in our world today, but also ensure a sustainable future we can all value and want to live into.

Just as how we're not doomsayers, neither are we starry-eyed idealists. As you can surmise from the extent of science-based research referenced throughout this book, combined with the numerous techniques for practical application, we are pragmatists. More so, we are pragmatists with intention. Our intention is to increase the wisdom of the decisions and actions taken in the world that affect us all. Our intentions have arisen as part of our Highest Expressions of compassion, courage and creativity. The pragmatics for achieving this is mBIT, our offering to you through this book.

Now, unless you're a powerful world leader, it's near impossible to directly affect changes on a global scale. However, we can all directly and indirectly contribute to collective change by elevating the consciousness from which we make our personal decisions and how we behaviorally respond and act in the world.

This is where you come in.

The freedom to choose

"Every man is condemned to freedom."

Jean-Paul Sartre

You are condemned to freedom. Regardless of your circumstances, you are free to choose your response. In fact, this is exactly what you do. And your choice of responses to whatever life presents you is based on what you know and don't know, what you are aware of or not aware of, and how you've patterned yourself to '*be*' on a habitual basis. The quality of your choices is affected by the level of your self-awareness and your intention. Is your intention to live from the Highest Expressions of your truest sense of self, or to live from default conditioning? You cannot not choose. Even the act of not choosing is a choice. It's the choice to live by circumstances rather than intention.

Many people live a default life as a form of reducing their cognitive dissonance. They may have moments when they get a glimpse of what it would be like to live a self-authored, fully expressed life, only to go out of coherence and succumb to a lack of courage, creativity and compassion. It all gets put into the '*too hard basket*' and they go on living the default conditioned life. You may be at risk of this now. The mBIT knowledge and methods you've learned in this book are transformative. Now that you are aware of them, you can choose to use them to make a real difference in your life and in the lives of others. Or you can choose not to. Either way, you are free and the choice is yours. You truly are condemned to freedom, you cannot not choose.

The only real and worthwhile question is, what are you going to choose? Will you choose to do nothing and live a default life that's hollow and meaningless? Or will you wisely choose a meaningful life filled with courageous, compassionate creativity? There's a world of difference in that choice. It's a matter of intention. The pragmatics are available. And your choice can make a real difference to the world that together we're all creating.

Authoring your life

Throughout this book we've talked about a concept called *'the authentic self'*, but now we'd like to share a secret with you…

There is no *'authentic self'*, no absolute, fixed, platonic ideal or intrinsic self that you must work to uncover. Your *'self'* is a fluid and changing process that emerges from the ongoing narrative of your life. In a complex process of feedback and feed-forward, you author the story of your *'self'* and your life. You create your *'self'* through a complex dance between thoughts, feelings, perceptions, beliefs, values, metaphors, expectations and a myriad of unconscious processes across all your neural networks. To talk about an *'authentic self'* is really just a shorthand way of describing this process of ongoing authoring of self and life. It's as the Buddhists so eloquently express it with their concept of *Anattā* or *'not-self'*, that "there ultimately is no such thing as a self independent from the rest of the universe."

If through reading this book you've come to understand the ideas and concepts on which mBIT is founded, then you'll realize just how powerful it is that you're able to author your own life. The skills you need to create and author a wise and generative self are those of the Highest Expressions. And it's through coherent states of compassion, creativity and courage that you give yourself the greatest chance of authoring an amazing self, an amazing life and an incredible and generative world. You are condemned to the freedom of authoring your '*self*' and your life, so make sure you choose a way of being that's wisest and most generative.

Neuro-genesis: evolving your self

"The principal activities of brains are making changes in themselves."

Marvin L. Minsky

As pointed out many years ago by psychologist Donald Hebb, and backed up by numerous cutting-edge scientific studies, when neurons fire together they grow new connections and '*wire*' together. Through a process called '*neurogenesis*' our brains grow new neurons and make new synaptic connections and new neural structures. One example of this was demonstrated with London taxi drivers. Researchers discovered that taxi drivers having learned the geographical complexities of driving around London had developed larger hippocampi, key regions of the brain responsible for visual-spatial memory. Another powerful example of brain plasticity, as shown in recent research, is the increase in frontal lobe connections of people who've learned and practiced loving-kindness meditation.

As described in Chapter 3, this process of neurogenesis not only occurs in the head brain, it's also been shown to occur in the gut and heart brains. This is an incredibly exciting finding with significant implications for you and your choice to use the mBIT methods in this book. The point is, by using mBIT on a regular basis, you can and will evolve new neural patterns and circuits within your brains! You will literally evolve yourself for greater neurological capabilities at higher orders of functioning.

"How we pay attention promotes neural plasticity, the change of neural connections in response to experience."

Daniel J. Siegal

The practice of compassion creates more neural compassion circuits throughout your brains. The practice of creativity creates more neural creativity circuits throughout your brains. And the practice of gutsy courage creates more neural courage circuits throughout your integrated and connected brains. You literally evolve yourself physically, mentally, emotionally and amplify your capacity for higher consciousness and ways of being.

Many of the individual and global challenges mentioned earlier are the result of both a lack of integration between all three brains, and most importantly, due to a lack of sufficient neural connections available for generating the levels of wisdom required for addressing these complex issues. So are we doomed to perpetually make un-wise decisions due to a deficiency in our neural patterning? Neurogenesis says no. Neurogenesis says there is hope. In fact there is more than hope. Not only can we intentionally grow new neural connections that enable us to process at higher levels of wisdom and address our existing global issues, we can generate new brain structures that have never been seen on this planet before.

And the pragmatics for this? It starts with every individual who cares about living a meaningful life. It starts with every person who wants to live a life that matters — a life that is worth living because it is being lived fully. Individuals who resonate with living a life that is courageous, creative and compassionate. Individuals like us, and if you've come this far reading this book, individuals like you.

Working wisely together to bring back balance

We now know that in addition to our head brain, we also have brains in our hearts and guts. We know these two other exceptional *'intelligences'* have their own important and unique functions and competencies. And when all of our intelligences operate together in states of *'Highest Expression'*, generative wisdom emerges.

While the science behind these new findings may be surprising, the implications and applications have been known for over 2500 years. As we stated back in Chapter 1, it's a case of modern neuroscience meeting ancient wisdom. But this is not just a matter of going *'back to the future'*. Through mBIT we now have far greater insight and precision in understanding how to put into practice the advice of ancient sages from varying disciplines. More than ever, the practicalities for reshaping our global dynamics are more immediately accessible than they've ever have been. And it starts with each and every one of us continually and intentionally choosing to *'be'* at our highest levels of expression for wise decision-making and living.

We have a vision we'd like to share. We didn't start this book with this vision in mind. But through the process of exploring and practicing mBIT and aligning our multiple brains via their Highest Expressions, this deeply mobilizing vision grew within our hearts, minds and lives, and has now come to passionately inspire and motivate us.

It's a vision of how each of us individually and together can create a world of generative wisdom — in our own lives, our family's lives and within and between all the organizations we are part of. Imagine great numbers of individuals in all areas of society consistently practicing alignment of their three brains, continually evolving themselves by connecting to their Highest Expressions, and continually emerging new levels of wisdom in their decision-making, goals, behaviors, and relationships.

Imagine some of these individuals as senior managers, executives and leaders of influential organizations or industries. Imagine how they would lead differently when their plans and decisions are based on a balanced integration of gutsy courage acted upon a creative strategy founded on heart-led values, along with a focus on ensuring quality relationships with customers, employees, and society in general.

Imagine what it would be like to live and work in organizations that are compassionate, creative and courageous; organizations that deeply value these virtues. The shift towards this is slowly starting. In the last decade there's been a growing awareness of the importance of heart based intelligence skills. Companies have started valuing and utilizing organizational processes such as *'Emotional Intelligence'* and *'Appreciative Inquiry'*. But this is just scratching the surface. The real power and wisdom comes when heart, head and gut intelligences are aligned and integrated. We need more than just heart and head, as the work on mBIT detailed in this book has shown. We need all three intelligences working together, aligned through Highest Expressions and applied in the world.

And it's not just within organizations. Imagine other individuals living from their Highest Expressions as parents who cultivate healthy, nurturing family environments through wise parenting that's informed by their three coherent intelligences. Imagine the positive flow-on effects with their children, their children's children, and so on.

Imagine other individuals who live together as couples. Imagine the quality of their relationships when one or both relate to each other through the Highest Expressions of who they are as individuals and who they are as a couple.

Now imagine if people everywhere in society were continually practicing on a daily basis making choices and living from their Highest Expressions rather than reacting from old conditioning. This is a vision of a world that self-organizes through a generative consciousness of compassion, creativity and courage. It's a vision of a world where generative wisdom is commonplace and increasingly becomes more the norm than the exception.

Is this a lofty *'pie in the sky'* ideal? Maybe, but based on what we've seen of the transformative power and the speed of results from mBIT methods, we believe this vision is highly possible and achievable in our lifetime.

It mainly requires that enough people become aware of the remarkable discoveries referenced in this book and begin practicing the simple processes of multiple brain integration and alignment through their Highest Expressions. We can accelerate the development of a wiser society by teaching mBIT/*mBraining* methods to our children from an early age and in schools, so this becomes second nature for them. We can bring these insights and skills to the way we conduct our businesses, our social organizations, our media, and of course, the holy-grail, our local, national and global politics. We recognize the latter is notoriously difficult to influence, however we're not naively suggesting that all politicians become *'enlightened'* through mBIT. All we're suggesting is that it only takes a few individuals in key areas of influence to simply practice living from the Highest Expressions of their truest sense of *'Being'*. By doing so, different decisions will be made and different actions will be taken by all levels of leaders.

Creating a wise and generative difference

If you, like us, want to create a better world, then we ask you to *'think global, and act local'* — start by applying the mBIT Roadmap and Toolkit to your own life. Align your brains and life around your Highest Expressions of your truest sense of self. Fill your life with integrated compassion, creativity and courage. Create a world — your world — that is worth living. One that inspires you. One that represents all you want to have and be. And then share your knowledge and skills with others. Bring the changes you want to create to all your relationships and all the organizations you're part of.

Let's all work together to make a wise and generative difference.

Acknowledgements

We would like to thank and acknowledge all the people who made this publication possible.

A big thank you to all the participants of our Action Research workshops and all those kind and generous people involved in our Case Study work and mBIT Coaching sessions. And in particular a special thank you to Ari Diskin for kindly hosting our workshops. Without everyone's wonderful support, connection and interest the mBIT model wouldn't be as grounded and integrated as you all helped us make it.

We'd also like to thank the following authors and researchers for their very kind permission to quote or reference their excellent work: Prof. Eugene Gendlin, Gavin de Becker, Joy Ainley, Stephen Elliot, The Institute of HeartMath, Mantak Chia, Will Scully, Mary O'Malley and Ken Marslew. We'd also like to acknowledge that Coherent Breathing® is a registered trademark of Coherence LLC and that HeartMath® is a registered trademark of the Institute of HeartMath.

We'd really like to share our appreciation and special thanks to Alex Heng, Sebastian Kaulitzki of SciePro.com and Alyssa and Murray Finlay of Artifact Design Group for all their fantastic art and graphics design work, and to Pauline Wong for her highly valued advice.

Lastly and most importantly, from deep in our hearts we'd like to thank the beautiful and wonderful ladies in our lives. Fiona, Cherie, Karis and Sachi, your love, support and encouragement have filled our lives with magic. Thank you.

Legal stuff

As indicated at the front of this publication, the authors and publisher have used their best efforts in preparing this book. This publication contains ideas, opinions, tips and techniques for improving wisdom and human performance. The materials are intended to provide helpful and useful material on the subjects addressed in the publication. The publisher and authors do *not* provide or purport to provide you with any medical, health, psychological or professional advice or service or any other personal professional service. You should seek the advice of your own medical practitioner, health professional or other relevant competent professional before trying or using information, exercises or techniques described in this publication.

The publisher and authors, jointly and severally, make no representations or warranties with respect to the accuracy, reliability, sufficiency or completeness of the contents of this publication and specifically disclaim any implied warranties or merchantability or fitness for any particular purpose. There are no warranties which extend beyond the descriptions contained in this paragraph. The accuracy and completeness of the information provided herein and the opinions stated herein are not guarantees, nor warranties to or towards the production of any particular result, and the advice and strategies contained herein may not be suitable for every individual.

You read this publication with the explicit understanding that neither the publisher, nor authors shall be liable for any direct or indirect loss of profit or any other commercial damages, including but not limited to special, incidental, punitive, consequential or other damages. In reading or using any part or portion of this publication, you agree to not hold, nor attempt to hold the publisher or authors liable for any loss, liability, claim, demand, damage and all legal cost or other expenses arising whatsoever in connection with the use, misuse or inability to use the materials. In jurisdictions that exclude such limitations, liability is limited to the consideration paid by you for the right to view or use these materials, and/or the greatest extent permitted by law.

About the authors

Grant Soosalu

Grant is an international Trainer, Leadership Consultant and Executive Coach with extensive backgrounds in Organizational Change, Training and Leadership Development. He has advanced degrees and certifications in Psychology, Positive Psychology, Applied Physics, Computer Engineering and System Development. He is a qualified Total Quality Management (TQM) Trainer, and has achieved Master Practitioner Certification in the behavioral sciences of Neuro Linguistic Programming (NLP) and Advanced Behavioral Modeling. More recently Grant was awarded a Graduate Coaching Diploma in the newly emerging field of Authentic Happiness Coaching.

Grant has wide ranging expertise and experience in the educational sector as a Lecturer, Coach, Training Developer and Facilitator. He also has extensive backgrounds in Business Development, Senior Technical Consulting and Project Management. Grant provides coaching and mentoring to numerous CEO's and Senior Executives.

Currently, Grant is a Consultant Lecturer at a leading Australian University where he runs workshops and programs on Social Media Marketing and the applications of Positive Psychology to Conflict Resolution, Risk Management and Organizational Change. Grant also runs a successful consulting company providing services to organizations predominantly in the finance sector.

Grant has published articles and papers in International Journals, in the fields of Coaching, Leadership, Philosophy, Applied Physics and Neuro Linguistic Programming.

Marvin Oka

Marvin is a highly sought after international consultant and speaker specializing in leading edge behavioral change technologies and research. Recognized as a world leader and authority in his field, Marvin has built an impressive track record helping organizations with strategic, systemic and cultural change. Marvin's clients range from private enterprises to government agencies throughout the world.

Marvin's professional background is in the innovative and groundbreaking field of Behavioral Modeling. This exciting field examines various forms of human talent, ability and expertise, and then seeks to create models and methods to replicate these forms of superior performance in others. Marvin is one of only five people in the world who have been recognized by his peers with the rare title of 'Certified Master Behavioral Modeler'. Additionally Marvin was one of the first five people to achieve the accredited status of a 'Certified NLP Master Trainer' in the field of Neuro Linguistic Programming (NLP), and at that time was the youngest ever to have reached this level of professional competency.

Born in Honolulu, Hawaii and now living in Australia, Marvin is one of the founding Directors and is on the board of the International NLP Trainers Association (INLPTA) based in Washington, DC, with representation in over 42 countries worldwide. Marvin is currently the Executive Director of Behavioural Modelling Research Pty Ltd.

References and resources

Extensive references, bibliography, suggested readings and additional resources for the work described in this publication can be found at:

www.mbraining.com

40850709R00212

Made in the USA
Charleston, SC
19 April 2015